INSTRUCTOR'S RESC
TO ACCOMPANY

SPANISH FOR BUSINESS

Patricia Rush
Ventura College

Patricia Houston
Pima Community College

PEARSON

Prentice
Hall

Upper Saddle River, New Jersey 07458

© 2003 by PEARSON EDUCATION, INC.
Upper Saddle River, New Jersey 07458

ISBN 0-13-110324-5

Printed in the United States of America

Contents

Teaching with Spanish for Business

Spanish for Business is designed to allow instructors to easily create and deliver pragmatic, "real-world" language and culture-training programs so that beginning students can master "need-to-know" language and put it to immediate use. The materials are designed to help the English-speaking workforce better serve the growing population of Spanish-speaking clients and employees who arrive with little or no English. In addition, the basic vocabulary, situations and cultural insights will provide a strong preliminary background for those students who eventually wish to major or minor in Spanish at a more-advanced level. The best part is that you, the instructor, do not need business background to successfully deliver the course.

Students will be presented key vocabulary in a comprehensible-input format, focusing on easily-mastered, core expressions. Art, realia, photographs and brief dialogues will reinforce needed terms for each occupational area, supported by brief grammar explanations presented in "chunks". Grammar practice will be embedded automatically in context. In class, students will focus on communicative survival using basic vocabulary essential to the topics that will enable them to utilize their Spanish in their job environment. Traditional scope and sequence has occasionally been modified to more accurately mirror the cultural and linguistic needs of a work setting; i.e. the subjunctive has been presented prior to the preterit because of its necessary use in situations where a business professional recommends or suggests a course of action to a client. Each chapter ends with *Síntesis* in which the chapter's grammar and vocabulary topics are synthesized in reading, writing, listening and speaking activities. *Algo más* offers cross-cultural insights significant to working with clients in its *Ventana cultural* section, accompanied by *A buscar* where students are sent to search out additional information connected to the chapter theme, frequently focused specifically on Hispanics. *A conocer* provides an opportunity for students to "meet" Hispanics who are successfully working in different areas of the business world. *En mis propias palabras* allows students to expand on their own experience as related to working with Hispanics in the business arena.

Whether the students are "non-traditional"—professionals already working in the field—or more traditional university or college students who want to contextualize the language requirement to meet a vocational, professional or career goal, true-beginning students will find that these materials provide a solid foundation in the basic skills of speaking, listening, reading and writing embedded in everyday workplace situations. High-beginner students will also find the materials excellent for structural review while acquiring routines and protocols of the workplace. In short, a "no-frills" book, supported by workbook and web activities, where rapid acquisition of the phrases and routines of the occupation is key to student success in the field (as opposed to success simply in the classroom). While language structure is considered essential, grammar will be less critical than "ready response" for communication. **Spanish for Business** represents two quarters/semesters of instruction in three or four credit courses. Production at a novice level is anticipated; students entering with previous training may produce at the low-intermediate step.

Components of the program

♦ **Text,** using realia-based materials to accompany content-based dialogues in major categories of business. Art spreads introduce appropriate vocabulary.

- **Website** includes tests with feedback for student work and links to websites categorized by theme.

- **Audio CD** for listening segments, dialogues and vocabulary lists from text in each chapter.

- **IRM** including tests for each chapter and final examinations for the two review chapters. Audioscript provided in this section.

- **Workbook** to provide additional practice and reinforcement of main concepts, as well as practical materials such as diagrams, forms, etc.

Sample Planning Guide

Spanish for Business readily lends itself to a two semester/quarter course. The first half of the book, covering *Para comenzar* through *Lección 6*, encompasses the first term; *Lección 7* through *Lección 12* are to be presented in the second. The final lesson in each half is a review of previous lessons, to prepare for the cumulative final exams which we have included.

Sample Lesson Plan

Each lesson should be taught over a two to three week period, depending on the number of class hours. There are two vocabulary and two grammar spreads in each module, thus representing a total of four vocabulary and four grammar segments in each lesson plus the *Síntesis* and *Algo más* sections. Module 1 would be the first week's lesson; Module 2 the second week's, with review segments from *Síntesis* and cultural input from *Algo más* presented prior to testing. Lesson 1, *Una entrevista,* could be presented as follows:

Week 1:

- *Buscando trabajo*

- Telling time: *La hora*

- *Preparando mi currículum*

- Introducing and describing yourself and others: **Ser** + *adjetivos*

Each vocabulary section begins with an art spread for initial vocabulary acquisition. Begin the presentation of this lesson's theme by using this art in a comprehensible-input format. Ask students to identify the name of our "applicant" as shown in the personal information form on p. 17. Continue to ask questions prompted by that form: *¿Cuál es el teléfono de Margarita? ¿Es soltera? ¿Cuál es su número de Seguro Social? ¿Su fecha de nacimiento? ¿Su ocupación?*

Activities A and B always recycle vocabulary just presented, and serve as background for material then introduced in the dialogues. For example, in Activity B students mechanically reproduce the vocabulary presented by role-playing a new employee and a receptionist gathering personal information, similar to what they saw in the art piece. After completing those opening activities, have students read the dialogue (or play the audio CD), followed by Activity C to check for comprehension. They learned "*apellido*" in the art, practiced in both A and B, and now use it again to answer questions based on the dialogue. These activities are appropriate for individual work (perhaps as previously-assigned homework), for entire class response, or for pair, small-group work even if the pair/group icons are not included.

The remaining activities in each vocabulary spread expand upon the content already presented, often using realia to provide the real-world focus and to assist students in applying what they just learned. On p. 20, students read a brochure on how to dress for success; they learn that they can read beyond what they can produce on their own (cognates are used throughout)—followed by another comprehension check. You may choose to present reading strategies, i.e. "It is not necessary to understand every word; read for overall meaning." You may also enhance cognate recognition by stressing commonalities, such as -ly = *-mente,* -ous = *-oso,* -ity = *-dad,* etc.

Estructuras presents our grammar explanation, recycling the same vocabulary and specifically tying it to the concept presented. Remember that some items will have been previously introduced lexically prior to their presentation as a grammar point (*Me gusta* is an example.) Students may read the explanation on their own at home; you may also choose to reinforce this explanation in class. The examples presented continue to utilize familiar words, and are followed by practice exercises to master the point taught, telling time in this case. For example, on p. 21 you see *La cita con el jefe es a las once.* "Cita" was introduced in the dialogue and *"a las once"* ties directly to the lesson explanation. *Llego a la oficina a la una* offers a sample cognate. Exercises usually include models as additional reinforcement, and specifically require students to apply what they just learned. Students are now prepared to do A, B and C orally in class; exercises may be written if desired.

The Workbook directly mirrors the text, so additional practice for this first vocabulary/grammar spread of Module 1, Lesson 1 may be assigned as independent work or for class use.

Preparando mi currículum, the second vocabulary presentation, should be presented in the same fashion. This spread ends with an interview activity for students to personalize their knowledge. The grammar in this section, *Introducing and describing yourself and* *others: **Ser** + adjetivos*, gives students confidence that they've learned a lot in a short time, for now they can talk about themselves and others.

The vocabulary for each module is recorded on the audio CD, so instruct students to study the list as well as to practice their pronunciation by listening/repeating each word. The website tests, with instant feedback for the student, divide each module into each of its segments—two vocabulary and two grammar parts—so students may check their progress piece-by-piece or wait until it's time for the lesson examination (provided in the IRM) to try their skills.

Week 2:

- *La entrevista*

- Asking for information: *Las preguntas*

- *Los recursos humanos*

- Describing people: *Los artículos*

Module 2 would be presented in similar fashion to Module 1, beginning with the art for vocabulary presentation, moving to the dialogue, following with the expansion material and then presenting the grammar, allowing students to practice both text and workbook material. Repeat for the second spread, again urging students to study the vocabulary list and listen to and repeat each word.

Week 3:

- *Síntesis* (recycles material from both modules, stressing listening, speaking, reading and writing)

- *Algo más* (provides a culturally significant reading, *Ventana cultural,* with additional opportunity for writing, *En mis propias palabras,* and a guided search for broader information tied to the topic in both the *A buscar* and *A conocer* sections.

- Lesson test (self-tests online for students and different instructor examinations in the Instructor's Resource Manual).

Síntesis opens with *A escuchar,* recorded on the audio CD (the audioscript is included in the IRM). There is always a comprehension check accompanying the listening segment. Now students recycle their vocabulary in reading and conversational segments, again relying on realia to reinforce our real-world concept, and encouraging students to "dare" to use their newly-acquired skills in guided conversations related to the lesson theme. *A escribir* provides a writing opportunity to further recycle material.

Algo más introduces material specifically geared to Hispanics in most cases. As the burgeoning population statistics show, Hispanics, now over 30 million, make up a growing segment in the United States and one of great significance. The *Ventana cultural* in Lesson 1 showcases the significance of speaking Spanish in today's world. Students then summarize what they read, giving them another opportunity to hone their writing skills, and an opportunity to check for comprehension by direct practice. Sharing their work with a classmate provides peer editing. *A buscar* sends them in search of more information in Spanish to enhance their connection to the language and its culture. As a suggestion, have students search for photo images of the Hispanics profiled in *A conocer* or to search for other prominent Hispanics, perhaps in their own community. The website offers an expanded list of links to whet their appetite for further research.

Expansion Opportunities

Spanish for Business provides the instructor with rich opportunities to lead students into further discussion and expansion of topics, depending on available time. Consider this example: *A escribir* in *Lección 5* asks the student to prepare a publicity campaign. Expand this activity into a student project by 1) showing a sample ad, 2) offering guidelines to follow, 3) allowing students to work together to create and revise their ad, and 4) presenting their finished presentation to the class.

While this text is designed with the beginning student in mind, many topics worthy of additional discussion are presented. *Sindicatos* and *maquiladoras, Lección 8,* trade agreements, immigrant labor, sweat shops, *Lección 9,* and environmental issues such as destruction of the rain forest, ecotourism, "Green" party issues, *Lección 10,* foster critical social analysis. By using media, print and video, the instructor can promote lively interaction to reinforce the real-world connection of language study.

Audioscript for A escuchar

Lección 1

RECEPCIONISTA:	Buenos días. Oficina de Recursos humanos. Soy Carmen, a sus órdenes.
CARLOS:	Buenos días, señorita. Me llamo Carlos Contreras. Soy secretario bilingüe, soy de México y busco empleo en su empresa.
RECEPCIONISTA:	Bueno, Sr. Contreras. Usted necesita enviar su currículum y una solicitud de empleo. Las solicitudes son electrónicas y están aquí, en nuestras computadoras. Hay disponible una cita el lunes a la una de la tarde.
CARLOS:	El lunes no es posible. ¿Hay citas los sábados? No trabajo los sábados.
RECEPCIONISTA:	¡Qué bueno! Hay una cancelación para el sábado próximo a las tres de la tarde. ¿Está bien?
CARLOS:	Está muy bien. ¿Necesito otros papeles?
RECEPCIONISTA:	Sólo su número de seguro social y su permiso para trabajar en Estados Unidos.
CARLOS:	Muchas gracias, señorita. Nos vemos el sábado.

Lección 2

MAMÁ:	Bueno.
LUCÍA:	Hola, mamá. Habla Lucía. ¿Cómo estás?
MAMÁ:	Ay, Lucía. Estoy cansada, pero bien. Y tú, hija, ¿cómo estás? Tienes la voz débil. No te escucho bien.
LUCÍA:	Es que estoy un poco enferma. No es nada. Llamo para hablarte de mi nuevo trabajo. Mañana es el primer día y estoy nerviosa.
MAMÁ:	Es normal, hija, pero tú aprendes rápidamente. Tranquila.
LUCÍA:	Mamá, tengo un nuevo apartamento. Es muy bonito. Tiene dos dormitorios, dos baños, una cocina grande y una sala con chimenea. Me mudo mañana.
MAMÁ:	¿Tienes ayuda de alguien?
LUCÍA:	Sí, mamá. Tengo un nuevo amigo del trabajo. Se llama Juan y su esposa se llama Iris. Tienen dos niños preciosos. Ellos alquilan un vehículo de mudanzas mañana para ayudarme.
MAMÁ:	Estoy contenta, hija. Pero tengo una pregunta, ¿tienes seguro de salud?
LUCÍA:	Sí, mamá, ahora tengo seguro de salud, dental, de vista y de inquilino. ¿Por qué?
MAMÁ:	Estoy preocupada. Si estás enferma tienes que visitar al médico. Hoy mismo.
LUCÍA:	¡Ay, mamá!

Lección 3

MAITRE:	Buenas tardes. Restaurante La Fuente. Paco Fuentes. ¿En qué puedo servirle?

ROLANDO:	¿Sabe usted si es posible hacer reservaciones para ocho personas esta noche?
MAITRE:	¿A qué hora desea la mesa?
ROLANDO:	Para las ocho y media.
MAITRE:	Si le gusta la música, tengo una mesa cerca de la orquesta.
ROLANDO:	No, gracias. Estamos celebrando una venta muy importante. Vamos a hablar de los detalles. ¿Hay una mesa más tranquila?
MAITRE:	Entonces, pongo una mesa en el patio. Allí no oyen nada.
ROLANDO:	¡Excelente! Entonces, tengo una reservación para ocho personas a las ocho y media de la noche.
MAITRE:	Y a las nueve, si todo va bien, yo traigo a la mesa una botella de champaña para animar la celebración.

Lección 4

ROLANDO:	¿Paco? Habla Rolando. Tenemos que hablar. ¿Tienes un momento?
PACO:	¡Claro, hombre! ¿Cuál es el problema?
ROLANDO:	Acabo de tomar una decisión importante. Como eres mi mejor amigo, tú debes saberlo primero. Esta noche durante la cena para celebrar el cumpleaños de Gina, voy a pedirle la mano en matrimonio.
PACO:	Imposible, hombre. Tomar la decisión de casarte no es tan fácil como tomar la decisión de comprar nuevos zapatos. ¿Cómo vas a proponerle matrimonio si no tienes un anillo?
ROLANDO:	Voy a tener un anillo de compromiso con un diamante solitario.
PACO:	¿Cómo es posible? ¿Cómo vas a encontrar un anillo antes de la cena?
ROLANDO:	Hay una joyería aquí con el mejor servicio al cliente del mundo. Acabo de hablar con el dueño que es tan romántico como yo. Él va a llevar una selección de anillos al restaurante quince minutos antes de la cena.
PACO:	Pues, ¿cómo piensas pagar un anillo de diamantes?
ROLANDO:	El joyero me va a conceder crédito. Voy a comprar el anillo a plazos.
PACO:	¡A plazos! Amigo, ésta es una decisión que vas a pagar por mucho tiempo. ¡Felicidades!

Lección 5

OPERADOR:	Bienvenido al centro de servicio al cliente Compre-su-ganga, su tienda favorita de Internet. Me llamo Rafael. ¿En qué puedo servirle?
CLIENTA:	Buenas noches, Rafael. Estoy navegando por Internet y veo que su sitio tiene una promoción de licuadoras. El anuncio dice que si uso mi tarjeta de crédito, hay un descuento adicional del 50%. Y el flete es gratis. ¿No es verdad?
OPERADOR:	Es verdad. Tenemos una promoción especial para los compradores que usan nuestra tarjeta.
CLIENTA:	Dice que el descuento se aplica al final de la transacción, ¿verdad?
OPERADOR:	Sí, señora. ¿Hay algún problema?

CLIENTA: Sí. El precio de la licuadora es $36.00. Yo debo pagar $18.00, incluyendo el flete. ¿Sí o no?

OPERADOR: Claro que sí, señora.

CLIENTA: Pues, mi cuenta final dice $82—$72.00 por la licuadora y $10.00 por el flete.

OPERADOR: Lo siento, señora. Hay un error. Tiene que hablar con el departamento de servicio al consumidor. Pero ahora son las ocho. Está cerrado. Vaya al sitio web y escríbales un e-mail explicando el problema.

CLIENTA: No. Mejor, cancele la licuadora. No quiero hacer todo esto.

OPERADOR: Lo siento, señora, no hay nadie aquí con autorización...

CLIENTA: [hangs up]

Lección 7

LUCÍA: Roberto, acabo de recibir las hojas de cómputo para calcular mis impuestos federales sobre la renta. Estoy confundida.

ROBERTO: Por eso paga usted a un contador. Yo estoy aquí para ayudar. ¿Cuál es la pregunta?

LUCÍA: Este año mis ingresos son completamente diferentes del año pasado. Además de mis inversiones, mi sueldo es $10,321 dólares más que el año pasado. Va a ser la primera vez que no voy a recibir un reembolso del IRS.

ROBERTO: Bueno. Primero tiene que preparar la lista de todos los ingresos, intereses y dividendos. Segundo, tiene que preparar la lista de todos sus gastos deducibles y tercero, tiene que traerme todo.

LUCÍA: Ese es el problema. Yo no sé qué gastos son deducibles y cuáles no lo son.

ROBERTO: Siga las instrucciones en mis hojas de cómputo. Después yo puedo preparar la planilla y calcular el impuesto que debe. Sólo entonces vamos a saber si recibe un reembolso o paga impuestos adicionales. Y para el año que viene, tenemos que pensar en organizar sus finanzas en un programa de computadora. Así, todo va a ser más fácil en el futuro.

Lección 8

MARÍA: ¿Vamos a la cafetería para comer? Quiero hablarte del supervisor nuevo.

CONSUELO: Sí, vamos. Pero primero, quiero lavarme las manos. Las tengo muy sucias porque la máquina no funciona bien. ¿Cómo es tu nuevo jefe? No lo conozco personalmente pero sé que tiene un carácter antipático.

MARÍA: ¡Ay! Consuelo, no es verdad. Sabe mucho de tecnología de maquinaria y sabe explicarla para que todos entendamos. Tiene mucha paciencia y nos escucha y nos ayuda con los problemas. Y hay otra cosa —cuando él tiene que tomar una decisión o resolver un problema de producción, nos pide ayuda a nosotros. Formamos un equipo excelente y todos nos llevamos muy bien.

CONSUELO: ¡Oye, mujer! No me digas que ahora te gusta tu empleo.

MARÍA: ¿Sabes, Consuelo? Por primera vez desde hace años, no me levanto con miedo de ir a la fábrica. Sí, en realidad, me gusta el empleo. ¡Imagínate!

Lección 9

SUSANA: Mi socia Laura y yo queremos poner un negocio de nutracéuticos: el primer producto es un dulce de chocolate con una fórmula que resulta excelente para el corazón humano. Laura está decidida a importar todo el cacao de Costa Rica.

ABOGADO: ¿Por qué quiere comprarlo de Costa Rica? Yo sugiero que compren el cacao de un distribuidor local. Así evitan los problemas con la aduana y los costos del transporte. No creo que el éxito de su empresa dependa del cacao importado.

SUSANA: Creo que tiene razón. Pero Laura dice que su amigo en Costa Rica tiene un producto orgánico —más rico en nutrientes. Y también es un producto que no causa problemas con el medio ambiente porque no se usa ningún pesticida y que nuestros productos respetan al consumidor y a la naturaleza.

ABOGADO: Personalmente sugiero que compren todos los ingredientes aquí. Pero si prefieren importarlos, recomiendo que tengan un buen abogado para ayudarlas. Y para mis amigas Susana y Laura y el chocolate nutracéutico, yo quiero ser el abogado.
Tengo mucha confianza en su empresa. Si no tienen capital para pagarme, quiero que sepan que puedo aceptar unas acciones en la nueva compañía.

Lección 10

SEÑORITA: Buenas noches. El señor Pérez, por favor.

SR. PÉREZ: Yo soy Daniel Pérez. ¿Con quién hablo?

SEÑORITA: Buenas noches, Sr. Pérez. ¿Cómo está usted esta noche?

SR. PÉREZ: Estoy muy bien, gracias. Pero, ¿quién habla?

SEÑORITA: Me llamo Juana López y soy una voluntaria de Ayuda Mundial, una organización sin ánimo de lucro que ofrece servicios de ayuda y rescate cuando ocurren desastres naturales. Su nombre salió en mi lista como una persona que hizo un donativo muy generoso el año pasado.

SR. PÉREZ: Perdone, señorita. No la escuché. No tenemos buena conexión. ¿Qué me dijo?

SEÑORITA: Le dije que su nombre y número de teléfono salieron en mi lista como una persona que hizo un donativo generoso...

SR. PÉREZ: ¿Usted dijo que yo hice un donativo a su organización el año pasado...?

SEÑORITA: Sí señor. Un donativo muy generoso. Le hablo para darle las gracias y para pedir su ayuda otra vez este año.

SR. PÉREZ: ¿Dónde trabajaron ustedes el año pasado? ¿Cómo usaron mi dinero?

SEÑORITA: Pues, no lo sé exactamente, señor, pero mandamos mucha comida y ropa a las víctimas del huracán Victoria en México y a las víctimas de las inundaciones en Brasil. Este año necesitamos más dinero que antes y llamé para pedir su ayuda otra vez.

SR. PÉREZ: ¿Ustedes no protegen el medio ambiente?

SEÑORITA: No, señor. Nosotros ayudamos a las víctimas de desastres naturales.

SR. PÉREZ: Lo siento, señorita. Tiene que hablar con el otro Sr. Pérez, mi hijo.

Él contribuye a las agencias que trabajan con desastres naturales. Yo sólo contribuyo a las caridades que benefician al medio ambiente. Él salió hace media hora.

Lección 11

MARÍA PATRICIA:	Bueno. Hola, Edith, ¡Precisamente en este momento estaba pensando en ti! ¿Cómo estás?
EDITH:	¿Cómo sabías que yo te llamaba? ¿Tienes una bola de cristal?
MARÍA PATRICIA:	Una bola de cristal, no. Sólo mi nueva identificadora de llamadas. Últimamente recibíamos muchas llamadas de vendedores que no me gustaban nada. Ayer la compañía de teléfonos me instaló la identificadora de llamadas y llamada en espera.
EDITH:	Te pones muy tecnológica. ¿Qué haces esta tarde?
MARÍA PATRICIA:	No sé. ¿Tienes alguna idea?
EDITH:	Esta mañana cuando iba a salir de la casa, noté que no tenía mi perfume. Cuando regresé al baño para ponérmelo, recordé que se me acabó ayer. Necesito comprar más. ¿Quieres ir de compras?
MARÍA PATRICIA:	¿Dónde?
EDITH:	No sé. Este perfume es difícil de encontrar.
MARÍA PATRICIA:	Yo recuerdo la última vez que necesitabas tu perfume. Fuimos de tienda en tienda y no lo pudimos encontrar. No quiero hacerlo otra vez. ¿Cuál es el número de tu Visa?
EDITH:	¿Mi Visa? ¿Por qué lo quieres?
MARÍA PATRICIA:	Porque mientras hablábamos, fui al sitio web de tu compañía de perfume, llené el formulario y pedí tu perfume. Lo hice todo menos pagarlo. Ahora… ¡tu tarjeta de crédito, por favor!

Examen: Para comenzar   Nombre_____

I. A escuchar

A. Conversaciones. Listen to the following spoken lines and select the most logical response.

1.   a. viernes

      b. lunes

      c. jueves

2.   a. Igualmente.

      b. Gracias.

      c. Adiós.

3.   a. Hasta mañana.

      b. No, lo siento.

      c. Es el ocho de noviembre.

4.   a. doce

      b. diez y ocho

      c. treinta y uno

5.   a. Muy bien.

      b. Nosotros

      c. Adiós.

B. ¿Cuál es? Match the items you hear with a logical choice from the items below.

a.   Hola.

b.   El dos de diciembre.

c. Regular.

d. De nada.

e. Con permiso.

A practicar

II. Vocabulario

A. A escoger. Choose the correct answer to respond to each one of the following questions.

1. Which subject pronoun would you use when talking about two clients?

   a. Ud.

   b. Uds.

   c. ellos

2. Which subject pronoun would you use when talking to two executives?

   a. Ud.

   b. Uds.

   c. ellos

3. Which subject pronoun would you use when talking about yourself and a friend?

   a. yo

   b. ella

   c. nosotros/as

4. Which of the following describes the word "tú"?

   a. formal

   b. informal

   c. plural

5. If you just bumped into a colleague behind the desk, what would you say?

    a. Gracias.

    b. Con permiso.

    c. Perdón.

B. A conversar. Choose the correct answer to each one of the following questions.

1. ¿Cómo saludamos a un amigo a las tres de la tarde?

    a. Buenos días.

    b. Buenas tardes.

    c. Buenas noches.

2. ¿Cómo está Ud.?

    a. Muy bien.

    b. Hasta luego.

    c. Igualmente.

3. ¿Cuál es la fecha de hoy?

    a. Son las diez.

    b. No hay clase los martes.

    c. Es el veinte de enero.

4. ¿Cuántos días hay en una semana?

    a. treinta

    b. siete

    c. los cognados

5. Si mañana es lunes, ¿qué día es hoy?

    a. Es lunes.

b. Es domingo.

c. Es miércoles.

C. A contestar. Answer the following questions in Spanish.

1. ¿Cómo se llama Ud.?

   _____

2. ¿Cómo está Ud.?

   _____

3. ¿Cuál es la fecha de hoy?

   _____

4. ¿Qué día es hoy?

   _____

5. ¿Cuántos son quince y seis?

   _____

III. A leer

Examen dental para niños y adultos
Incluye:
- Examen oral completo
- Todos los rayos X necesarios
- Diagnóstico y consulta individual

$10 (tarifa normal $50)
 Nuevos pacientes solamente
Horario: De lunes a viernes de las 8 a las 5
Oferta vence el 31 de agosto de 2004

A. A comprender. Read the advertisement and then decide if these statements are **Cierto** or **Falso.**

1. _____ El examen dental es para adultos y niños.

2. _____ El costo incluye los rayos X.

3. _____ La oferta es para pacientes nuevos solamente.

4. _____ La oficina está abierta los domingos.

5. _____ Es posible ver al dentista a las siete de la tarde.

B. A escribir. Write an ad for a business, listing days and hours that the office is open, as well as what products/services are available.

_____

_____

_____

_____

_____

_____

Script for A escuchar A

1. Hoy es miércoles. ¿Qué día es mañana?

2. Mucho gusto.

3. ¿Hay citas los sábados?

4. ¿Cuántos son catorce y cuatro?

5. Buenas noches.

Script for A escuchar B

6. Perdón.

7. Gracias.

8. Buenos días.

9. ¿Cuál es la fecha de hoy?

10. ¿Cómo está Ud.?

I. A escuchar

A. Conversaciones. Listen to the following questions and select the most logical answer.

1.   a. Son las nueve.

      b. A las once.

      c. 842-0906.

2.   a. Es la una.

      b. A las tres.

      c. 459 Calle Real.

3.   a. El señor Peralta.

      b. En su oficina.

      c. La señora Gómez.

4.   a. Sí, por favor, con su permiso para trabajar.

      b. No, no tengo seguro.

      c. A sus órdenes.

B. La solicitud de empleo. Complete the blanks on the job application.

Nombre _____

Edad _____ Estado civil _____

Número de Seguro Social _____

Teléfono particular _____

Dirección _____

_____

A practicar

II. **Vocabulario**

A. A completar. Complete the following form with your personal information.

Apellido(s) _____	Nombre _____	Sexo _____
Edad _____ Fecha de nacimiento _____	Estado civil _____	
Número de Seguro Social _____	Email _____	
Dirección _____	Teléfono particular _____	
_____	Teléfono del trabajo _____	

B. A trabajar. Identify the job title described here.

1. un maestro de niños _____

2. un instructor para atletas _____

3. un jefe de una empresa o nación _____

4. un/a asistente administrativo/a _____

5. una persona que contesta el teléfono y "recibe" a los clientes _____

C. A nombrar. Identify these things found in an office.

1. una mesa y ocho _____

2. la parte de la computadora que produce los documentos en papel _____

3. un "mapa" visual de la organización del personal de la compañía

   _____

4. un formulario de información personal de un candidato para un empleo

   _____

III. Gramática

A. En la oficina. Fill in the correct form of the verb **ser** in the present tense.

En la oficina de la Directora de Recursos Humanos, yo 1._____

recepcionista y contesto las llamadas telefónicas. Ella 2._____ una jefa

excelente. Ustedes 3._____ recepcionistas y trabajan mucho. Tú, Elenita,

4._____ mi colega (*co-worker*) favorita.

B. Los candidatos. Write the correct form of the indicated adjective.

La primera candidata es 1._____ (extrovertido) y tiene mucha experiencia. El

otro candidato es 2._____ (serio). Los dos candidatos son

3._____ (inteligente) y 4._____ (trabajador). La decisión no es

5._____. (fácil)

C. En la oficina. Fill in the correct form of the definite article.

En 1._____ oficina usamos 2._____ teléfono, 3._____ computadoras y 4._____

publicaciones financieras para analizar 5._____ problemas.

D. Preguntas. Write the appropriate question word.

1. ¿_____ es la entrevista?   Es el 12 de mayo.

2. ¿_____ está la compañía?   En Santa Bárbara.

3. ¿_____ es el director?   El Sr. Peralta.

4. ¿_____ es necesario llamar?   Porque el director quiere verificar la

hora.

IV. A leer

Solicitamos empleados bilingües.

Somos una empresa multi-nacional con oficinas en más de veinte ciudades exóticas. Si usted es bilingüe (español/inglés), honesto y trabajador y desea un futuro con promociones rápidas, llame al número (800) 555-9900 para hablar con uno de nuestros agentes. Ofrecemos sueldos y prestaciones excelentes a los candidatos seleccionados.

No se necesita experiencia.

A. A comprender. Read the advertisement and then decide if these statements are **Cierto** or **Falso.**

1. _____ Solicitan empleados que hablen francés.

2. _____ Hay oficinas en más de 30 ciudades exóticas.

3. _____ Los candidatos no necesitan experiencia.

4. _____ Los candidatos seleccionados reciben buenos sueldos y prestaciones.

5. _____ Es necesario tener un currículum para hablar con un agente.

B. A escribir. Write one or two sentences in Spanish explaining this ad in your own words.

_____

_____

_____

_____

_____

Script for A escuchar A

1. ¿Qué hora es?

2. ¿A qué hora es su cita?

3. ¿Dónde está el director?

4. ¿Necesita Ud. mi número de seguro social?

Script for A escuchar B

Me llamo Roberto Gómez. Tengo 28 años. Soy soltero. Mi número de seguro social es

516-07-2314. El teléfono de mi casa es 315-0611. Mi dirección es número 9 Avenida

Ventura en Las Vegas, Nevada.

I. A escuchar

A. Conversaciones. Listen to the following activities and select the problem they are meant to resolve.

a. tengo frío   b. tengo calor   c. tengo hambre   d. tengo sueño   e. tengo sed

1._____

2._____

3._____

4._____

5._____

B. A contestar. Answer the following questions in Spanish with complete sentences.

    1. _____

    2. _____

    3. _____

A practicar

II. Vocabulario

    A. A completar. Fill in the blanks with the word/s that best answer/s the following descriptions. For some, there may be more than one possibility.

    1. Los beneficios que las compañías ofrecen a sus empleados son

    _____.

    2. Una persona que ayuda a las familias a encontrar la casa ideal y facilita la compra

    es un _____.

3. Si quiero comprar una casa voy al banco por un préstamo especial que se llama

una _____.

4. Si voy al dentista no pago nada porque tengo un _____.

5. Si voy al médico normalmente tengo un _____ de $5.00.

B. Acciones. Tell what activities you would do in the following places, situations or

with the following things. Use the **yo** form of the verb.

1. En McDonald's _____.

2. Con mi teléfono, _____.

3. Yo _____ agua.

4. Cuando cambio de una casa o apartamento a otro, _____.

5. Yo _____ la televisión.

III. Gramática

A. El verbo *estar* y los adjetivos. Write the correct form of the verb **estar** in the

present tense along with the appropriate form of the indicated adjective.

Mi jefe y yo 1. _____ _____(preocupado) por uno de los

empleados en nuestro departamento porque él 2. _____

_____(enfermo). Su esposa 3._____ _____

(contento) porque él tiene un seguro de salud excelente y no hay problema

económico. 4. Pero todos nosotros _____ _____ (nervioso) hoy

porque esperamos las noticias del hospital. Los otros empleados del departamento,

sus amigos, 5. _____ _____ (listo) para ayudar.

B. Los verbos que terminan en -ar, -er, -ir. Write the correct form of the verb in the

present.

Un día típico en la oficina

En la sala de espera, una señorita le pregunta a la recepcionista, "¿Ustedes 1.

_____ (recibir) pagos con tarjeta de crédito?" "Claro que sí, señorita," es

la respuesta. Hay otro cliente que no 2._____ (comprender) qué

información necesita escribir en el formulario. Las recepcionistas

3._____ (ver) la lista de citas de hoy. 4. Las secretarias

_____ (buscar) los archivos que el jefe necesita. La directora 5.

_____ (preparar) los reportes de los nuevos empleados.

La operadora 6. _____ (recibir) muchas llamadas. Ella 7.

_____ (contestar) inmediatamente si es posible.

Después de otro día difícil, yo 8._____(correr) en la playa para aliviar

mi tensión y mi compañero y yo 9. _____(tomar) té de yerba buena

(mint). Él me pregunta, "¿A qué hora 10. _____(regresar) tú mañana?

C. Expresiones con *tener*. Write the correct form of the verb **tener** in the present and

an expression to logically finish each sentence.

1. Necesito un vaso de agua. Yo…

2. Marisa ve un monstruo en su dormitorio. Ella…

3. Son las 10 de la mañana. Tengo una reunión con mi jefe a las 10:15 pero hay

mucho tráfico. Yo….

4. Tengo que terminar este reporte para mañana. Ahora son las 4 de la mañana y yo…

5. Mis amigos van a la pizzería. Ellos…

D. A contestar. Answer each question in Spanish with a complete sentence.

1. ¿Está contento/a con su vida?

   _____

2. ¿Qué come Ud. por la mañana?.

   _____

3. ¿Tiene usted seguro dental?

   _____

4. ¿Tiene hambre en este momento?

   _____

5. ¿Vive en una casa o en un apartamento?

   _____

IV. A leer

Programa ¡Buen Viaje!:

Los seguros de auto para los turistas en Estados Unidos

Los seguros de autos son sumamente importantes. No intente usar un auto en Estados Unidos sin tener cobertura. Las agencias que alquilan autos siempre ofrecen seguros para daños contra impacto o colisiones y contra robo, pero normalmente las tasas en estas agencias son muy altas. Es posible comprar seguros de corto plazo en otras agencias de seguros. También hay muchas agencias de viajes, como American Express, que venden seguros automovilísticos para turistas entre los servicios que ofrecen. Y cuando usa su tarjeta de crédito para alquilar su auto, es posible que el seguro sea gratis.

Si usted necesita mapas o guías turísticas para disfrutar de su viaje, las agencias que alquilan los autos frecuentemente dan mapas y guías gratis. ¡Buen viaje!

A. A comprender. Read the brochure and then decide if these statements are **Cierto** or **Falso.**

1. _____ Este programa se llama "Buen Viaje".

2. _____ Tener seguros de auto en Estados Unidos no es importante.

3. _____ En las agencias que alquilan autos los seguros son gratis.

4. _____ Muchas veces venden seguros de auto en las agencias de viajes.

5. _____ Es posible recibir mapas y guías gratis.

B. A escribir. Write two sentences in Spanish explaining this article about car insurance for tourists.

_____

_____

_____

_____

Script for A escuchar A

1. Bebo mucho agua.

2. Necesito un suéter.

3. Como en McDonald's.

4. Necesito más aire acondicionado.

5. Una siesta, por favor.

Script for A escuchar B

1. ¿Cuáles son dos servicios importantes que hay que conectar en una casa nueva?

2. ¿Vive usted en una casa o apartamento?

3. ¿Tiene usted seguro de salud?

Examen: Lección 3   Nombre_____

I. A escuchar

A. Reservaciones. Listen to the following phone call making reservations and answer the questions.

1. ¿Cómo se llama la secretaria?

    a. Colega

    b. Adriana

    c. Roberto

2. ¿Por qué celebran el jefe y el cliente?

    a. Hay un contrato importante.

    b. Es su cumpleaños.

    c. No hay trabajo.

3. ¿Por qué es difícil reservar una mesa en un buen restaurante?

    a. No hay nadie en la ciudad.

    b. Hay varias conferencias y exposiciones en la ciudad.

    c. No hay comida.

4. Hay un restaurante con una mesa disponible para 22 personas…

    a. a las seis.

    b. a las ocho.

    c. a las once.

B. A contestar. Answer the following questions in Spanish with complete sentences.

1._____

2._____

3._____

A practicar

II. Vocabulario

A. A completar. Fill in the blanks with the word/s that best complete/s the idea. For some, there may be more than one possibility.

1. Cuando una persona viaja a otro país, necesita su _____ para demostrar su identidad y ciudadanía.

2. Hoy es el 30 de junio. Estamos preparando los reportes financieros de la actividad económica de los últimos 12 meses. Hoy termina el año _____.

3. Tengo todos los documentos importantes organizados en carpetas en orden alfabético en mi _____.

4. Mi jefe va a una _____ de productos industriales en Dallas para ver todas las innovaciones de nuestra industria.

5. Los jefes de los departamentos de nuestra empresa están preparando los _____ para el año que viene. Estas son las proyecciones de los gastos e ingresos de cada departamento.

B. Definiciones. Write the definition of each of the following words or phrases or use it in a sentence that demonstrates the meaning.

1. el pasajero

2. el equipaje

3. un avión

4. el boleto

5. los asistentes de vuelo

III. Gramática

A. En el avión. Write the present progressive form of the verb.

Nosotros 1._____ _____(esperar) al piloto de nuestro vuelo. Él

2._____ _____(hablar) con el co-piloto. Yo 3._____

_____(leer) la revista: Sky Mall. Un asistente de vuelo 4._____

_____(poner) toallas calientes (*hot towels*) en las mesitas de primera clase.

En la cabina de turistas, los asistentes de vuelo 5._____

_____(hacer) café.

B. *Ser* vs. *estar*. Provide the correct present tense form of **ser** or **estar**.

Yo 1._____ María Elena Cervantes y 2._____ de Madrid. En

este momento, 3._____ en la sala de espera de un aeropuerto internacional

con muchos otros pasajeros. 4. Nosotros _____ esperando nuestro avión que

tiene problemas mecánicos. Los agentes 5._____ simpáticos y eficientes,

pero nosotros, en este momento 6._____ cansados, nerviosos y frustrados.

Aquí viene el piloto con un anuncio. Él nos dice: "Buenas noticias, señores pasajeros, el

avión ahora 7. _____ listo para abordar. Favor de presentar su tarjeta de

embarque al agente.

C. ¿Adónde vamos? We're organizing our agenda for the day. Fill in the correct form of

ir in the present tense.

Nosotros 1._____a la oficina esta mañana, pero tú 2._____ a la

reunión con los nuevos clientes. Yo 3._____ a la agencia de viajes antes de

regresar a casa y los ejecutivos de México 4. _____ al hotel.

D. ¿Qué van a hacer? Answer each of the following questions in Spanish with a complete sentence, using **ir a + infinitive.**

1. ¿Qué va a hacer el profesor después de clase?

_____

2. En su imaginación, ¿adónde va a viajar usted?

_____

E. La rutina diaria. Provide the correct form of the verb in the present tense.

Yo 1._____(salir) para la oficina a las ocho. Primero, yo 2.

_____(hacer) café y lo 3. _____ (llevar) a

los ejecutivos. Estamos muy ocupados todo el día. Algunos ejecutivos no hablan español,

pero muchos clientes sí. El intérprete 4._____ (traducir) la

información de los clientes. Yo 5. _____ (saber) que ellos

necesitan aprender español y que toman clases cada semana. Mientras las recepcionistas

6._____ (poner) los papeles en el archivo, ellas 7.

_____(oír) música suave. Así termina otro día.

IV. A leer

Restaurante La Fuente

Comida Auténtica de Sonora, México

La comida exquisita de Sonora ahora está aquí en Washington.

Preparamos todos nuestros platos de carnes, pescados y quesos a la parrilla (*on a grill*).

Hacemos todas las tortillas y las salsas frescas cada día en nuestra cocina.

Nuestros platos son los típicos de México.

Hay servicio completo de bar.

Hay menú de niños.

Escuche su música favorita el sábado y domingo con el famoso Mariachi La Fuente. Abierto los siete días a la semana desde las once de la mañana hasta las once de la noche.

Para su reservación, llame al (555) 907-3636

Aceptamos todas las tarjetas de crédito.

A. Cierto o falso. Read the above advertisement and then decide if each of these statements is **Cierto (C)** or **Falso (F).** If the statement is false, rewrite it to make it true.

_____1. La Fuente tiene comida española.

_____2. No está abierto los sábados ni domingos.

_____3. Hay música todos los días.

_____4. No aceptan Visa ni Mastercard.

_____5. No tienen vino ni cerveza.

B. A escribir. Think about your favorite restaurant and write an ad for it using the model above. If you don't know the details, make them up!

_____

_____

_____

_____

Script for A escuchar A

Soy Adriana, una secretaria en una empresa muy famosa. Esta noche mi jefe y un cliente importante van a celebrar un contrato muy importante. Ellos y 20 colegas quieren comer en un restaurante elegante con buena música latina para la fiesta. Estoy llamando a varios restaurantes para hacer reservaciones. El problema es que ahora hay varias conferencias y exposiciones aquí en esta ciudad y los restaurantes no tienen espacio. Bueno. Aquí hay un restaurante con una mesa disponible para 22 personas—¡a las once de la noche!

Script for A escuchar B

1. ¿Cuál es su restaurante favorito?

2. ¿Necesita hacer reservaciones?

3. ¿Dónde van Uds. a comer esta noche?

I. A escuchar

A. Conversaciones. Listen to the following 2 dialogues and indicate which one is better customer service (**mejor**), and which one is worse (**peor**).

1. _____

2. _____

B. A contestar. Answer the questions you hear with complete sentences in Spanish.

1._____

2._____

3._____

A practicar

II. Vocabulario

A completar. Fill in the blanks with the letter of the word that best fits the descriptions given in the following sentences.

a. comprar   b. garantizar   c. flete   d. ¡trato hecho!   e. negociar   f. mayorista

g. minorista   h. vender   i. a plazos   j. al contado   k. reembolso   l. vendedor

1. ___ un empleado que explica los beneficios de los productos al cliente

2. ___ una tienda que compra de las fábricas y vende al público

3. ___ el acto de aceptar dinero por un producto

4. ___ la frase que indica que dos personas aceptan los términos de un contrato

5. ___ comprar una cosa con un depósito y pagos mensuales

6. ___ comprar una cosa con la cantidad total del dinero inmediatamente

7. ___ el costo del transporte y entrega de los productos

8. ___ la promesa de una compañía de reemplazar un producto defectuoso

9. ___ el dinero que recibe un cliente cuando devuelve (*returns*) un producto

10. ___ el distribuidor de productos a las tiendas minoristas

III. Gramática

A. ¿De quién es? Provide the correct possessive adjective to match the person/s indicated in the sentence.

1. Es el coche de **Ángela**. Es _____ coche.

2. **Nosotros** tenemos un negocio mayorista. _____ negocio es pequeño.

3. **Mi mecánico** garantiza el trabajo. _____ garantía está vigente por noventa días.

4. **Yo** tengo dos hijos. _____ hijos son vendedores.

5. **Los señores** piden un reembolso. _____ reembolso no incluye el flete.

6. Es la limusina de **unas celebridades**. Es _____ limusina.

B. Los verbos irregulares. Provide the correct form of the verb in the present tense as you complete this conversation between two customers and a sales person.

1. VENDEDOR: ¿_____ (poder-yo) ayudarlos, señores?

2. CLIENTES: Nosotros _____ (querer) devolver este radio.

3. VENDEDOR: Claro. Está bien. ¿ _____ (tener) ustedes el recibo?

4. CLIENTES: _____ (pensar-yo) que está en la bolsa. Aquí está.

5. VENDEDOR: ¿ _____ (preferir) ustedes recibir crédito o un reembolso?

6. CLIENTES: _____ (preferir-nosotros) un reembolso, por favor.

C. Los comparativos. Some of you are discussing your favorite stores during a lunch-time break. Make the appropriate comparisons of *more than, less than* or *the same as*, as indicated.

1. El Almacén Mayo es moderno. El Almacén Centavo no es moderno.

2. El Almacén Mayo tiene 3 pisos. El Almacén Centavo tiene 5 pisos.

3. Hay 50 vendedores en el Almacén Mayo. Hay 50 vendedores en el Almacén Centavo.

4. El Almacén Mayo da muchos descuentos. El Almacén Centavo da muchos descuentos

también.

5. El Almacén Mayo es bueno. El Almacén Centavo es excelente.

IV. A leer

Clientela contenta… aumento de ventas

La transformación de atención al cliente en oro…

Con un cliente contento y satisfecho al terminar una transacción con un representante de servicio, su compañía tiene:

- un cliente que probablemente vuelve para comprar más….Ventas repetidas
- un cliente que probablemente va a comunicar su satisfacción a sus amigos… **Ventas nuevas**
- unos empleados también contentos y listos para vender… **Ventas internas…**
- **Más clientes, Más ventas, Más satisfacción…Más dinero.**

Si usted quiere que su compañía tenga más ventas repetidas, más ventas nuevas y más ventas internas, necesita a nuestros expertos de **Profe Profits.** Nuestros "profesores de profesionales" ofrecen productos, servicios y clases para mejorar la comunicación con los clientes. Nos especializamos en reducir el estrés para el vendedor y el cliente y a la vez aumentar las ventas para su organización.
Llámenos hoy mismo para organizar su clase y mañana habrá
más ventas, más ventas, más ventas…

Profe Profits es una división de **Telefortuna.** Se habla español e inglés.

A. Cierto o falso. Read the advertisement and then decide if each of these statements is **Cierto (C)** or **Falso (F)** according to the claims made.

1. _____ Más ventas son el resultado de la satisfacción del cliente al terminar una transacción.

2. _____ El lema *(motto)* de Profe Profits es: "Más estrés, más fortuna".

3. _____ Profe Profits es una compañía que da clases en técnicas para resolver problemas y reducir las ventas.

4. _____ Profe Profits ofrece clases en francés, inglés y ruso.

5. _____ TeleFortuna es una división de Profe Profits.

B. A escribir. Write a brief summary (three to five lines) in your own words of what this ad is about.

_____

_____

_____

_____

_____

_____

_____

Script for A escuchar A

1. REPRESENTANTE: Me llamo Ricardo. ¿Cuál es su problema? Un momento, tengo

otra llamada. ¿Puede usted esperar un momento? Gracias.

CLIENTE: Pues…

(momentos después)

REPRESENTANTE: Su problema por favor.

2. REPRESENTANTE: Buenas tardes, bienvenido a TeleFortuna. Me llamo José. ¿En

qué puedo servirle?

CLIENTE: Tengo un producto nuevo de ustedes que no funciona. Estoy furioso. Con el

dinero que pagué y las horas que tengo invertidas…Quiero un reembolso.

REPRESENTANTE: Siento mucho que tenga problemas. A ver si puedo ayudar.

Primero, ¿está bien conectado a la electricidad?

CLIENTE: ¿Electricidad? No, no lo conecté. Un momento. Sí, ¡ahora funciona! Soy

idiota. Perdone usted…

REPRESENTANTE: No se preocupe. Es un problema común. Si me necesita para otra

cosa me llamo José.

Script for A escuchar B

1. ¿Qué piensa usted hacer después de esta clase?

2. ¿Prefieren ustedes comprar de minoristas o mayoristas? ¿Por qué?

3. ¿Por qué es importante la buena atención al cliente?

Nombre_____

I. A escuchar

A. Compras por teléfono. Listen to the following conversation between a customer and a customer service representative and answer the following questions.

1. ¿Qué busca el cliente?

    a. información sobre computadoras

    b. información sobre lavadoras

    c. el número de teléfono del operador

2. ¿Por qué necesita esperar el cliente?

    a. El operador tiene que comer.

    b. El operador tiene que hablar con su amigo.

    c. El operador tiene una computadora lenta.

3. ¿Cuál es el número del catálogo que tiene el cliente?

    a. dos mil

    b. A382

    c. 38

4. ¿Por qué no compra la computadora el cliente?

    a. Porque las computadoras de esta compañía no funcionan bien.

    b. Porque necesita otro catálogo.

    c. Porque no quiere hablar con la supervisora.

B. A contestar. Answer the following questions in Spanish with complete sentences.

1._____

2._____

3._____

4._____

A practicar

II. Vocabulario

A. Acciones. Fill in the blanks with the letter of the word that best completes the idea.

     a. cocinar b. ahorrar c. limpiar d. terminar e. vender

  1. ___ pagar menos dinero a causa de un descuento o liquidación

  2. ___ aceptar dinero a cambio de un producto

  3. ___ completar una tarea o trabajo

  4. ___ preparar comida

  5. ___ lavar

B. La tecnología. Identify these descriptions of computer parts and components with the appropriate word in Spanish.

1. El _____ es la parte donde veo la información que está en mi computadora.

2. El _____ tiene los botones que toco para escribir los documentos que aparecen en el monitor.

3. Para abrir un programa, muevo el _____ y hago clic.

4. El _____ usa una línea telefónica para conectar mi computadora con Internet.

5. Dentro de la computadora, el _____ _____ guarda todos los programas de mi computadora y toda la información que escribo.

III. Gramática

A. El servicio al cliente. Form commands for the following verbs in the **usted** form, telling your client what to do—he's already nervous about working with technology!

Señor Cruz, todo va a salir bien. Primero, 1. _____ (abrir) las

cajas con las computadoras y 2. _____ (sacar) los componentes.

Ahora, 3. _____ (buscar) los números de identificación en el CPU. 4.

_____ (escribir) los números en la tarjeta de registro antes de

conectar la computadora. 5. _____ (poner) Ud. la tarjeta en un lugar

seguro hasta más tarde. 6. _____ (conectar) los cables del mismo

color. 7. Después de prender la computadora, _____ (leer) las

instrucciones en la pantalla. 8. _____ (disfrutar) de su nueva

computadora.

B. Mandatos para su familia. Now, use commands in the **ustedes** form to tell his

children what to do or not to do with the computer.

1. Niños, no _____ (tocar) la computadora con las manos sucias.

2. No _____ (comer) ni 3. _____ (beber) cerca de

la computadora.

4. No _____ (pelear).

5. No _____ (buscar) sitios para adultos en la Web.

C. Conteste. Mr. Cruz' wife has some questions for you. Use the **usted** command to

answer them.

1. ¿Pongo el disquete aquí?

Sí, señora, _____ el disquete aquí.

2. ¿Escribo e-mails con este programa?

Sí, señora, _____ su e-mail con este programa.

3. ¿Compro la garantía ampliada?

Sí, señora, _____ la garantía ampliada.

4. ¿Pido ayuda al técnico?

Sí, señora, _____ ayuda al técnico.

5. ¿Hago clic aquí?

Sí, señora, _____ clic aquí.

D. Afirmativo⇒negativo. A coworker always disagrees with you, even if you're right.

Change these sentences to the negative, anticipating what she'll say in advance.

1. Alguien está en la sala de espera.

2. La señora Limón siempre pide más ayuda.

3. Veo algo serio en el disco duro.

4. Los operadores también pueden ayudar.

5. El técnico va a hacer algunas pruebas a la computadora.

IV. A leer

Cómo escoger a un proveedor de electricidad

Si usted está listo para buscar un nuevo proveedor de electricidad, simplemente siga las siguientes instrucciones.
Llame o haga clic—llame gratis al 1 866-797-4839, o visite www.poderdeescoger.org para solicitar una lista de los proveedores de electricidad.

Compare—Póngase en contacto con uno o más de los proveedores de electricidad que ofrecen servicio en su área para obtener la etiqueta de información sobre electricidad, que le ayudará a comparar las ofertas.

Escoja—Después de comparar las ofertas, tome una decisión informada, según sus necesidades. Usted no necesita ponerse en contacto con su proveedor actual para informarle de su selección.

* * *

Un mensaje importante de la Comisión de Servicios Públicos de Texas.

A. Cierto o falso. Read the brochure on choosing a supplier of electricity and then decide if each of these statements is **Cierto (C)** or **Falso (F).**

1. _____ Los residentes de Texas ahora tienen la oportunidad de seleccionar su compañía de electricidad.

2. _____ Es posible informarse por Internet.

3. _____ Es fácil comparar los costos de las diferentes compañías—solamente una llamada.

4. _____ Es importante ponerse en contacto con la compañía actual.

5. _____ Es un proceso muy complicado para el consumidor.

B. A escribir. Prepare a four-point summary of how someone in Texas may choose his or her power company.

_____

_____

_____

_____

_____

_____

Script for A escuchar A

CLIENTE: Estoy leyendo su nuevo catálogo y veo que ustedes tienen buenas computadoras con descuentos del 60%. Quiero más información, por favor.

OPERADOR: Espere un momento, por favor. Mi computadora está lenta en este momento. Ahora. Dígame, por favor el número del catálogo.

CLIENTE: Es el A382. Quiero información de la computadora en la página 23.

OPERADOR: Otro momento, por favor. No encuentro el catálogo en mi computadora. ¿Es el catálogo A382?

CLIENTE: Sí. Es el número de mi catálogo. ¿Ahora lo tiene usted?

OPERADOR: No. Mi computadora no funciona bien. Espere y llamo a mi supervisor para la información que usted quiere.

CLIENTE: No. Mejor no. Ya tengo exactamente la información que necesito. Las computadoras de ustedes tienen muy buen precio. Pero es obvio que no funcionan. Adiós.

Script for A escuchar B

1. ¿Compra usted algunos productos por medio de catálogos o Internet?

2. ¿Dónde nota usted la influencia latina en nuestra cultura?

3. Para usted, ¿es interesante estudiar las campañas de publicidad?

4. ¿Normalmente compra usted garantías ampliadas con los productos electrónicos?

Examen final: Lecciones PC-5   Nombre_____

I. A escuchar

A. **¿Necesita ayuda?** Listen to the following descriptions of properties for rent/sale, then select the appropriate one for each tenant/buyer from the group given.

1.____   a. Un hombre joven, soltero, que viaja mucho

2. ____   b. Una señora vieja, sola, con poco dinero

3. ____   c. Una familia con tres hijos de 4, 6 y 8 años

4. ____   d. Un matrimonio sin hijos; los dos son ejecutivos que dan fiestas

                elegantes para sus colegas

5. ____   e. Una señorita, maestra, a quien le gusta cocinar y trabajar en el jardín

B. **La tarjeta garantizada Visa.** Listen to the passage and then decide if these statements are **Cierto** or **Falso**. If the statement is **Cierto**, mark "A". If it is **Falso**, mark "B".

6. Se acepta esta tarjeta en más de 19 millones de negocios.

7. La tarjeta garantizada Visa sólo se usa en Estados Unidos.

8. Se puede pagar automáticamente.

9. El comprador acepta responsabilidad por todas las compras.

10. Es necesario hablar con un representante para solicitar la tarjeta.

II. A leer

A. Movimercado

Programa de servicio a domicilio—ofreciéndole siempre más servicio, más calidad, más comodidad, más confianza, más seguridad.

MOVIMERCADO ofrece mucho más que buenos precios; ahora hacemos sus compras y se las llevamos a su casa--¡una solución perfecta para usted, que ya está muy ocupado!

Elija entre las siguientes opciones:
a) Pedidos por teléfono: Surtimos su pedido completo desde la comodidad de su hogar, asegurando al 100% la calidad de todos nuestros productos. Tiempo de entrega: 3 horas. Incluso puede solicitar una hora exacta de entrega. Se aplica una mínima cuota (fee) por entrega, dependiendo de la zona.

b) Pedidos urgentes: Un máximo de 10 artículos.
¡Reciba su pedido en 45 minutos!

Formas de pago:
• Efectivo
• Tarjetas de crédito
• Cheques

Horarios: De lunes a domingo de 8:00 a 20:00 incluyendo días festivos
Llame a **MOVIMERCADO**: 1 800 250.3664 o vía Internet: www.movimercado.net

---

Cierto o falso. Read the above passage and then decide if each of these statements is

Cierto o Falso. If the statement is **Cierto**, mark "A". If it is **Falso**, mark "B".

11.   Movimercado le entrega sus productos directamente en su casa.

12.   El tiempo de entrega para un pedido urgente es de tres horas.

13.   Hay dos maneras de hacer un pedido.

14.   Se puede pagar con tarjeta de crédito solamente.

15.   Movimercado está cerrado los días festivos.

B. ¿Hay un problema?

**SuAlmacén le ofrece servicios que le permiten
hacer devoluciones y cambios de formá rapida y sencilla.**

Política de devoluciones y cambios

Para cualquier devolución o cambio debe presentarse un recibo de compra
fechado durante los 90 días anteriores a la devolución.
Todo artículo para devolución o cambio debe entregarse nuevo, sin usar y
con todos sus materiales de empaque y accesorios. Algunos artículos no
pueden devolverse si están abiertos, como discos de música, películas, juegos
de vídeo, software y artículos coleccionables. Algunos artículos están sujetos a
un cargo del 15% por manejo de inventario, entre ellos están las cámaras de
vídeo, las cámaras digitales, los aparatos DVD portátiles y otros artículos
electrónicos portátiles.

¿No encuentra su recibo?

SuAlmacén puede buscar en su sistema las compras que usted hizo en los
últimos 90 días.
Si va a comprar un regalo (gift), podemos darle un recibo de regalo.

En caso de devolución o cambio después de los 90 días, le ofrecemos la
garantía del fabricante y asistencia con las reparaciones si llama al
1 800 303.0307 o por Internet: **www.sualmacen.com**

A escoger. Choose the correct answer to complete the following sentences.

16.   Las devoluciones en SuAlmacén son _____.

   a.   imposibles y abiertas

   b.   nuevas y anteriores

   c.   rápidas y sencillas

17. Es necesario tener _____.

   a.   un recibo

   b.   una película

   c.   un inventario

18. Hay un cargo del 15% por _____.

   a.   juegos de vídeo

   b.   manejo de inventario

   c.   materiales de empaque

19. No pueden devolverse _____.

   a.   discos de música

   b.   cámaras digitales

   c.   aparatos DVD portátiles

20. Para las compras de hace más de 90 días, SuAlmacén ofrece _____.

   a.   recibo de regalo

   b.   accesorios

   c.   garantía del fabricante

A practicar

III. Vocabulario

A escoger. Choose the correct answer to complete the following sentences.

21. ¿Cómo saludamos a un amigo a las diez de la mañana?

    a. Buenos días.

    b. Hasta mañana.

    c. Buenas noches.

22. Hoy es lunes. ¿Qué día es mañana?

    a. jueves

    b. viernes

    c. martes

23. El primer mes del año es _____.

    a. octubre

    b. enero

    c. diciembre

24. Ocho y catorce son _____.

    a. veintidós

    b. diecinueve

    c. treinta

25. ¿Cómo está Ud.?

    a. Muy bien.

    b. Hasta luego.

    c. Perdón.

26. ¿Qué hora es?

    a. A las once.

    b. Son las nueve.

    c. El siete de junio.

27. ¿Cuál es su dirección?

    a. 564-77-8192

    b. (347) 961-0905

    c. 67 Calle Real, Los Gatos CA 95133

28. ¿Cuál es su apellido?

    a. soltera

    b. Margarita

    c. Ilisástigui

29. Mi seguro dental y mi seguro de salud son dos de mis _____.

    a. vacaciones

    b. prestaciones

    c. solicitudes

30. ¿Cómo se llama el préstamo especial para comprar una casa?

    a. la hipoteca

    b. el gasto

    c. el hipódromo

Emparejar. You need to explain some concepts to a client who needs insurance. Match the following words in **Columna A** to the most logical description in **Columna B.**

Columna A	Columna B
31. la prima	a. la persona que tiene seguro
32. el riesgo	b. el cálculo de la cantidad de dinero que cuesta algo
33. la cotización	c. el dinero que una persona paga por los seguros
34. el asegurado	d. los problemas o peligros posibles

Cierto o falso. You have a client that is full of misinformation. Read the following statements that she makes and declare whether each one is **Cierto** (A) or **Falso** (B).

35. La hipoteca es un préstamo para comprar un automóvil.

36. Mi agente de bienes raíces me ayuda con la compra de los seguros.

37. Me mudo cuando cambio de una casa a otra.

38. El copago es para el seguro de salud.

39. Si tengo sed, necesito dormir.

A escoger. Choose the correct answer to complete the following sentences.

40. Para tener calefacción en la casa necesito_____.

    a. el gas o la electricidad

    b. un refrigerador

    c. un teléfono

41. Los socios tienen ganas de almorzar.

    a. Tienen calor.

    b. Tienen sueño.

    c. Tienen hambre.

42. La acción de transmitir información por medio de pluma y papel: _____.

a. beber

b. escribir

c. ver

43. Muchas industrias presentan sus nuevos productos al mercado durante _____

anual de la industria.

   a. el presupuesto

   b. la carpeta

   c. la exposición

44. Otra palabra para exposición es _____.

   a. escándalo

   b. feria

   c. café

Sí o no. An inexperienced traveler has several questions for you before leaving for the

airport. Answer the questions with **Sí** (A) or **No** (B).

45. ¿Es necesario pasar por el control de seguridad?

46. ¿Me permiten tener 5 maletas dentro del avión?

47. ¿Es importante abrocharse el cinturón de seguridad?

48. Al llegar a mi destino, ¿tengo que facturar el equipaje?

A escoger. Select the correct answer for our traveler.

49. En el hotel, la persona que lleva mis maletas a la habitación es:

   a. el mesero

   b. el asistente de vuelo

   c. el botones

50. Nuestra habitación está en el piso 15. Debemos subir en el _____.

    a. automóvil

    b. camión

    c. ascensor

Emparejar. You need to explain some concepts to a foreign guest. Match the following

words in **Columna A** to the most logical description in **Columna B.**

<u>Columna A</u>	<u>Columna B</u>
51. la propina	a. donde los huéspedes mandan la ropa sucia
52. el mesero	b. la persona que sirve la comida
53. el desayuno	c. cereal, pan tostado, huevos, leche, café...
54. la lavandería	d. la parte del hotel donde los huéspedes reciben servicios personales, como masajes
55. el spa	e. el dinero que usted paga para agradecer el buen servicio

Cierto o falso. Your same misinformed client is back. Read the following statements that

she makes and declare whether each one is **Cierto** (A) or **Falso** (B).

56. _____ La garantía es para protegerme contra productos o labor defectuosos.

57. _____ Una empresa que vende al público es una mayorista.

58. _____ El calzado es ropa interior.

59. _____ Si yo quiero comprar algo y pagarlo poco a poco cada mes, compro a plazos.

60. _____ La ciencia de la mercadotecnia se basa, en gran parte, en las estadísticas.

IV. Gramática

A escoger. Choose the correct answer to complete the following sentences.

61. ¿A qué hora es su cita con el director?

    a. Son las dos.

b. A las tres.

c. El martes.

62. Yo _____ secretaria.

   a. eres

   b. soy

   c. es

63. _____ ejecutivas son muy trabajadoras.

   a. Los

   b. La

   c. Las

64. El jefe recomienda _____ presupuesto estricto para el departamento.

   a. un

   b. una

   c. la

65. La recepcionista es _____.

   a. alto

   b. simpática

   c. jóvenes

66. ¿Quién es el Director de Recursos Humanos?

   a. En la oficina.

   b. Es muy inteligente.

   c. El señor muy alto.

67. El dinero es _____.

a. rojo

b. roja

c. verde

68. Tú _____ español.

    a. hablo

    b. hablas

    c. hablamos

69. Él y yo no _____ el informe.

    a. comprenden

    b. comprendes

    c. comprendemos

70. Después de trabajar todo el día, yo _____ sueño.

    a. estoy

    b. tengo

    c. soy

Una historia. You and your co-worker opened up the store this morning. Choose the letter of the verb that best completes the exciting story.

a. va a llamar   b. está   c. sabe   d. estoy hablando   e. ponemos

Mi amiga y yo abrimos la tienda todos los días. Esta mañana yo 71._____ con el jefe por teléfono. Mi amiga acaba de empezar a trabajar aquí y no 72._____ dónde poner las cosas. Ella y yo las 73._____ en su sitio después de terminar la llamada. El jefe dice que 74._____ más tarde para verificar que todo va bien. Él 75._____ en el aeropuerto porque va a una exposición.

La historia sigue. Your boss calls back to see how things are going and you're not happy with your friend's performance. Choose the letter of the comparison that best completes the sad story.

a. tantas   b. mejor   c. más   d. menos   e. tanto como

Ay, señor, estoy preocupada. Rosario no trabaja 76. _____ yo. Yo hago

77._____ que ella. Ella no tiene 78._____ responsabilidades como yo y

trabaja 79. _____ horas que yo. Yo quiero más dinero porque soy 80._____

que ella.

A escoger. Choose the correct answer to complete the following sentences.

81. El micrófono no sirve y yo no _____ bien.

    a. oigo

    b. produzco

    c. salgo

82. Los clientes no _____ al vendedor muy bien y por eso no tienen mucha

confianza.

    a. conocen

    b. conducen

    c. saben

83. Juan, debes a llamar a _____ secretaria porque ella tiene la información.

    a. mis

    b. tu

    c. nuestro

84. ¿De quién es el automóvil? ¿Del Sr. Ríos?

a. Sí, es de él.

b. Sí, es de ella.

c. Sí, es de Ud.

85. Una buena garantía con la compra de un auto es _____.

    a. importantísima

    b. peligrosísimo

    c. mayor

86. Hay tres clientes aquí. El joven está enojado, la señora está más enojada y el señor es

_____.

    a. la más enojada

    b. enojadísimas

    c. el más enojado

87. Señora, _____ aquí, por favor.

    a. venga

    b. viene

    c. vengo

88. El cliente tiene sed.

    a. Búsquele un refresco.

    b. Ponga la mesa, por favor.

    c. Dígale adiós.

89. Los señores que compran la computadora están nerviosos.

    a. No se preocupen.

    b. Paguen en la caja.

c. Vayan al cine.

90. Él tiene una computadora defectuosa.

a. No le diga la verdad.

b. Investigue el problema.

c. No se vaya.

Emparejar. Match the following words in **Columna A** to the most logical sentence in **Columna B.**

Columna A	Columna B
91. puedo	a. El técnico_____ una computadora menos complicada.
92. dicen	b. Nosotros _____ más información.
93. pedimos	c. Los técnicos _____ la verdad—necesita un monitor nuevo.
94. entienden	d. A veces los clientes no _____ las instrucciones bien.
95. recomienda	e. Yo no _____ instalar mi computadora. ¡Es muy difícil!

Problemas económicos. The whole company is gathered in the cafeteria to hear the news about the company's future. Select the appropriate word to complete each sentence.

a. nadie   b. alguien   c. también   d. algunos   e. ninguna

Todos los empleados están aquí. 96._____ miembros del sindicato están sentados en una mesa. No habla 97._____ porque todos están pensando en el futuro de su compañía después de los anuncios. Hay unos ejecutivos esperando en el pasillo 98._____. 99._____ habla por teléfono celular. El Presidente les dice a sus empleados, "No les voy a decir 100._____ mentira *(lie)*. Tenemos problemas graves. Pero les aseguro que por el momento todos tienen su empleo."

Script for A escuchar A

1. Casa nueva con 4 recámaras y 3 baños. Cerca de una buena escuela primaria y un parque público.

2. ¡Viva la vida de los ricos y famosos en este palacio! Piscina, cancha de tenis, sala y comedor enormes en un buen barrio

3. Casa móvil en un parque para personas mayores con buena seguridad

4. ¡Atención, cocineros! Casa pequeña con cocina fabulosa y patio con muchas flores y plantas

5. Condominio de una recámara, amueblado, moderno—con un baño

Script for A escuchar B

Tarjeta garantizada Visa

Para establecer o mejorar su crédito después de un problema, solicite hoy su Tarjeta garantizada Visa. Su tarjeta le ofrece:

- Aceptación en todo el mundo en más de 19 millones de negocios

- Su línea de crédito desde $300 a $5,000

- Beneficios como premios de viaje

- Tranquilidad y seguridad con protección de pago y pago automático

- Usted no asume ninguna responsabilidad por compras sin autorización realizadas por Internet, por teléfono o en un negocio

Nadie sabe que su tarjeta está garantizada y se usa como una tarjeta de crédito tradicional. Es un buen paso hacia el buen crédito. Visite a su representante o simplemente complete y envíe esta solicitud hoy.

I. A escuchar

A. Conversaciones. Listen to the following questions that Mr. González asks his personal banker and select the most logical answer.

1.   a. Usted puede abrir una cuenta de ahorros.

       b. Usted puede gastar más dinero en la ropa.

       c. Usted puede comprar más cosas para la casa.

2.   a. Usted puede quedarse en casa.

       b. Usted puede comprar cheques de viajero.

       c. Usted debe usar sus inversiones.

3.   a. Se venden en todos los bancos.

       b. Se vende en el café.

       c. Se venden en la Bolsa.

4.   a. Usted necesita un entrenador personal.

       b. Usted necesita un corredor de seguros.

       c. Usted necesita un contador.

5.   a. No, $5,000 es mucho dinero.

       b. No, $500 es mucho dinero.

       c. No, $50,000 es mucho dinero.

       d. No, $5,050 es mucho dinero.

B. A contestar. Answer the following questions in Spanish with complete sentences.

1. _____

2. _____

3. _____

4. _____

5. _____

A practicar

II. Vocabulario

A. A escoger. Choose the correct answer to complete the following sentences.

1. Yo quiero ahorrar dinero rápidamente. Voy a _____.

    a. dormir mucho

    b. retirar dinero

    c. sacar dinero del Cajero Automático

    d. comprar un certificado de depósito

2. Quiero mantener muy líquido mi dinero. Voy a _____.

    a. invertir en bienes raíces

    b. comprar un certificado de depósito de 36 meses

    c. comprar bonos municipales

    d. abrir una cuenta de ahorros

3. Acabo de heredar $100,000. Quiero arriesgarlo todo con la posibilidad de ganar una fortuna. Quiero invertir en _____.

    a. compañías establecidas tradicionales

    b. cuentas corrientes sin intereses

    c. compañías nuevas con mucha promesa

    d. una compañía en bancarrota por el fraude

4. "El sueldo tributable" quiere decir _____.

a. los activos

b. los pasivos

c. el respeto

d. los ingresos ajustados para el cálculo de los impuestos

5. No quiero tener tanta deuda. Tengo que _____.

    a. aumentar el uso de mis tarjetas de crédito

    b. preparar y seguir un presupuesto

    c. levantar pesas

    d. calcular los impuestos

B. Antónimos. Match each action from **Column A** with its **opposite** from **Column B**.

Columna A	Columna B
1. _____ pasivos	a. arriesgar
2. _____ proteger	b. retirar
3. _____ depositar	c. activos
4. _____ ingresos	d. gastos

III. Gramática

A. A escoger. Choose the correct answer to complete the following sentences.

1. Las cuentas corrientes _____ para mantener líquidos los fondos.

    a. usa

    b. se usa

    c. se usan

    d. usan

2. No me _____ arriesgar mi dinero.

a. gusta

b. gusto

c. gustan

d. gustas

3. Acabo de heredar mucho dinero. **No** voy a _____.

    a. invertirlo

    b. declararme en bancarrota

    c. buscar un buen corredor de inversiones

    d. preparar una merienda

4. Un ingreso personal de _____ dólares es elevado.

    a. diez

    b. dos mil

    c. dos millones de

    d. doscientos noventa

5. Su portafolio tiene _____ (6,771) acciones diversificadas

    a. cinco mil setecientos setenta y una

    b. siete mil seiscientos setenta y uno

    c. seis mil setecientos sesenta y un

    d. seis mil setecientas setenta y una

IV. A leer

Situación de fantasía. Read the following paragraph and then complete the activities.

You are the financial advisor in this situation.

María Elena acaba de decirle a usted, su banquero personal, que está deprimida porque quiere reducir su deuda y no puede. Ella tiene un nuevo coche deportivo y va de compras mucho con sus amigas. No tiene un presupuesto. Tiene varias tarjetas de crédito que han alcanzado su límite; sólo puede pagar el mínimo cada mes. Trabaja muchas horas como secretaria en una oficina grande y siempre sale a almorzar o tomar cócteles con sus compañeros de trabajo. Ella dice que normalmente no pide las comidas más caras, pero a veces cree que merece algo especial. Después del trabajo siempre está muy cansada y no quiere buscar otro trabajo de tiempo parcial. Ella necesita ayuda. Quiere cambiar su situación económica, pero no quiere cambiar su rutina ni sus costumbres (habits). Usted es su banquero y ella necesita sus consejos. Tiene que hacerle unas recomendaciones después de hacerle unas preguntas.

A. ¿Qué le gusta? Ask María Elena if she likes the following things.

MODELO: tener muchas deudas

¿Le gusta tener muchas deudas?

1. los presupuestos

2. los intereses altos en las tarjetas de crédito

3. declararse en bancarrota

4. la disciplina

5. el plan para ahorrar dinero

B. Recomendaciones. Now, as her advisor you have to make recommendations to help her to get in shape. Explain to María Elena what one does with the things or activities or problems on the list.

MODELO: el presupuesto

Se hace para vigilar y proteger el dinero.

1. los almuerzos *brown-bag* (de casa)

2. la disciplina

3. los intereses altos en las tarjetas de crédito

4. un plan para ahorrar dinero y cancelar las deudas

5. la bancarrota

Script for A escuchar A

1. ¿Qué puedo hacer para ahorrar dinero?

2. Voy a viajar a Argentina y quiero protección para mi dinero. ¿Qué puedo hacer?

3. ¿Dónde puedo comprar cheques de viajero?

4. No tengo un buen sistema en mi negocio para mis activos y pasivos. ¿Qué debo hacer?

5. Tengo más de $50,000 en mi cuenta corriente. ¿Está bien allí?

Script for A escuchar B

1. ¿Cómo puede una persona ahorrar dinero?

2. Identifique dos tipos de cuentas bancarias.

3. Si el contador le dice a un cliente que hay problemas con "la liquidez", ¿qué puede hacer?

4. Si una persona tiene dos cuentas de ahorros y cada cuenta tiene setecientos cincuenta dólares, ¿cuánto dinero tiene en total?

5. ¿Cuáles son inversiones con muchos riesgos?

I. A escuchar

A. Conversaciones. Listen to the following description of a daily routine and answer the following questions.

1. Las actividades de esta persona, ¿representan más el estereotipo de un hombre o una mujer?

2. ¿A qué hora se levanta todos los días laborales?

3. Identifique tres actividades que hace antes de despertar a su esposo/a y a sus hijos.

4. ¿Dónde trabaja esta persona?

5. ¿Qué trae cada día de la fábrica?

B. A contestar. Answer the following questions in Spanish with complete sentences.

1. _____

2. _____

3. _____

4. _____

5. _____

A practicar

II. Vocabulario

A. A completar. Fill in the blanks with the word/s that best complete/s the idea.

1. Un grupo de trabajadores que se organiza para resolver conflictos laborales forman un

_____.

2. Un negocio que forma parte de una cadena pero tiene dueños independientes y locales

es una _____.

3. Si los trabajadores tienen que ducharse y ponerse los uniformes antes del turno, van al

_____.

4. La instrucción que reciben los trabajadores en las técnicas modernas para el trabajo es

la _____.

5. Pequeños grupos de gerentes, supervisores y trabajadores que forman grupos para

resolver problemas de producción son _____.

B. Definiciones. Write the definition of each of the following words or phrases or use it

in a sentence that demonstrates the meaning.

1. la gerencia

2. el almuerzo

3. la cosecha

4. la fuerza laboral

5. las plagas

C. Sinónimos. Match each action from **Column A** with a word that means the same from

Column B.

Columna A	Columna B
1. ____ apoyarse	a. bañarse
2. ____ ducharse	b. ponerse la ropa
3. ____ regar	c. ponerse furioso
4. ____ enojarse	d. dar agua
5. ____ vestirse	e. ayudarse

III. Gramática

A. Los verbos reflexivos. Fill in the blanks with the correct present tense form of the reflexive verb.

1. Muchas veces Sandra _____ _____ (despertarse) a las cinco para limpiar la casa.

2. Primero, yo _____ _____ (levantarse) y después, _____ _____ (bañarse).

3. Nosotros _____ _____ (acostarse) a las once de la noche.

4. Muchas madres _____ _____ (preocuparse) por sus hijos cuando van a la guardería (*day care*).

5. Tú siempre _____ _____ (dormirse) durante el almuerzo.

B. ¿Reflexivo o no? Read the following sentences, decide if the verb should be used in the reflexive form or not, and fill in the blank with the appropriate form.

1. Las supervisoras _____ (lavar/lavarse) las máquinas cada semana.

2. Primero, yo _____ (vestir/vestirse) a los niños, después yo

_____.

3. Ustedes _____ (acostar/acostarse) a las once de la noche.

4. Todos los empleados _____ (lavar/lavarse) las manos antes de entrar en el centro de producción.

5. El nuevo empleado _____ (despertar/despertarse) a medianoche porque está preocupado por la estabilidad de su trabajo.

C. ¿Saber o conocer? Use the correct form of **saber** or **conocer** to complete the following sentences.

1. Yo siempre leo los artículos de la producción. Yo _____ mucho del mantenimiento de las máquinas en la fábrica.

2. Mi hermana es amiga de mi supervisor. Ella lo _____ muy bien.

3. Yo no _____ dónde está la cafetería de la fábrica.

4. Yo _____ muy bien a mi supervisora. Cuando grita (*yells*), yo

5._____ si es en serio o si está bromeando.

D. Complemento directo. Use a direct object pronoun to tell if you need the following things.

MODELO: más tiempo

No lo necesito.

1. coche nuevo _____

2. otra supervisora _____

3. otros sándwiches _____

4. un sindicato _____

5. dinero _____

E. La rutina de la mañana en su casa. Using at least five reflexive verbs, describe the morning routine at your house.

_____

_____

_____

_____

_____

IV. A leer

Los robots y el empleo

Hay muchas personas que no quieren ver la automatización de nuestras fábricas porque tienen miedo de perder su trabajo ante un empleado mecánico. Pero poco a poco los robots actuales empiezan a realizar funciones muy peligrosas para aliviar a sus contrapartes humanas.

Por ejemplo, hay una compañía que se llama ActivMedia Robotics. Ellos acaban de anunciar un robot que se especializa en la protección y la seguridad. Se llama el robot Smart Patrol—o sea, en español—Patrulla inteligente y se usa como guardia o policía automatizada que inspecciona y vigila situaciones potencialmente peligrosas. Dice el anuncio que este robot apoya al personal de seguridad y aumenta la productividad al ofrecerles más ojos, más oídos, más piernas y más brazos. También dice el anuncio: "La patrulla inteligente es el robot de seguridad del futuro. Navega la ruta de seguridad que usted indica, cambia la ruta con un clic y se detiene para observar por rutina o por otro clic. Proporciona imágenes visuales de su ruta, sonido y otra información importante." Yo tengo mucha curiosidad acerca de los robots policías. Me interesa saber si ellos a veces gritan "¡manos arriba!" cada vez que ven algo sospechoso (*suspicious*).

A. A contestar. Choose the most logical answer based on the reading.

1. Este artículo habla a favor de _____.

   a. la policía   b. los robots

   c. las fábricas   d. los peligros

2. Muchas personas tienen miedo de los robots porque _____.

   a. son sospechosos   b. la automatización pone en peligro los trabajos

c. son policías   d. son caros

3. La patrulla inteligente proporciona _____ .

   a. mucho dinero   b. acceso visual a eventos remotos

   c. empleos   d. amor

4. El robot se controla con un _____ .

   a. clic   b. grito

   c. beso   d. pistola

B. A escribir: Write a three sentence summary of the core information in the above article.

_____

_____

_____

Script for A escuchar A

Todos los días laborales me levanto a las cinco de la mañana y mientras duerme el resto de mi familia, yo limpio la casa y empiezo a preparar la cena que vamos a comer por la noche. Cada día sigo la misma rutina. Limpio, cocino y entonces leo el periódico y tomo mi café. A las siete, despierto a mi esposa y a mis hijos. Ellos se levantan, se bañan y se visten mientras yo les preparo el desayuno. A las ocho, ellos salen de la casa para sus clases o trabajo y entonces yo me baño, me afeito y me visto. Llevo un uniforme todos los días a mi empleo, así que no hay muchas decisiones que tomar en cuanto a la ropa que me pongo cada día. Trabajo en una fábrica moderna donde procesamos y empaquetamos productos agrícolas. Mi jefe es una persona muy generosa y todos los días salgo de la fábrica con una buena cantidad de las frutas o de las verduras que procesamos en ese momento. La mañana siguiente, cuando me levanto a las cinco, otra vez limpio la casa y empiezo a preparar la cena con las verduras o las frutas que traigo a la casa.

Script for A escuchar B

1. Normalmente, ¿a qué hora se levanta usted?

2. ¿Cuáles son tres actividades que forman parte de su rutina cada mañana?

3. Identifique partes de una fábrica moderna.

4. ¿Conoce usted a un chef profesional?

5. ¿Sabe cultivar la tierra?

Examen: Lección 9   Nombre _____

I. A escuchar

A. Conversaciones. Listen to the following questions and select the most logical answer.

1.   a. la aduana, las divisas, las zonas francas

        b. ensamblar, explorar, estudiar

        c. problemas económicos, camiones frigoríficos, los corredores

2.   a. su pelo, su coche y su yate

        b. las visas, los recursos humanos, los proveedores locales

        c. los camarones, las comidas, las enchiladas

3.   a. divisas

        b. el medio ambiente

        c. aranceles

4.   a. un yate

        b. un carrito de golf

        c. un semi-remolque frigorífico

5.   a. consultorio

        b. bufete

        c. visa

B. A contestar. Answer the following questions in Spanish with complete sentences.

1. _____

2. _____

3. _____

4. _____

5._____

A practicar

II. Vocabulario

A. Síntomas. Match the problems from **Column B** with the appropriate expert from

Column A.

Columna A   **Columna B**

1. __ Tengo que pasar productos por la frontera.   a. abogado

2. __ Necesito las divisas actuales de los pesos mexicanos.   b. corredor de aduana

3. __ Necesito comprar ingredientes locales.   c. banquero

4. __ Necesitamos ayuda con las visas y documentos.   d. gerente de maquila

5. __ Tenemos una fábrica en el extranjero. Necesito un   e. proveedor

    administrador.

B. Definiciones. Write the definition of each of the following words or phrases or use it

in a sentence that demonstrates the meaning.

MODELO: aranceles

Los aranceles son una clase de impuestos internacionales.

1. zona franca

2. el extranjero

3. un bufete

4. el medio ambiente

5. un banco comercial

III. Gramática

A. El subjuntivo. Use the correct form of the verb in the subjunctive.

1. El experto insiste en que ustedes _____ (pensar) más.

2. Yo recomiendo que tú _____ (hacer) una cita con un abogado.

3. Mi socio teme que nuestro negocio _____ (perder) dinero.

4. Yo quiero que mis empleados _____ (trabajar) más.

5. Es importante que nosotros _____ (ir) a conocer el parque industrial.

6. El dueño no cree que ellos _____ (tener) problemas con la aduana.

7. Ojalá que el camión frigorífico _____ (llegar) pronto.

8. Es difícil que el abogado _____ (poder) arreglar los papeles para mañana.

9. Los agentes de aduana prohíben que los camiones _____ (salir) del almacén.

10. Es importante que los trabajadores _____ (tener) todos sus documentos.

B. Subjuntivo o indicativo. Read the following sentences and fill in the blank with the indicated form of the indicative or the subjunctive, according to the context.

1. Es evidente que ustedes _____ (tener) excelentes planes para la maquiladora.

2. Siento que su negocio _____ (sufrir) problemas económicos.

3. Yo creo que el agente _____ (buscar) la causa de las demoras (*delays*).

4. Nosotros recomendamos que ustedes _____ (buscar) otro parque industrial.

5. Tú insistes en que los camioneros _____ (ir) directamente a la fábrica.

6. Es dudoso que los componentes _____ (llegar) para mañana.

7. Es verdad que yo_____ (tener) problemas con inmigración.

8. Quizás _____ (venir) los abogados inmediatamente.

9. Es triste que usted no _____ (saber) qué hacer para ayudar a los empleados que pierden su trabajo.

10. Estamos contentos de que tú _____(estar) aquí hoy.

C. Recomendamos que... You and a colleague are lawyers talking to two partners who would like to investigate moving their assembly plant to Mexico. Complete the following sentences as indicated.

Recomendamos que ustedes....

1. **visitar** varios parques industriales.

2. **conocer** a nuestros administradores en México.

3. **hacer** una cita con el abogado.

4. **buscar** un banco comercial.

5. **asistir** a una reunión de la Comisión de Libre Comercio.

IV. A leer

El futuro de la economía global

A lo largo de la frontera de Estados Unidos con México, en los dos lados de la línea,vemos un creciente número de parques industriales que invitan la cooperación binacional y multinacional. El sistema maquiladora ofrece oportunidades enormes para el desarrollo económico de las empresas y de los trabajadores que sepan aprovechar los nuevos mercados que se abren. La expansión rápida de las economías de México y Centroamérica ofrece mercados lucrativos para los productos de tecnología en tales campos como: la electrónica para el consumidor; la tecnología y equipo para el medio ambiente; la óptica y las ciencias biológicas, entre otros. Para las personas que hablan dos o más idiomas y saben moverse en varias culturas y protocolos, el mundo del comercio internacional—aquí mismo en nuestra frontera con México—es una puerta de oro.

A. A contestar. Answer the following questions based on the reading.

1. ¿Dónde vemos un creciente número de parques industriales?

2. ¿Cuáles son algunas de las industrias que crecen rápidamente?

3. ¿Qué sistema ofrece oportunidades?

4. ¿Quiénes pueden pasar por "la puerta de oro"?

B. A escribir: Write a three sentence summary of the core information in the above article.

_____

_____

_____

Script for A escuchar A

1. ¿Cuáles son tres palabras asociadas con el comercio internacional?

2. ¿Qué necesita arreglar un comerciante antes de trasladar su negocio al extranjero?

3. ¿Cuál de estas palabras significa una clase de impuestos internacionales?

4. ¿Cuál de estas formas de transporte es la mejor para transportar productos perecederos?

5. Yo tengo que consultar a mi abogado. Mañana tengo cita con él en su...

Script for A escuchar B

1. ¿Qué recomienda usted que haga una persona que piensa trasladar su negocio al extranjero?

2. ¿Cuáles son dos medios de transporte a larga distancia?

3. ¿Cuáles son dos documentos oficiales que necesita una persona que quiere viajar al extranjero por razones de turismo o comercio?

4. ¿Qué es un inmigrante?

5. ¿Quiere usted trabajar en el extranjero? ¿Por qué?

I. A escuchar

A. Conversaciones. Listen to the following telephone solicitations and tell if the call is to sell a product or service **(vender),** solicit donations for a non-profit organization **(donativos)** or to influence social or political decisions **(política).**

1. ____

2. ____

3. ____

B. A contestar. Answer the following questions with complete sentences.

1. _____

2. _____

3. _____

4. _____

A practicar

II. Vocabulario

A. Emparejar. Find the word or phrase from **Column A** that has the **opposite** meaning from one in **Column B**.

Columna A	Columna B
____ 1. mantener	a. apoyar
____ 2. voluntario	b. donar dinero
____ 3. anteayer	c. empleado
____ 4. recaudar fondos	d. transformar
____ 5. protestar	e. pasado mañana

B. ¿Qué quiere decir? Write the definition of each of the following words or phrases or use it in a sentence that demonstrates the meaning.

1. movimiento del pueblo

2. medio ambiente

3. donativo

4. caridad

5. ayer

III. Gramática

A. El tiempo pretérito. Read the following story and fill in the blanks with the correct form of the verb in the preterit tense.

Ayer yo (1) _____ (sentirse) mal cuando (2)_____ (oír) las noticias. Hubo otro desastre natural en este país: un terremoto (*earthquake*). Después de sentir unos temblores ligeros, muchas personas (3). _____ (sentir) temblores muy fuertes por varios minutos. Hubo muchos daños y heridos. Cuando yo (saber) (4) _____ lo que pasó, (5) _____ (buscar) el número de teléfono de la Cruz Roja y yo (6)_____ (hacer) una cita para donar sangre. La recepcionista me (7) _____ (decir) que afortunadamente muchas personas (8)_____ (tener) la misma reacción. Yo (9)_____ (ir) inmediatamente al centro de donaciones donde la enfermera me (10)_____ (hacer) unas pruebas. Después, ella (11) _____ (darme) un vaso de jugo, un donut y una sonrisa enorme para decir "gracias."

B. Después del desastre. Match the subjects and verbs in the preterit tense to tell what happened after the disaster.

1. Los equipos de rescate/trabajar/día y noche

2. El personal médico/no dormir/nada

3. El Presidente/venir/a ver la destrucción

4. Muchas personas/traer/flores

5. Muchas familias/buscar/a sus parientes

6. Un niño/tener/ una incisión/muy profundo

7. La Cruz Roja/dar/ropa y comida

8. Una mamá/dormir/en el hospital cerca de sus hijos

9. Varias organizaciones sin ánimo de lucro/pedir/donativos en la calle

10. La humanidad/sentir/solidaridad

IV. A leer

Yo soy escritor profesional. Normalmente paso más de sesenta horas a la semana sentado frente a mi computadora buscando las palabras exactas para expresar lo que necesito decir. Para mí, es una carrera ideal: trabajo en mi casa—en pijama si quiero—las horas que quiero trabajar y en los proyectos que quiero hacer. A veces escribo ficción, a veces escribo sobre el medioambiente y los desastres naturales, a veces escribo sobre política. Tengo una vida perfecta, sin estrés. Mentira. Sí, hay una cosa en mi vida que me causa mucho estrés: las llamadas a todas horas de los "tele-vendedores". Piden donativos para caridades auténticas y sospechosas. Quieren vender servicios de teléfono, hipotecas, ventanas, drogas (no sé si son legales o ilegales). Quieren mi opinión sobre este producto o aquel asunto político. Y siempre son *tan* simpáticos. "Hola, señor, me llamo Antonio. ¿Cómo estamos hoy? ¿Disfrutando de un día tan bonito?" ¡Ayyyyy! Normalmente me pongo furioso. Pero ayer, cuando me llamó una señorita—con la voz muy dulce—no pude más. Yo le contesté:

"Hola, Ana Fimbres, estoy de muy buen humor. Hace buen tiempo. Acabo de ganar millones de dólares en la lotería. Y, en realidad, en este momento estoy muy ocupado con mi abogado planeando los donativos enormes que voy a hacer a mis caridades favoritas. No puedo hablar ahora. Pero si me das tu número de teléfono de casa, yo te llamo a las seis o siete de la tarde."

Ella estaba tan sorprendida que sólo pudo decirme: "Yo no puedo darle mi número de teléfono particular." Le contesté: "¡Aja! Tú no quieres que nadie te moleste (*bother*) en casa. Ahora sabes precisamente como me siento yo!" Clic.

A. Cierto o falso: Indicate whether the following statements are **Cierto (C)** or **Falso (F).** Correct the ones that are false.

1. _____ El escritor está muy contento con su vida, con una excepción.

2. _____ Trabaja en una oficina enorme al lado de muchos tele-vendedores.

3. _____ Le gusta mucho hablar y conversar con las personas que llaman para pedir donativos o vender productos y servicios.

4. _____ Ana le pide al escritor su número de teléfono para llamarlo a las 6 o 7.

5. _____ Ana le da su número al escritor con mucho entusiasmo.

B. A escribir. Write a three or four line summary what the writer did to the telemarketer for "revenge." Explain why it was effective.

_____

_____

_____

Script for A escuchar A

1. Buenas noches. ¿Señora Cosme? Me llamo Margarita Sánchez y llamo de parte de la

Asociación de Mejora de la Educación. Necesitamos su apoyo en la próxima elección

para nuestro candidato pro-educación…

2. Buenas tardes, llamo del Centro de Investigación del Consumidor. Quiero pedir su

opinión sobre su servicio telefónico de larga distancia comparado con el servicio que yo

les puedo ofrecer…

3. Bueno, quiero hablar, por favor, con el señor de la casa. Yo represento al grupo:

"Niños Pobres." Nosotros damos casa, comida y medicinas a niños en naciones pobres.

Por sólo $15 al mes… cincuenta centavos al día, usted puede salvarle la vida a un niño

pobre.

Script for A escuchar B

1. ¿Cuáles son dos caridades u organizaciones sin ánimo de lucro que usted apoya?

2. ¿Hace usted donativos de dinero, productos o tiempo?

3. ¿Por qué son importantes los voluntarios?

4. Escriba una lista de tres cosas que usted hizo el once de septiembre, 2001.

Nombre_____

I. A escuchar

A. Conversaciones. You are a customer service representative in a very busy technology call center and are often asked to recommend solutions to clients trying to enter the world of virtual reality and commerce. Listen to the following requests for help and match them to the recommended actions.

A. Al cliente _____ usted le responde: "Usted necesita verificar la disponibilidad del dominio y registrarlo."

B. Al cliente _____ , usted le responde: "Para que su dominio tenga más presencia en la Web, yo recomiendo que se inscriba con varios motores de búsqueda internacionales y compre una bandera de publicidad que va a aparecer en muchos sitios cuando la gente navegue por Internet."

C. Al cliente _____ , usted le responde: "Yo creo que usted debe llamar al banco directamente y reportarlo. Después ellos pueden cambiar su contraseña. Cuando tenga una nueva, no se lo diga a nadie. Es un secreto."

D. Al cliente _____ , usted le responde: "El nombre de usuario es usted—es el nombre ficticio que usted seleccionó para identificarse."

E. Al cliente _____ , usted le responde: "Su impresora rueda de margarita tiene una tecnología muy vieja. Es casi imposible comprar componentes. Usted debe comprarse una impresora nueva—tipo láser. Son muy rápidas."

B. A contestar. Answer the following questions with complete sentences.

1. _____

2. _____

3. _____

4. _____

5. _____

A practicar

II. Vocabulario

A. A completar. Choose the answer that best completes the statement or answers the

question.

1. Si quiero investigar un tema por Internet, tengo que poner _____ en el espacio

del buscador.

      a. una bandera de publicidad

      b. las palabras claves

      c. el correo electrónico

2. ¿Qué hizo usted cuando supo que su dominio estaba disponible?

      a. Fui inmediatamente al hospital.

      b. Fui inmediatamente al registro.

      c. Usted iba a su tienda virtual.

3. Para asegurar la seguridad de su identidad en Internet, usted debe tener _____ y

_____ difíciles de reconocer.

      a. una bandera de publicidad / una presencia en los motores de búsqueda

      b. un nombre de usuario / una contraseña

      c. un enlace / una palabra clave

4. Ahora que viajo mucho por mi empleo, necesito tecnología portátil. Pienso comprarme

_____.

a. un servidor de 5 toneladas

b. una pantalla sensible

c. un Palm

5. Tengo varias computadoras primitivas y nuevas. Mi _____ es una maravilla de la tecnología. Mi _____ tiene mucha nostalgia.

a. llevable con pantalla sensible

b. zapato

c. Lisa con disquetes de 8"

B. Definiciones. Write the definition of each of the following words or phrases, or use it in a sentence that demonstrates the meaning.

1. dominio

2. tienda virtual

3. contraseña

4. C2C

5. un punto com

III. Gramática

A. ¿Qué hacía usted? You and several other people all happened to be working in a technology call center when the computers went down. Use the imperfect tense to tell what each person was doing.

1. Yo/hablar con una clienta histérica

2. Los representantes de ventas/tomar los datos de los nuevos clientes

3. El gerente/ir a su oficina

4. Los estudiantes en la clase de entrenamiento/estudiar para el examen final

5. Algunos empleados/volver del almuerzo

6. Mis amigos/mirar el horario *(schedule)* para la semana

7. María Patricia/soñar con su nuevo refrigerador con pantalla sensible

8. Edith y Óscar/tener una reunión con su supervisor

9. Uno de los señores de la limpieza/estar distraído y causó el problema al desconectar la electricidad

10. El presidente de la compañía/disfrutar de sus vacaciones en el yate

B. ¿Imperfecto o pretérito? Read the following paragraph and use either the imperfect or the preterit form of the verb to logically complete the story.

Hace muchos años, cuando yo 1. _____ (ser) niño, yo 2. _____ (vivir) con mi familia en un pueblo. El pueblo, muy tranquilo, no 3. _____ (tener) muchos servicios. No 4. _____ (haber) muchos teléfonos ni televisión. Las comunicaciones 5. _____ (ser) difíciles. Un día, mientras mi mejor amigo y yo 6. _____ (caminar) a la escuela y 7._____ (hablar) de los planes para el fin de semana, de repente él me 8. _____ (decir): "No me siento bien" y se desmayó *(fainted)*. Sin teléfono, yo 9. _____ (estar) solo con la emergencia. Yo no 10. _____ (saber) qué hacer, pero 11. _____ (empezar) a darle resucitación RCP como en el cine. Muy pronto yo 12. _____ (escuchar) su respiración. ¡Qué alivio! Nunca voy a olvidar esa emergencia sin posibilidades de ayuda. Ahora nunca salgo de la casa sin mi teléfono celular.

IV. A escribir. When you were young you and your family did things very differently from now because of technology. Think of at least four changes technology has made in your life and explain the way you used to do them and how you do them now.

MODELO: *Cuando era joven, íbamos al banco para hacer las transacciones. Ahora vamos a un cajero automático o al sitio web.*

_____

_____

_____

_____

_____

_____

V. A leer

Una carta

Estimada Sra. Álvarez,

Acabo de recibir la noticia de que el portal empresarial Guiacom se vende por falta de recursos. Como usted sabe, Guiacom era uno de nuestros primeros portales empresariales con sectores de hospedaje web, agencias de viajes, áreas de mercadeo, un motor de búsqueda y correo electrónico. Además, tenía una sección completamente dedicada a las ventas " b2b" .

Si a usted o a alguno de sus socios les interesa explorar la posibilidad de comprar Guiacom, el precio de venta es 60.000 € e incluye el website, el dominio y la marca registrada Guiacom. Favor de comunicarse conmigo si quiere más información.

A contestar: Answer the following questions with complete sentences.

1. ¿Por qué se vende Guiacom?

2. ¿Qué clase de negocio es?

3. ¿Cuáles son algunos de los servicios que ofrece Guiacom a los clientes?

4. ¿Cuál es el precio?

5. ¿Qué incluye el precio?.

Script for A escuchar A

Cliente 1. Disculpe usted, yo tengo una impresora muy cara tipo rueda margarita. Es muy lenta; produce una página cada minuto. Y también necesito componentes pero no los encuentro en las tiendas. ¿Qué debo hacer?

Cliente 2. Hola. Yo tengo una idea fantástica para una tienda virtual en la Red. Pensé en un nombre fabuloso para mi dominio. Quiero reservarlo antes que otra persona lo tome. ¿Qué recomienda usted que haga?

Cliente 3. Acabo de poner mi nombre de usuario y mi contraseña para conectarme con mi banco electrónico y me dijo que otra persona ya estaba conectada con mi cuenta. ¡Es imposible! Yo soy el único usuario. ¿Qué debo hacer?

Cliente 4. Yo monto una tienda-e nueva y quiero mucha presencia en la Web. ¿Qué debo hacer para que los clientes me conozcan?

Cliente 5. Yo no comprendo nada de este correo electrónico. La pantalla quiere mi nombre de usuario. ¿Qué es esto?

Script for A escuchar B

1. ¿Cuáles son dos extensiones de dominios muy comunes?

2. Cuando usted era joven, ¿tenía una computadora? ¿Qué marca era?

3. La última vez que usted usó su computadora, ¿qué hizo?

4. ¿Alguna vez compró usted algo por Internet? ¿Fue fácil o difícil la transacción?

5. La tecnología cambia todo. Identifique dos actividades que hace por computadora ahora que no hacía antes. Antes de tener la computadora, ¿cómo hacía usted estas cosas?

Nombre_____

I. A escuchar

A. Cierto o falso. Listen to the passage and then decide if each of these statements is

Cierto or **Falso.** If the statement is **Cierto**, mark "A". If it is **Falso**, mark "B".

1. _____ Anthony Muñoz es jugador profesional de béisbol.

2. _____ Es nieto de inmigrantes mexicanos.

3. _____ Para él, su herencia mexicana no es importante.

4. _____ Su papel como modelo para niños latinos es una responsabilidad seria.

5. _____ Cree que hay muchas oportunidades para los hispanos en deportes,

negocios, política y espectáculos.

B. Preguntas. Listen to the advertisement and select the most logical answer for each

question.

6. ¿Qué es PROMONET.com?

    a. una guía de televisión

    b. una agencia de publicidad

    c. una lista de direcciones de empresas

7. ¿A cuántas empresas representan en su base de datos?

    a. 6,300

    b. 63,000

    c. 630

8. ¿Cuál es el porcentaje de errores?

    a. 5%

    b. 15%

c. 50%

9. ¿Cuál es la única limitación?

    a. nombre, dirección, código postal, teléfono, fax y e-mail

    b. usar la lista solamente una vez

    c. no pasar la lista a otros

10. ¿Qué se debe hacer para recibir más información?

    a. pulsar Información

    b. pulsar Visitar Web

    c. usar su servidor

II. A leer

MiBanco es su banco
¿Quiere tener todas sus cuentas en un banco y recibir el servicio personal que merece?
Necesita estar con nosotros, porque MiBanco es SU banco.

Cuentas de cheques, ahorros y más
MiBanco es su conexión con nuestra extensa familia de servicios financieros. Usted tiene
acceso online GRATIS con el líder de la nación en transacciones bancarias por Internet en
www.mibanco.com. Claro que también puede aprovechar nuestro servicio excelente en
cualquier sucursal por toda la nación, donde no tiene que esperar y no paga ninguna
cuota (*fee*) por nuestros servicios al cliente.

¿Qué ofrecemos?
Cuentas de cheques
    • Protección contra sobregiro (*overdraft*)
    • No hay cargos con:
        • Depósito directo
        • Balance diario mínimo de mil dólares
        • Pagos automáticos a su hipoteca o línea de crédito
Cuentas de ahorros
    • Intereses con tasas competitivas
Tarjetas de crédito MiBanco
Tarjetas de cajero automático
Seguro para autos, seguros de vivienda y de vida
Cuenta MiBanco Express

    • Sólo $10 por envíos a México hasta $1,000
    • Transferencia directa de su cuenta MiBanco a la cuenta Banamex de su beneficiario
    • Acceso las 24 horas por medio de cajeros automáticos o vía telefónica

¡Venga hoy a su sucursal de MiBanco más cercana y abra su cuenta!

Cierto o falso. Read the brochure and then decide if each of these statements is **Cierto** or **Falso.** If the statement is **Cierto**, mark "A". If it is **Falso**, mark "B".

11. Es posible hacer sus transacciones bancarias en persona o por Internet.

12. El balance mínimo de cuenta de cheques para no pagar cargos es $100.

13. MiBanco ofrece un interés más alto que Wells Fargo en su cuenta de ahorros.

14. Se puede solicitar un seguro de vivienda de MiBanco.

15. Banamex en México acepta transferencias de dinero de su cuenta de MiBanco.

B. Inscríbase para votar

Información para los votantes

1. Tiene que ser ciudadano de Estados Unidos.

2. Tiene que ser residente de New Jersey.

3. Tiene que tener 18 años de edad o más el día de la próxima elección.

4. Usted NO puede estar en la prisión ni en libertad condicional debido a una condena por un delito mayor.

5. Para votar en cualquier elección específica tiene que estar inscrito 29 días antes de dicha elección. Recibirá una Tarjeta de notificación a los votantes que confirmará su inscripción. Si NO recibe esta tarjeta, llame al secretario del condado/registrador de votantes.

6. Si usted desea recibir una tarjeta para votantes ausentes por correo, tiene que presentar una solicitud por escrito a la oficina del secretario del condado/registrador de votantes por lo menos 7 días antes de la elección. Después del plazo de 7 días usted puede solicitar y votar mediante una tarjeta para votantes ausentes en dicha oficina, en persona o a través de un representante autorizado.

7. Para obtener información electoral, llame al número que se indica a continuación: Teléfono 1 800 654-2781

Tiene que volver a inscribirse cada vez que se mude a otra residencia.
Conserve esta sección para su información.

Emparejar. Read the above information and then match each item with its appropriate selection.

a. registrador   b. ciudadano   c. tarjeta   d. votante   e. elección

16. Si usted no recibe su Tarjeta de notificación a los votantes debe hablar con el _____ de votantes.

17. Hay que inscribirse para votar veintinueve días antes de la _____.

18. Este boletín tiene información para el _____.

19. Se usa una _____ para sus selecciones de candidatos.

20. No se puede votar sin ser _____.

A practicar

III. Vocabulario

A. A escoger. Choose the letter that best answers the following questions.

21. ¿Cuál es un riesgo de inversión en acciones como Enron y WorldCom?

a. una cuenta corriente   c. un extraterrestre

b. un estado mensual   d. la bancarrota

22. ¿Qué se hace con un corredor?

a. Se descubre la esperanza.   c. Se heredan millones.

b. Se ejecutan transacciones.   d. Se toma cuando se tiene un dolor.

23. Para mejorar el _____ es necesario que mejore la economía.

a. extranjero   c. estacionador

b. desempleo   d. cantinero

24. Para el buen futuro de la compañía es importante el _____ de un plan muy

detallado.

a. desarrollo   c. plazo

b. parentesco   d. retiro

25. El dinero que se gana en acciones y bonos es _____.

a. el euro   c. el dividendo

b. el billete   d. la ventaja

26. Recibí una _____ y ahora tengo el título de vice-presidente. ¡Gano mucho más

dinero!

a. penalidad   c. promoción

b. ruta   d. deducción

27. Para saber el saldo en mi cuenta de ahorros tengo que _____ todos los

depósitos.

a. presentar   c. bailar

b. pintar   d. sumar

28. La _____ es el sueldo que se paga a los empleados.

a. nómina   c. casilla

b. moneda   d. fortuna

B. A emparejar. You need to find new ways to explain some concepts to a client. Match

the following words in **Columna A** to the most logical description in **Columna B.**

<u>Columna A</u>	<u>Columna B</u>
29. la huelga	a. el sitio para los niños de los empleados
30. la maquinaria	b. las horas que uno trabaja
31. la guardería	c. un paro de trabajo
32. el turno	d. el equipo de una fábrica

C. ¿Qué necesito? Explain what you will need in order to balance the activities by

matching the verbs in **Columna A** to the verbs in **Columna B.**

<u>Columna A</u>	<u>Columna B</u>
33. enojarse	a. unir
34. despertarse	b. calmarse
35. ponerse	c. quitarse
36. pelearse	d. dormirse

D. El análisis. You are a professional problem-solver working with companies experiencing problems related to growth, providing advice as to their expansion goals. Make suggestions by identifying the conditions they describe and choosing from the following list.

a. la unión

b. el traductor

c. la escasez

d. el enfoque

37. No sabemos si debemos abrir una maquiladora en la República Dominicana o no.

38. Es difícil encontrar aquí los productos agrícolas que necesitamos .

39. Los empleados están completamente desorganizados y no tienen disciplina.

40. Muchos de los empleados no hablan inglés.

E. Consejos. You are working with clients interested in purchasing a food-processing factory. Identify the items they describe from the following list.

a. la limpieza

b. la panadería

c. el ganadero

d. la plaga

41. Estamos muy preocupados por la posibilidad de una infestación de insectos.

42. El gobierno tiene muchas restricciones en cuanto a las condiciones en la fábrica, especialmente en esta área.

43. La granja de este señor es enorme—él dice que nos vende parte de su tierra.

44. ¿Se puede comprar fácilmente por aquí azúcar, maíz?—la frescura de lo que preparamos es muy importante para nosotros.

F. Cierto o falso. You have a client that is full of misinformation. Read the following statements that she makes and declare whether it is **Cierto** or **Falso**. If the statement is **Cierto**, mark "A". If it is **Falso**, mark "B".

45. La frontera es donde ensamblamos los componentes.

46. La zona franca es el nombre oficial de las maquiladoras.

47. Los aranceles son los impuestos internacionales.

48. Un camión grande de por lo menos 18 ruedas es un puerto.

49. Un vehículo terrestre que transporta productos perecederos *(perishable)* a temperaturas muy bajas se llama camión frigorífico.

50. El medio ambiente es el ecosistema de una región.

51. Los comestibles orgánicos son productos para comer con ingredientes medicinales.

52. Un bufete es el proceso de trasladarse a otro país para vivir.

G. El gobierno. As a volunteer, you are always asked to help people understand "the system." Match the proper word from the list below to each situation.

a. audiencia   b. acusador o fiscal   c. citación judicial   d. criminal

53. Una _____ ocurre cuando un gran jurado decide que hay evidencia para un tribunal oficial.

54. Cuando el Congreso necesita investigar a una persona u organización, hay una _____.

55. La persona a quien se acusa de un crimen es el _____.

56. En un caso civil la persona que hace la acusación es _____.

H. La tecnología. As a sales clerk in a large retail computer chain, you are always asked to help customers understand today's technology. Match the item they need to understand its meaning.

57. contraseña a. el proceso de crear SU nombre de Internet

58. usuario b. las conecciones a sitios web

59 registro de dominio c. la palabra secreta que permite acceso

60. enlaces d. la persona que maneja la computadora

IV. Gramática

A. En la oficina. As the CEO's administrative assistant in a busy insurance office, you are responsible for making certain that the employees carry out the boss' instructions and answering client questions.

Answer the following questions by choosing the most logical answer.

61. ¿Dónde puedo comprar las sillas?

    a. Se venden en Office Depot.   b. Se vende en Costco.

    c. Compre unos archivos.   d. No la necesitan.

62. Cliente: ¿Cuándo puedo hablar con el director?

    Usted: Él acaba de llamar por teléfono _____.

    a. mañana   b. hace un minuto

    c. en media hora   d. antes de comer

63. Usted: ¿Por qué no terminó usted el proyecto?

    Empleado: Porque los datos _____.

    a. no me gustaron   b. no me gustó

    c. no te gusta   d. no te gustan

64. Cliente: El director dice que leyó la historia de mi multa por tomar alcohol—ya pagué $2,000. ¿Eso es un problema?

Usted: Una multa de _____ dólares es alta.

a. doscientos   b. doscientas

c. dos mil   d. dos millones

B. Las reacciones del/de la director/a. During a discussion with your boss you make the following statements. Mark each statement with an **A** if s/he likes the statement or with a **B** if s/he doesn't.

Le gusta (A)   No le gusta (B)

65. Acabo de preparar los contratos para la construcción del edificio nuevo.

66. Mi sueldo es muy bajo para el trabajo que hago—quisiera un aumento.

67. Las computadoras nuevas que compramos eran bastante caras.

68. En mi país, Colombia, es costumbre empezar las reuniones con un poco de conversación personal antes de empezar a hablar de negocios.

C. Las compras. Sometimes the customers in your store feel the need to explain to you why they are buying the items they have selected. Choose the most logical answer to finish their explanation.

69. Yo compro un reloj despertador. Me gusta _____.

a. levantarse temprano   b. levantarte temprano

c. levantarme temprano   d. acostarme temprano

70. Este café descafeinado es para mi hermana. Tiene insomnio y no puede _____.

a. dormirme   b. dormir

c. se duerme   d. me duermo

71. Este lápiz labial es para mi hija. Es actriz en la telenovela más popular en Suramérica.

    a. Se maquilla todos los días. b. Me maquillo todos los días.

    c. Se afeita todos los días.   d. Me afeito todos los días.

72. En mi casa, compramos mucho champú y acondicionador. Todos nosotros

_____.

    a. se lavan el pelo mucho   b. nos lavamos el pelo mucho

    c. te lavas el pelo mucho   d. nos bañamos mucho

73. Siempre compro estos pañuelos.

    a. Las uso para limpiar las ventanas. b. Los uso para limpiar las ventanas.

    c. Lo uso para limpiar las ventanas.   d. La uso para limpiar las ventanas.

74. ¡Ay de mí! Yo iba a comprar muchas cosas pero no tengo dinero.

    a. Lo dejé en casa.   b. Los dejé en casa.

    c. Me dejé en casa.   d. Las dejé en casa.

75. Quiero comprar este equipo para hacer ejercicio, pero no _____ usarlo.

    a. sé   b. conozco

    c. sabe   d. conoce

76. El Sr. González es un jefe excelente. ¿Lo _____ usted?

    a. sé   b. conozco

    c. sabe   d. conoce

D. El subjuntivo. As a counselor in an employment agency, you must often make

recommendations, suggestions and judgments regarding the clients. Finish the following

statements with one of these three clauses:

a. hablar con el director   b. hable con el director   c. habla con el director

77. Es importante que Ud. _____ ahora mismo.

78. Sugiero que Ud. _____ .

79. Es evidente que Ud. _____ con frecuencia.

80. Ud. necesita _____ hoy.

81. Dudo que Ud. _____ hasta mañana.

82. La ley insiste en que _____ .

83. Ud. quiere _____ .

84. Ojalá que _____ .

E. Una historia. You and your co-worker opened up the store this morning. Choose the letter of the verb that best completes the exciting story.

a. hizo   b. llegamos   c. fui   d. pudimos

Nosotros _____ (85) a las ocho de la mañana. Una persona _____ (86) ruido.

Nosotros no _____ (87) ver nada. Yo _____ (88) a llamar a la policía.

F. El resto de la historia. Finish the story by choosing the appropriate verbs.

a. supimos   b. dije   c. vino   d. puso

Yo le _____ (89) al operador que había un robo en la tienda.

La policía _____ (90) rápidamente y el sargento les _____ (91) esposas

(handcuffs) a los criminales. Entonces, nosotros _____ (92) que los criminales eran

muy peligrosos.

G. De niña. Finish this story by filling in the blanks with the letter that represents the

correct form of the imperfect or preterit tense according to the context.

De niña, cada vez que yo _____ (93. a. miraba b. miré) la televisión, mi mamá me

_____ (94. a. decía b. dijo) "Mi hija, tienes que terminar tu tarea." Siempre me

_____ (95. a. gustaba b. gustó) el programa de Barrio Sésamo y mi madre me

_____ (96. a. permitía b. permitió) mirar la televisión solamente una hora al día.

Un día, yo _____ (97. a. decidía b. decidí) no ir a la escuela. Yo _____ (98.

a. ponía b. puse) el termómetro en la lámpara para calentarlo y después yo _____

(99. a. llamaba b. llamé) a mi mamá. Al leer el termómetro—105 grados—ella me

_____ (100. a. decía b. dijo) que tenía que ir inmediatamente a la escuela.

Script for A escuchar A

Una entrevista con Anthony Muñoz

En los 13 años que Anthony Muñoz lleva jugando fútbol americano para los Cincinnati Bengals fue elegido 11 veces para el *Pro Bowl*, nombrado en 1980 para el equipo *All-Decade* y el equipo *All-NFL* en honor del 75 aniversario. Recibió el honor de *Offensive Lineman* por tres años y jugó dos veces en el *Super Bowl*. Es miembro del *Pro Football Hall of Fame* y recibió un premio de *Hispanic Heritage.* Trabaja con niños en Estados Unidos y México.

PERIODISTA: ¿Su familia es de México?

ANTHONY MUÑOZ: Sí, mis abuelos inmigraron de México a Estados Unidos.

PERIODISTA: ¿Cómo cambió su vida desde su niñez?

ANTHONY MUÑOZ: De niño, nunca pensé en la posibilidad de cenar con el presidente
                              Bush, el presidente Fox de México y sus esposas en la Casa
                              Blanca, ni de hablar enfrente de grupos de 100 a 500 personas.

PERIODISTA: ¿Usted cree que su herencia mexicoamericana es importante?

ANTHONY MUÑOZ: Es muy importante mantener mi historia y es un honor para mí
                              ser un modelo para niños hispanos. Es una responsabilidad de
                              mucha importancia.

PERIODISTA: Gracias por hablar conmigo. ¿Tiene algún comentario final?

ANTHONY MUÑOZ: Sí, creo que hay muchas oportunidades en el siglo XXI para los
                              hispanos, no sólo en deportes, sino también en negocios, política
                              y todo tipo de espectáculo.

Script for A escuchar B

Nosotros somos PROMONET.com. Si necesitan una buena base de datos de empresas con e-mail para ofrecer sus productos o dar a conocer su empresa, les ofrecemos nuestra base de datos con 63.000 empresas, incluyendo nombre, dirección, código postal, teléfono, fax y e-mail. Garantizamos un máximo de errores del 5%. Pueden usar esta base de datos cuantas veces deseen; la única limitación es no pasarla a otros grupos. Podemos enviar su correo desde nuestro servidor. Si desean recibir más información pulsen el botón INFORMACIÓN; si quieren visitar nuestra web pulsen VISITAR WEB.

Spanish for Business
Answer Key for Exams

Para comenzar

A escuchar:
A. Conversaciones: 1. c 2. a 3. b 4. b 5. c.
B. ¿Cuál es? a. 8, b. 9, c. 10 d. 7 e. 6

A practicar:
II. Vocabulario:
A. A escoger. 1. c 2. b. 3. c. 4. b. 5. c
B. A conversar. 1. b 2. a 3. c. 4. b. 5. b.
C. A contestar: Answers 1-4 will vary. 5. veintiuno/veinte y uno

D. A leer:
A. A comprender: 1. C. 2. C. 3. C. 4. F. 5. F.
B. A escribir: Answers will vary.

Lección 1
I. A escuchar:
A. Conversaciones. 1. a. 2. b. 3. b. 4. a
B. La solicitud de empleo: Nombre: Roberto Gómez. Edad: 28, Estado civil: soltero; Número de seguro social: 516 07 2314; Teléfono: 315 0611; Dirección: 9 Avenida Ventura, Las Vegas, Nevada.

A practicar:
II. Vocabulario:
A. A completar: Answers will vary.
B. A trabajar: 1. profesor, 2. entrenador, 3. presidente/administrador/director, 4. secretario/a, 5. recepcionista.
C. A nombrar: 1. sillas; 2. impresora; 3. organigrama; 4. solicitud.

III. Gramática
A. En la oficina: 1. soy 2. es 3. son 4. eres
B. Los candidatos: 1. extrovertida 2. serio 3. inteligentes 4. trabajadores 5. fácil
C. En la oficina: 1. la 2. el 3. las 4. las 5. los
D. Preguntas: 1. Cuándo 2. Dónde 3. Quién 4. Por qué

IV. A leer.
A. A comprender: 1. F 2. F 3. C 4. C 5. F
B. A escribir: Answers will vary.

Lección 2
I. A escuchar:
A. Conversaciones: 1. e 2. a 3. c. 4. b 5. d
B. A contestar: Answers will vary.

A practicar:
II. Vocabulario:
    A. A completar: 1. prestaciones 2. agente 3. hipoteca 4. seguro 5. copago
    B. Acciones: 1. como 2. llamo 3. tomo/bebo 4. me mudo 5. veo

III. Gramática
A. El verbo *estar*... 1. estamos preocupados 2. está enfermo 3. está contenta 4. estamos nerviosos 5. están listos
B. Los verbos... 1. reciben 2. comprende 3. ven 4. buscan 5. prepara 6. recibe 7. contesta 8. corro 9. tomamos 10. regresas
C. Expresiones con *tener*. 1. tengo sed 2. tiene miedo 3. tengo prisa 4. tengo sueño 5. tienen hambre
D. A contestar: Answers will vary.

IV. A leer.
A. A comprender: 1. C 2. F 3. F 4. C 5. C
B. A escribir: Answers will vary.

Lección 3
I. A escuchar.
A. Reservaciones: 1. b 2. a 3. b 4. c
B. A contestar: Answers will vary.

A practicar:
II. Vocabulario:
A. A completar: 1. pasaporte 2. fiscal 3. portafolios 4. exposición 5. presupuestos
B. Definiciones. Answers will vary.

III. Gramática
A. En el avión. 1. estamos esperando 2. está hablando 3. estoy leyendo 4. está poniendo 5. están haciendo
B. *Ser* vs. *estar*. 1. soy 2. soy 3. estoy 4. estamos 5. son 6. estamos 7. está
C. ¿Adónde vamos? 1. vamos 2. vas 3. voy 4. van
D. ¿Qué van a hacer? Answers will vary.
E. La rutina diaria. 1. salgo 2. hago 3. llevo 4. traduce 5. sé 6. ponen 7. oyen

IV. A leer.
A. Cierto o falso. 1. F 2. F 3. F 4. F 5. F
B. A escribir. Answers will vary.

Lección 4
I. A escuchar:
A. Conversaciones: 1. peor 2. mejor
B. A contestar: Answers will vary.

A practicar:
II. Vocabulario
A completar: 1. l 2. f 3. h 4. d 5. i 6. j 7. c 8. b 9. k 10. f

III. Gramática
A. ¿De quién es? 1. su 2. Nuestro 3. Su 4. Mis 5. Su 6. su
B. Los verbos irregulares: 1. Puedo 2. queremos 3. Tienen 4. Pienso 5. Prefieren 6. Preferimos
C. Los comparativos: (there are other possibilities)
1. El Almacén Mayo es más moderno que el Almacén Centavo.
2. El Almacén Mayo tiene menos pisos que el Almacén Centavo.
3. Hay tantos vendedores en el Almacén Mayo como en el Almacén Centavo.
4. El Almacén Mayo da tantos descuentos como el Almacén Centavo.
5. El Almacén Mayo es peor que el Almacén Centavo.

IV. A leer.
A. Cierto o falso: 1.C 2.F 3.F 4.F 5.F
B. A escribir. Answers will vary.

Lección 5
I. A escuchar:
A. Compras por teléfono: 1.a 2.c 3.b 4.a
B. A contestar: Answers will vary.

A practicar:
II. Vocabulario:
  A. Acciones: 1.b 2.e 3.d 4.a 5.c
  B. La tecnología: 1. monitor 2. teclado 3. ratón 4. módem 5. disco duro

III. Gramática
A. El servicio al cliente. 1. abra. 2. saque 3. busque 4. Escriba 5. Ponga 6. Conecte 7. lea 8. Disfrute
B. Mandatos para su familia: 1. toquen 2. coman 3. beban 4. peleen 5. busquen
C. Conteste: 1. ponga 2. escriba 3. compre 4. pida 5. haga
D. Afirmativo > negativo: 1. Nadie está... 2. La señora Limón nunca pide... 3. No veo nada... 4. Los operadores tampoco pueden... 5. El técnico no va a hacer ninguna prueba....

IV. A leer:
A. Cierto o falso: 1. C 2.C 3.F 4.F 5.F

B. A escribir. Answers will vary.

Lecciones PC-5

1. c	35. b	69. c
2. d	36. b	70. b
3. b	37. a	71. d
4. e	38. a	72. c
5. a	39. b	73. e
6. a	40. a	74. a
7. b	41. c	75. b
8. a	42. b	76. e
9. b	43. c	77. c
10. b	44. b	78. a
11. a	45. a	79 d
12. b	46. b	80. b
13. a	47. a	81. a
14. b	48. b	82. a
15. b	49. c	83. b
16. c	50. c	84. a
17. a	51. e	85. a
18. b	52. b	86. c
19. a	53. c	87. a
20. c	54. a	88. a
21. a	55. d	89. a
22. c	56. a	90. b
23. b	57. b	91. e
24. a	58. b	92. c
25. a	59. a	93. b
26. b	60. a	94. d
27. c	61. b	95. a
28. c	62. b	96. d
29. b	63. c	97. a
30. a	64. a	98. c
31. c	65. b	99. b
32. d.	66. c	100. e
33. b	67. c	
34. a	68. b	

Lección 7
I. A escuchar:
A. Conversaciones: 1.a 2.b 3.a 4.c 5.c
B. A contestar: 1. Answers will vary.
                    2. Answers will vary.
                    3. Answers will vary.

4. mil quinientos

5. Answers will vary.

A practicar:

II. Vocabulario:

A. A escoger: 1.d 2.d 3.c 4.d 5.b

B. Antónimos: 1.c 2.a 3.b 4.d

III. Gramática

A. A escoger: 1.c 2.a 3.b 4.c 5.d

IV. A leer:

A. ¿Qué le gusta? 1. le gustan 2. le gustan 3. le gusta 4. le gusta 5. le gusta

B. Recomendaciones: 1. Se comen 2. Se necesita 3. Se evitan 4. Se hace 5. No se pone en bancarrota.

Lección 8

I. A escuchar:

A. Conversaciones: 1.una mujer 2. a las cinco 3. limpia, cocina y lee el periódico 4. una fábrica 5. frutas o verduras

B. A contestar: Answers will vary.

A practicar:

II. Vocabulario:

A. A completar: 1. sindicato 2. franquicia 3. vestidor 4. capacitación 5. comisiones

B. Definiciones: Answers will vary.

C. Sinónimos: 1. e 2. a 3. d 4. c 5. b

III. Gramática:

A. Los verbos reflexivos: 1. se despierta 2. me levanto / me baño 3. nos acostamos 4. se preocupan 5. te duermes

B. ¿Reflexivo o no? 1. lavan 2. visto / me visto 3. se acuestan 4. se lavan 5. se despierta

C. ¿Saber o conocer? 1. sé 2. conoce 3. sé 4. conozco 5. sé

D. Complementos directos: 1. Lo necesito. 2. (No) la necesito. 3. Los necesito. 4. (No) lo necesito. 5. Lo necesito.

E. La rutina de la mañana... Answers will vary.

IV. A leer:

A. A contestar: 1. b 2. b 3. b 4. a

B. A escribir. Answers will vary.

Lección 9

I. A escuchar:

A. Conversaciones: 1. a 2. b 3. c 4. c 5. b
B. A contestar: Answers will vary.

A practicar:
II. Vocabulario:
A. Síntomas: 1. b 2. c 3. e 4. a 5. d
B. Definiciones: Answers will vary.

III. Gramática
A. El subjuntivo: 1. piensen 2. hagas 3. pierda 4. trabajen 5. vayamos 6. tengan 7. llegue 8. pueda 9. salgan 10. tengan
B. Subjuntivo o indicativo: 1. tienen 2. sufra 3. busca 4. busquen 5. vayan 6. lleguen 7. tengo 8. vengan 9. sepa 10. estés
C. Recomendamos que...: 1. visiten 2. conozcan 3. hagan 4. busquen 5. asistan

IV. A leer:
A. A contestar: 1. la frontera de Estados Unidos con México 2. la electrónica para el consumidor, la tecnología y equipo para el medio ambiente, la óptica y las ciencias biológicas 3. maquiladora 4. las personas que saben operar en dos o más idiomas y navegar varias culturas y protocolos
B. A escribir. Answers will vary.

Lección 10
I. A escuchar:
A. Conversaciones: 1. política 2. vender 3. donativos
B. A contestar: Answers will vary.

A practicar:
II. Vocabulario:
A. Emparejar: 1. d 2. c 3. e 4. b 5. a
B. ¿Qué quiere decir? Answers will vary.

III. Gramática
A. El tiempo pretérito: 1. me sentí 2. oí 3. sintieron 4. supe 5. busqué 6. hice 7. dijo 8. tuvieron 9. fui 10. hizo 11. me dio
B. Después del desastre: 1. trabajaron 2. durmió 3. vino 4. trajeron 5. buscaron 6. tuvo 7. dio 8. durmió 9. pidieron 10. sintió

IV. A leer.
A. Cierto o falso. 1. C 2. F 3. F 4. F 5. F
B. A escribir. Answers will vary.

Lección 11

I. A escuchar:
A. Conversaciones: A. 2 B. 4 C. 3 D. 5 E. 1
B. A contestar: Answers will vary.

A practicar:
II. Vocabulario:
A. A completar: 1. b 2. b 3. c 4. c 5. a / c
B. Definiciones: Answers will vary.

III. Gramática
A. ¿Qué hacía usted? 1. hablaba 2. tomaban 3. iba 4. estudiaban 5. volvían 6. miraban 7. soñaba 8. tenían 9. estaba 10. disfrutaba
B. ¿Imperfecto o pretérito? 1. era 2. vivía 3. tenía 4. había 5. eran 6. caminábamos 7. hablábamos 8. dijo 9. estaba 10. sabía 11. empecé 12. escuché
C. A escribir: Answers will vary.

IV. A leer:
A. A contestar: 1. por falta de recursos 2. un portal empresarial 3. hospeaje de web, agencias de viajes, áreas de mercadeo, un motor de búsqueda y correo electrónico 4. 60.000 € 5. el website, el dominio y la marca registrada Guiacom

Lección 12 Review 7-11

1. b	23. b	45. b
2. a	24. a	46. b
3. b	25. c	47. a
4. a	26. c	48. b
5. a	27. d	49. a
6. c	28. a	50. a
7. b	29. c	51. b
8. a	30. d	52. b
9. c	31. a	53. c
10. a	32. b	54. a
11. a	33. b	55. d
12. b	34. d	56. b
13. b	35. c	57. c
14. a	36. a	58. d
15. a	37. d	59. a
16. a	38. c	60. b
17. e	39. a	61. a
18. d	40. b	62. b
19. c	41. d	63. a
20. b	42. a	64. c
21. d	43. c	65. a
22. b	44. b	66. b

67. b	79. c	91. d
68. b	80. a	92. a
69. c	81. b	93. a
70. b	82. b	94. a
71. a	83. a	95. a
72. b	84. b	96. a
73. b	85. b	97. b
74. a	86. a	98. b
75. a	87. d	99. b
76. d	88. c	100. b
77. b	89. b	
78. b	90. c	

Synopsis of the Spanish for Business Companion Website

http://www.prenhall.com/rush

The Spanish for Business Companion Website is an online study guide coupled with links to websites grouped according to theme. The site allows students to practice, reinforce, and further explore the vocabulary, structures, and content topics of each *lección*.

Example of links by theme:

Job listings   Empleos

http://www.empleosprofesionales.com/   Site features news articles, search for jobs and opportunity to sign on for job postings.

http://www.empleosweb.com.ar/   Post your resume for distribution to over 250 Human Resources departments and firms.

http://www.empleoscr.com/   Job search for Costa Rica, including section for foreigners looking for work in that country.

http://www.laborum.com/   Search for jobs in Latin America by country.

http://www.cvfuturo.com.ve/   Businesses and individuals can post job information for Venezuela, Mexico and Colombia.

http://www.empleosmx.com/   Job postings for Mexico.

http://www.americaonline.com.mx   See employment opportunities with AOL in Mexico.

http://www.empleos.cjb.net/   Secretaries, cooks, manicurists, sales positions… in Venezuela.

franchises.

Language Practice for Students

Each *lección* includes testing sections offering online practice. Tests are then sent directly

to the Prentice Hall server for immediate correction. Hints are provided to enable students

to consult the text for reference to a particular vocabulary segment or grammar point.

Examples from *Lección 1:*

Módulo 1

Vocabulario B. Preparando mi currículum

[Hint: p. 23-24]

Choose the item from **Column B** that meets the needs of **Column A**.

Columna A	Columna B
1. Un recepcionista debe ser _____ para hablar con el público.	a. honesto
2. En Estados Unidos, ser _____ ayuda mucho porque muchas personas hablan español.	b. bilingüe
	c. realista
3. Coca-Cola es una compañía _____.	d. internacional
4. El joven desea *(wants)* ser presidente; es muy _____.	e. ambicioso
5. Un criminal no es _____.	

Módulo 1

Estructuras B. Introducing and describing yourself and others: Ser + adjetivos

[Hint: p. 27-28]

1. En la oficina del señor Ortega yo _____ recepcionista.

a. es

Coaching: Incorrecto. Review the forms of **ser.**

b. eres

Coaching: Incorrecto. Review the forms of **ser.**

c. soy

Coaching: ¡Correcto!

2. Ustedes _____ administradores.

a. somos

Coaching: Incorrecto. Review the forms of **ser.**

b. son

Coaching: ¡Correcto!

c. es

Coaching: Incorrecto. Review the forms of **ser.**

3. La candidata es _____.

a. simpática

Coaching: ¡Correcto!

b. simpático

Coaching: Incorrecto. Review adjective agreement.

c. simpáticas

Coaching: Incorrecto. Review adjective agreement.

4. La situación es _____.

a. serio

Coaching: Incorrecto. Review adjective agreement.

b. difíciles

Coaching: Incorrecto. Review adjective agreement.

c. grave.

Coaching: ¡Correcto!

5. Los ejecutivos son _____.

a. trabajador

Coaching: Incorrecto. Review adjective agreement.

b. trabajadores

Coaching: ¡Correcto!

c. trabajadoras

Coaching: Incorrecto. Review adjective agreement.

Acknowledgements

My thanks to Mum and Dad for all their encouragement, for the inspiration of their gardens and for sowing the gardening seed for me. I am particularly indebted to Elizabeth van Herk for her ability to organise my busy schedule so efficiently, and for typing and checking this book while keeping up a steady flow of blueberry muffins! Thanks also to Karin Robin for extra typing, to Robyn Holloway for lending her garden and time, and to everyone who provided recipes. I am grateful for assistance from Roger Spencer of the Royal Botanic Gardens, Melbourne; Kuranga Native Plant Nursery in Ringwood; Chandlers' Nursery at The Basin; Golden Ray Lilium Gardens at Olinda; and Gardenworld Nursery in Springvale. For help with the photograph of the flower colour wheel, thanks to Fiona White of Flowers Vasette in Fitzroy. And to all the people at Lothian Books, who make writing a book a pleasure, thanks for their expertise in cajoling and enthusing me, and for producing the finished work.

A Lothian Book

Thomas C. Lothian Pty Ltd
11 Munro Street, Port Melbourne, Victoria 3207

Copyright ©Jane Edmanson 1995
First published 1995

National Library of Australia
Cataloguing-in-publication data:

Edmanson, Jane.
Jane Edmanson's favourite plants.

Includes index.
ISBN 0 85091 706 9.

1. Gardening. 2. Plant selection. I. Title.
II. Title: Favourite Plants.

635

Cover and text design by Lynn Twelftree
Photographs by Jane Edmanson
Illustrations by Gillian Haag
Typeset in Perpetua by Image Makers, South Melbourne
Printed and bound in Singapore by Imago Productions (F.E.) Pte. Ltd.

Cover photographs

Front cover: *The magnificent pink and white, tulip-shaped flowers of* Magnolia × soulangeana.

Front flap and back cover: *The porcelain grape vine (*Ampelopsis brevipedunculata*) with its highly ornamental mauve, turquoise and lilac berries.*

Inset: Grevillea *'Robyn Gordon', one of the most popular Australian shrubs of all, flowers for most of the year.*

Inside front cover: *My mother's walled garden in Mildura, where wisteria and classic roses such as* Rosa *'Clair Matin' cover a pergola, while shrub roses, poppies and many perennials proliferate in the garden beds.*

Back cover inset: Jane Edmanson

Back flap inset: *The perfume of the boronia characterises the Australian spring. These are the pinkish red, bell-shaped flowers of* Boronia heterophylla.

Inside back cover: *A tranquil Australian native garden where kangaroo paws (*Anigozanthos spp.*) complement tufty sedge plants and rocks by a peaceful pond (photograph by Ted Rotherham).*

JANE EDMANSON'S
Favourite Plants

A LOTHIAN BOOK

Contents

Climbers, creepers, groundcovers, screeners . . . 85

Pots, tubs and hanging baskets 109

Foliage, flowers and ferns for shady spots 119

Plants that like it hot and dry 143

Introduction

I can't tell you how often people ask me what my favourite plant is. It doesn't matter if it is on radio, at garden talks or just meeting the general public, I am always asked this question. Well, it is much more difficult to answer than it would seem because I have so many favourites. I like miniature plants, big plants, colourful flowering plants and flowerless plants. I like plants from exotic places and I like plants that are truly Australian. I like bizarre plants, simple cheery plants and romantic plants with fragrant flowers and soft, scented leaves.

Apart from their beauty of form, colour, texture and fragrance, I also take delight in what plants can provide. Cooking and eating things from the garden is just one of the bonuses — making herbal vinegars, pickled capsicums, a string of garlic, lavender hanging in bunches, ornamental gourds lying decoratively in a bowl, nuts, berries and seeds collected in a basket and a vase of flowers just picked … These are just some of the gifts from the garden that give me special pleasure.

And gardening doesn't only benefit the gardener, since much of its attraction lies in sharing with other people. I like to give a simple posy of flowers or leaves picked with special thoughts of the person I am giving it to — perhaps for a birthday, to say congratulations or just to say I'm thinking of you.

Another easy way of getting and giving pleasure is to grow a cutting or a seedling to give away. My garden is full of memories from older relatives, friends or neighbours, and plants given to me by others often become my favourites.

My mother has always been my garden mentor. She has always had a fine garden; well, more than one. I can remember her suburban garden and two gardens in Mildura in the Sunraysia district of northern Victoria. Her interest affected me immeasurably, even when I was a small child.

The earliest of my mother's gardens that I can remember had many plants, including a bed of azaleas by the front door. On the edge of the pathway masses of freesias popped up every spring. I was too young to recognise these as precious treasures, and probably my earliest gardening memory is of my mother's face when she caught me 'weeding' her freesia patch.

In one corner of the same front garden there was a big old crab apple, origin unknown, name unknown. We children used to sit in the branches and gorge ourselves on its delicious fruit. That is why I have always thought of crab apples as very useful, as well as wonderfully ornamental, trees in the garden.

At the back of the garden there was an area that we called 'the mound' — the children's area, where we had cubby houses and played soldiers. It was screened from view by a magnificent Cootamundra wattle (*Acacia baileyana*) and I was always impressed by its grey leaves and yellow flowers in spring. Perhaps this is where my love for our native plants originated.

The weeping form of Cootamundra wattle (*Acacia baileyana*) looks very striking in full flower. I remember a beautiful Cootamundra in one of my mother's many beautiful gardens.

In more recent years, since my parents have retired, they have moved to a smaller house and garden than the rambling ones of my childhood. Their current garden is enclosed by a wall. One side is divided into four beds with roses, perennials and small fragrant plants edging the paths. Around the walls are more climbing roses and interesting shrubs such as quince, medlar and flowering crab apples. There is always something to pick — one winter I counted thirty-six different plants that could have provided at least some little flower for a posy. And of course, it's not only flowering plants that attract my mother. She makes great use of foliage plants and grows scented geraniums, lemon verbena, creeping thyme and sage to add to her gift posies.

From my mother's gardens I learnt to appreciate the beauty of plants all year round, not only in their peak, flowering seasons. She has a great sense of plant association and knows how to group plants according to their likes and dislikes, soil conditions and growth habits, as well as their visual effect. Attractive and successful combinations I remember are *Ceanothus* 'Blue Pacific' underplanted with clumps of grey-leaved *Dianthus* 'Fragrant Pink', a delightful effect in spring; hellebores massed underneath a lovely old spreading claret ash; and a bed of native ajugas (*Ajuga repens* 'Jungle Beauty') with deep mauve flower spikes matching, in tone and flowering time, the soft mauve wisteria hanging from the pergola overhead.

She and Dad now live in Mildura, where I was born. If you are a gardener in this district you really know about the heat, and often about frost and drought as well. That is the kind of gardening that many Australians have to face. It is not only inland Australians who must be aware of drought, even 'spoilt' gardeners like me who live in areas with higher rainfalls have to be much more water-wise these days.

My father, being a citrus farmer in the Sunraysia district, was intensely aware of the salinity problem, especially in the Murray River environs, even in the early days. He saw the devastating effects of salinity, erosion and soil degradation and has passed this knowledge on, as a farmer, to me as a horticulturist. Both he and Mum have always had an affinity with the seasons and I think they have passed this on to their children and grandchildren in turn. Barbecues out in the countryside and bushwalking always made us aware of nature and gave us all a love of the outdoors. I still love these open-air activities.

One of my great joys was discovering the beauty of native plants. It happened when I was a secondary school teacher at Dimboola High School. Dimboola is a very small country town which was made notorious by the Jack Hibberd play of that title. The town is on the edge of the Little Desert, and in spring the desert was filled with flowers — hakeas, the tiny flowers of the bush peas and milkmaids and native orchids. I still find it exciting to come across a native orchid when I'm bushwalking.

It took one of the schoolchildren to open my eyes to the particular beauty of our native flora. A thirteen-year-old boy, who hadn't in any way been an outstanding performer in the classroom, astonished me with his knowledge of the long, complex botanical names of the local plants. On our bush walks and orienteering days (I was the part-time Physical Education instructor) we would venture out into the Little Desert and be thrilled by the native plant life, especially the orchids. Most Australian native plants are not strident in colour; they have a delicate beauty that is not so obvious to everybody's eyes. Of course there are the spec-tacular displays of flowers in early spring, but I think the treasures are in the smaller flowers which take time and patience to focus on. Through getting to know Australian native plants I have discovered their beauty and, more importantly, their role in the ecosystem. It is this fragile balance that we must learn to treasure.

It was a natural progression for me to develop an awareness of botanical drawings. I have always been interested in this wonderful art form, from the work of early botanists such as Joseph Banks, who

The flowering crab apple, *Malus floribunda*, is prolific in early spring. This is one of the hardiest flowering plants in my parents' garden.

accompanied James Cook on his voyages, and Ferdinand Bauer to contemporary botanical artists such as Celia Rosser, whose banksia paintings are famous all over the world, and Helen Leitch, whose lovely drawings of endangered flora carry a strong environmental message.

My love of plants and gardening extends into other fields. I love reading gardening books, in particular those about the early plant explorers. In my spare time I do some needlework, usually with a floral theme. I get a lot of pleasure when I see flowers or foliage used as a theme for interior decoration, even if this is something as simple as a cushion embroidered with a variety of herbs.

Another of my passions is travelling, both within Australia and overseas. I am always fascinated to see different lifestyles and cultures, landscapes and natural wonders, and of course this includes the flora and fauna wherever I go. One of my greatest thrills was to come across a forest of daphne, indigenous to Nepal where I was doing some trekking, and rhododendrons as tall as trees, in the Nepalese foothills. Closer to home, on a visit to Mungo National Park in the desert inland from Mildura, I spotted the *Pittosporum*

phillyreoides, a beautiful tree with pendulous branches and tough enough to live out in the desert. I had great pleasure in growing a few seeds from this graceful, willow-like tree.

My own inner city garden is fairly small and it is impossible to grow everything I'd like to. No gardener is ever content! We all need to be reminded that we can't have it all. I grow a mixture of things that I love: camellias in pots, roses, herbs, liliums, azaleas, wax plants and helichrysum. And, of course, the beautiful Chinese golden rain tree (*Koelreutaria paniculata*) outside my kitchen is a great pleasure in all seasons. I grow my vegetables in a generous neighbour's garden and we share the produce. Many people I meet have, like me, only small spaces in which to garden, and this is obviously a modern trend, but even a small patio or balcony with container-grown plants can give very satisfying results through careful selection of suitable plants for decoration and use.

I feel lucky to be able to do something I enjoy so much, and to be able to share it with the many gardeners, experienced and just beginning, I meet in my work. Every day I learn something new and pleasurable.

As you will see from this book, I've found it impossible to include all my favourite plants, but there comes a time when we all have to be selective. I've tried, with those plants which are included, to show their individual qualities and requirements, their practical and creative uses and their beauty and fascination.

Heaven-scent: Fragrance in the garden

Of all the many beautiful and interesting characteristics of plants, their fragrance is the most evocative. Our eyes might see the garden but our noses can often tell us about plants before we catch sight of them, and fragrances have strong associations. A halved passionfruit practically transports you to a tropical paradise, while, for me, the smell of jonquils brightens up winter. The fragrance of sweet peas seems to turn the clock back, and gardenias always speak to me of weddings. And what a pleasure it is to have a daphne by the back door, or to rub the leaves of a lemon-scented verbena every time you pass by.

Boronia

Something that strikes me above all about our native plants, in particular, is that so many of them have a wonderful fragrance, yet there was a mistaken belief in the past that they lacked both colour and perfume. One of the most desirable native plants with strong perfume is the boronia—its fragrance is almost a symbol of the Australian spring. Once you smell boronia it is never forgotten (although there are some poor unfortunate people who just do not have the right nose to enjoy its perfume).

The brown boronia (*Boronia megastigma*) is the best known, with its tiny cup-shaped flowers in yellow and dark brown. It is

The glorious, heady fragrance of *Michelia doltsopa* is as stunning as its spectacular creamy white flowers, set against deep green foliage. Unlike deciduous magnolias, most evergreens in the magnolia family are fragrant.

grown commercially as a cut flower, as well as for its scent. There are many forms of brown boronia; a new one recently introduced into nurseries is *B.* 'Royale'. It is quite compact in its growth so there is no need to prune it, and it has larger flowers and a stronger perfume than the normal brown boronia. It is ideal as a feature in a tub near the entrance to your house, as it grows in the shape of a ball. Take it indoors while it's in flower; the perfume will fill the air for more than four weeks.

A form of boronia that I just love is *B. m.* 'Jack Maguire's Red'. Another colour variation of boronia is a yellow one, *B. m.* 'Lutea', with sweetly scented, yellow bell flowers.

There are many other boronias bred for their improved performance in the garden. *B. heterophylla* is better known as the red boronia, with deep pink, bell-shaped flowers, and again a lovely perfume that is slightly different from the fragrance of the brown boronia.

A new cultivar of *B. heterophylla* is 'Just Margaret'. It was originally selected as a cut flower variety by Margaret Pringle (hence the name) on a flower farm in New Zealand. It has finely divided light green foliage which is also fragrant, and masses of soft pink flowers.

As you hunt around in nurseries and garden centres, you will find many different boronias, each with its own charm. Specialist native nurseries and branches of the Society for Growing Australian Plants can give you more information.

MAINTAINING BORONIAS

Boronias won't grow well unless they are given the right conditions. They need good drainage, preferably a light sandy soil, and plenty of mulch around them. Mulch, like leaf litter in the natural bush where boronias originate, will keep their roots cool. If these conditions are provided a boronia should live for many years.

- Grow boronias in sandy soils, or at least soil that is light and free draining. They will do well on a slight mound with plenty of well-rotted compost mixed into the soil, particularly in heavier soils.

- They can grow in full sun or light shade as long as their roots do not bake or get too hot in summer. Leaf litter or compost over the surface of the soil, covering the roots, is a great help.

- Some boronias need pruning after flowering to improve

Many people say that the fragrance of the brown boronia (*Boronia megastigma*) is one of the best in the plant world, and it is never reproduced well as talcum powder or in a scent bottle. Each spring it is worth having a plant in a pot near the door, so you can enjoy its fragrance.

The lime-yellow flowers of *Boronia megastigma* 'Lutea' are attractive and again have a lovely, Australian fragrance.

the plant's bushiness and shape. Immediately the flowers finish, cut off 10 cm of growth from the top of the stems.

- They will grow in pots which can be brought indoors for their fragrance, but make sure you use a good quality potting mix and keep them moist in dry times.
- They last well indoors as cut flowers.

Daphne, a winter favourite

There is probably no more popular plant in southern Australia than the daphne, with its glorious sweet scent when the shrub is in full flower. For me daphne is practically synonymous with Melbourne's chilly, wet winters, and I am always cheered when I smell its perfume. I will never forget the huge bush that my grandmother grew near her back door. It seemed a never-ending supply of lovely fragrance to put into vases indoors or to give to visitors. Her daphne bush was growing in exactly the right position to give such rewards: in a spot that received morning sun and afternoon shade, well protected from hot summer sun and cold winter winds. So, if you want to plant a daphne, a sheltered, east-facing spot is ideal.

Daphnes also like to grow in well-drained soil, as their leaves will yellow and fall off if their roots are too wet. In heavy clay soils, where water can hang around the plant's roots, make sure you mix plenty of organic matter, such as compost or rotted leaves, into the soil. If you add organic matter your soil will be more acidic, which suits the daphne. Even in sandy, well-drained soils it will never hurt to incorporate a couple of shovelfuls of compost before planting.

You often see daphne shrubs growing in pots or containers, and this is a sensible idea, especially if you do not have the ideal position or soil. With a good quality, well-drained potting mix in the tub, you can guarantee that the roots will not be sitting in water. Never leave the saucer filled with water as the plant can easily get root rot.

It is best to fertilise a plant in a container every month or so with a liquid fertiliser or a small teaspoon of slow-release fertiliser sprinkled around the soil surface in spring. Give plants in the ground some granules of slow-release fertiliser in spring and again in autumn for good healthy growth and flowers.

PROPAGATING DAPHNE

People love to propagate daphne. The best time to take cuttings is in late December through to February. Take several 10-cm shoots, remove the lower leaves, leaving a few at the top, and insert the cuttings into a pot filled with propagating sand mixed with coconut fibre. Put a plastic bag over the top of the pot, making a mini-hothouse, and leave it under a leafy shrub outside for 6–8 weeks. By then you may have a few cuttings with roots, and you can repot each one. They make a very special present.

HOW TO GROW DAPHNE

Best position Plenty of afternoon shade, so an easterly position with morning sun is ideal. Daphne can be grown in the ground or in a container.

Soil type Daphne does not like lime, but will grow well with plenty of compost or well-rotted animal manure mixed into the soil or added to the soil surface.

Drainage If water is not freely draining the plant can get root rot, so make sure it is growing in well-drained soil or potting mix.

Feeding After flowering, feed a daphne bush with animal manure — either the pelletised variety or well-rotted material — or with a specific fertiliser formulated for daphnes, camellias and rhododendrons.

Pruning If the bush has grown straggly, prune after flowering or simply by cutting the flowering stems to take indoors.

Pests and diseases Spray with white oil for scale and sooty mould. If leaves start to hang down limply, this may mean daphne virus has struck — pull the plant out and burn it. Do not plant a new daphne bush in the same spot.

It is a pretty common problem to find daphne leaves going yellow over winter. Don't worry, as long as the plant is not suffering from poor drainage which causes wet feet. Don't feed until after flowering, and then you could try some iron chelates, a product which supplies the extra iron that the daphne may need, especially in clay soils that can lock up iron. Most nurseries and garden centres will supply iron chelates in powder or liquid form.

By snipping off flower stems 10–15 cm long to bring indoors for a vase, you will have pruned your daphne. They generally do not need much more pruning attention unless you have a straggly plant with long, leggy growth and minimal foliage. Take off the tips with clean secateurs in early September to encourage buds down the stem to bush out to form a more compact bush.

Don't let the plant dry out in summer. Keep the surrounding soil moist with mulch. Never allow the mulch to pile up too close to the trunk; leave about 10 cm clear as breathing space around the base.

Daphne can occasionally suffer from insect problems such as scale. This is a sap-sucking insect that also causes black sooty mould over the leaves. To eradicate the scale and mould, spray with Clensel, a safe, detergent-like spray, or Malascale, a chemical spray that should be handled carefully. Do not forget to read the instructions.

Always choose clean, healthy specimens when you are buying a daphne bush. The label should guarantee that the plant is 'virus free'. Daphne virus can knock the plant, causing its leaves to go 'leathery' and hang down forlornly. Worse still, there is no cure. You just have to say good-bye to the plant and try again.

VARIETIES OF DAPHNE

Daphne × burkwoodii certainly rivals the best known *D. odora* for fragrance. It has clusters of light pink to white flowers all over the bush, which grows to approximately 90 cm high. The fragrance is not as heady as *D. odora*, but light and spring-like. This variety flowers in October, much later than the common daphne.

Other fragrant varieties are *D. cneorum* and *D. mezereum*. You may have to hunt for them in specialist nurseries, but you will be greatly rewarded.

D. odora is the best known, with probably the most pungent fragrance. Its flowers are deep purplish-pink to white.

The glorious gardenias

One of the sweetest scented flowers is the gardenia, which never fails to delight a passer-by with its luxuriant tropical fragrance. This evergreen shrub comes from southern Africa and tropical Asia, so a gardener can only admire its courage in growing and flowering in the cool winter of southern Australia.

Several varieties are available. The most popular is the double-flowering form, *Gardenia augusta* 'Florida'. *G. thunbergia* is a small tree, and a little more unusual nowadays, but you might find it in old gardens planted up to 60 years ago.

All gardenias must have rich, well-drained soil with lots of leaf mould around the roots. Given a position that is semi-shaded and sheltered, they will grow well, but obviously the warmer the position the better the plant will thrive and flower. A heated glasshouse, or an easterly aspect where the morning sun can reflect off the house walls, will give the plant the heat it needs. If the temperature is not high enough the flower buds will drop off. The plant must not dry out, so keep it well mulched to retain moisture. Gardenias can also be grown in containers with correctly drained potting mix.

Lavender

Of all the old-fashioned cottage garden plants, lavender never fails to give flowers and fragrance to a sunny spot, and it never fails to remind me of old aunts and butterflies. It is a very nostalgic plant! Lavender bushes can find a spot in any garden and are, of course, perfect for a cottage-style garden. A clump or hedge of lavender acting as a pathway border gives a feeling of heritage to a period house.

Lavender is probably one of the toughest plants. It withstands extremes of heat and drought, as well as blasts of wind. The only environmental hazard it hates is to have its roots in permanently boggy or wet soils, in which case it will drop dead without hesitation. Lavender is often used in large landscape projects as it is

There are many varieties of lavender with their splendid 'old world' fragrance. This one, *Lavandula angustifolia* 'Hidcote', has dense spikes of deep-purple flowers massed all over, and aromatic leaves. It grows well as a border plant, and can be grown into a small hedge to 90 cm high.

so hardy, able to withstand long periods of neglect and lack of water.

Pick the sunniest position in the garden; the lavender will love it. If grown in a spot with poor light it will grow straggly, with little fragrance in the leaves and few flowers. Soils with lime in them are perfect for growing these shrubs.

VARIETIES

Lavender is simply lavender to most of us, but to an ever-growing band of enthusiasts, there are many different varieties. 'Lavender blue, dilly-dilly, lavender green', as the old rhyme goes, reminds us that it has flowers of blue/mauve and green; there are also pink and white varieties. There are actually around twenty-five different lavender varieties, and the number is still growing.

The commonest is English lavender (*Lavandula angustifolia*) with the truest blue flowers and compact, narrow foliage. It is used commercially for oil, and in the home garden is a neat, compact grower. Other English lavenders come in the form of the white-flowering variety 'Alba'; the small-growing, pink form, 'Rosea'; 'Munstead' which has mauve-blue flowers on a dwarf bush; and 'Hidcote', another dwarf variety growing to approximately 60 cm with deeper coloured lavender spikes.

Lavender originates from Mediterranean countries, growing well in the rocky outcrops and limestone soils of this area. Both the French and Italian varieties have adapted well to Australian conditions for that reason. In fact, Italian lavender (*L. stoechas*) is a noxious weed if grown outside metropolitan areas in Victoria. It is a pretty flower with showy purple bracts that look as if they have wings attached, but it self-seeds readily and if left unchecked it can spread quite rapidly, causing a great deal of harm in rural areas.

French lavender, *L. dentata* 'Allardi', is a highly perfumed shrub. In my own garden, when it was left for a season un-trimmed, it grew rampantly to more than 1.5 m high. Even though it looked a bit straggly, it produced a magnificent lot of flowers for picking. If left on the bush these long graceful wands of light blue spikes waft around attracting bees and butterflies galore.

The green lavender is *L. viridis*. It is a more compact grower with a leaf of an unusual lime green colour, as is the fragrant flower.

SPICY LAVENDER POTPOURRI

Potpourri, a mixture of fragrant flowers and leaves, can perfume a linen cupboard, a wardrobe, a bathroom or an entire house, and it is very easy to make.

To prepare lavender as the main ingredient in potpourri, cut the flower spikes and hang the bunches upside-down in the laundry or garage to dry, or spread them out on a rack, wire frame or jumper drier, or on newspaper in an airy spot (but away from draughts). They will dry in a few weeks with the air circulating around them. Once dry, strip the flowerheads off and throw away the sticks (or use them as fire starters).

To the tiny flowerheads add a variety of fragrant flowers or leaves and mix them with spices or a few drops of essential oils (available from health food shops).

One of my favourite potpourri recipes is a mix of lavender and spices:

3–4 cups dried lavender flowers
2 cups dried lavender leaves
2 teaspoons ground cloves
2 teaspoons ground cinnamon
2 teaspoons orris root
(it helps 'fix' the fragrances)
4 drops lavender oil

Mix all the ingredients together, adding the lavender oil last. Store in a big jar, preferably ceramic (an old bread crock is good) for two weeks. Stir with a wooden spoon every day to allow the aromas to mix and blend. Place the potpourri in smaller bowls around the house. Every time you pass by, give them a little stir to disperse the fragrance.

PRUNING AND PROPAGATION

Once the flowers have finished, give the lavender a hard prune to encourage strong, bushy growth. Start pruning when the plant is young to prevent it becoming weak and spindly in the centre. If your lavender looks as if it is over the hill, it may be best to propagate a new plant. You can take cuttings from young growth at any time, but spring or autumn will probably give the best results. Tip cuttings or heel cuttings of the laterals are the best pieces to use. Take cuttings 5–7 cm long, use some rooting hormone powder to encourage quicker root growth and place the cuttings in a mix of 75 per cent coarse sand and 25 per cent peat moss or coconut fibre. Keep the cuttings well watered and they should strike within six to eight weeks.

By taking cuttings you can ensure that an ancient bush of lavender continues to give pleasure in your garden. It is invaluable to have a little pot of lavender in the potting area, just in case an old favourite turns up its toes.

Lilac *(Syringa spp.)*

Many old gardens contain a lilac. Their delicious perfume wafts through the air to reach you way before your nose reaches the flower. I love the soft, lavender-coloured ones. They make good partners to the creamy white verburnum (*Viburnum opulus* 'Sterile') as they flower at the same time.

Of course, there are many species and varieties of lilac available, in single or double flowers ranging from deep mauve to pink, white or red. But I think it is their perfume and soft appearance that make them such a lovely garden plant.

In areas with cold winters (they don't take to heat or humidity) lilacs will flower on for years, not really needing much attention, apart from removing the spent flowerheads and annual feeding with a complete fertiliser. Keep them moist, especially in dry times, and mulch over the root surface. They will eventually reach 3–4 m high, but can be pruned to 2 m.

One of the most popular varieties of the Oriental lily is *Lilium* 'Stargazer', which flowers in summer with a rich red colour and a white edge. I grow these lilium bulbs in pots to bring close to the house, or indoors, when they are in full flower, just for a few days so guests can appreciate them.

Liliums

Whenever I walk into a florist shop I find the wafty fragrance of the liliums enticing, no matter what time of year. Liliums are such popular cut flowers that they are widely grown in controlled hot-house conditions, hence their availability all year.

There are the Oriental lilies (*Lilium auratum*), with enormous flowers often 15–20 cm across, in pink, white or cream, spectacular as cut flowers. Other liliums with a scent that nearly overwhelms are the Madonna lily (*L. candidum*), with pure white, waxy flowers in summer, and the November or Christmas lily (*L. longiflorum*) with white trumpet flowers that herald the Christmas season.

Lily of the valley
(Convallaria majalis)

Lily of the valley will remind me forever of Paris where, on 1 May, every corner store, florist and market sells little bunches of lily of the valley which it is customary to give away to friends. Parisians go out to the forests to pick these wonderfully fragrant posies. Lily of the valley has a never-to-be-forgotten fragrance, and one that is never truly replicated in powder and soap.

Lily of the valley can be bought in pots in flower, or more usually as 'pips', little budded roots ready to be planted in autumn. They will spread, once established successfully, to cover quite a large area.

Choose a relatively sheltered spot with morning sun, not too hot as they need cool conditions. Dig in loads of rotted animal manure, leaf mould and rotted-down lawn clippings, as they like this kind of rich soil.

One of the pleasantest gardening tasks I have ever had was helping two elderly gardeners clear out their patch of lily of the valley. They had a huge area along an east-facing fence, about 1.5 m wide and 10 m long, filled with a mass of these beautiful plants. It had been growing there for thirty years and was now popping up

POLLEN STAINS FROM LILIUMS

Always nip off the stamens in the middle of the lilium flowers as they are covered with thick golden or brown pollen that can stain clothes and furnishings. If pollen does get onto clothing, don't rub it. Simply cover with talcum powder and then brush off. It will come off cleanly.

Even just a few sprigs of lily of the valley (*Convallaria* spp.) have a glorious fragrance.

through their lawn. We spent several hours digging it up and separating the clumps. There was plenty to give away, and it still keeps popping up. Their secret was to grow Solomon's seal (*Polygonatum*) amongst the lily of the valley — the two seemed most compatible. Solomon's seal grows to a little less than 1 m high, while lily of the valley spreads over the ground to only a few centimetres high. They both give a very spring-like effect with their fresh green leaves.

Luculia gratissima

Luculias are good plants to have in any garden because they flower in the winter months when you are often short of colour. Luculias have wonderful bunches, up to 15 cm across, of pink flowers with a magnificent scent. There is also a variety with white flowers, *L. grandiflora*, also sweetly scented.

Luculias can be grown in many positions in the garden, though it is best to put them in a protected spot where frosts cannot cut them back. Many gardeners have success when they plant a luculia against a house or a fence, out of range of full sun. Give them a good mulching so they don't dry out in summer, and enrich the soil with plenty of animal manure or blood and bone.

When the plants are young they will respond well to tip pruning to produce a bushy plant. Luculias will grow to approximately 3 m high by 2 m wide. After the bush has finished flowering, cut the stems back by a third.

Native frangipani
(*Hymenosporum flavum*)

An evergreen tree that is one of my favourites for its rich fragrance is the native frangipani. In early summer, particularly at dusk, its perfume fills the air. Its flowers are creamy at first and age to a deep yellow.

This tree originates in the rainforests of northern New South Wales and Queensland, but it has adapted well to growing in many other climates, from hot and dry to milder areas. In a larger garden, native frangipanis can be grown in a clump, spaced closely at about 1 metre apart, for a very impressive effect. They will grow to approximately 10–15 m in ideal conditions, but in cooler climates grow to approximately 8 m.

Left to their own devices, native frangipanis can shoot up to the heavens and become very straggly, so tip prune them when they are young so they grow denser and thicker. At planting time, a teaspoon of slow-release fertiliser especially formulated for native plants can be put around the plants, and give them plenty of water as they grow. Mulch around the surface, though not close to the main trunk, to keep moisture around the roots.

One of my very favourite trees is *Hymenosporum flavum*. This native plant has a magnificent perfume and its cream-yellow flowers contrast well with the glossy green leaves.

Perennials, for nostalgic fragrance

*T*here are many perennial plants with a fragrance that takes me straight back to early childhood days, so maybe they should be in a nostalgia list. The aromas of cherry pie, violets, carnations and wallflowers are typical of these old-fashioned plants. They have made a great comeback with the resurgence of cottage-style gardens and, if you can arrange it, a few doves coo-cooing in the garden wouldn't go astray.

A fragrant Australian native garden

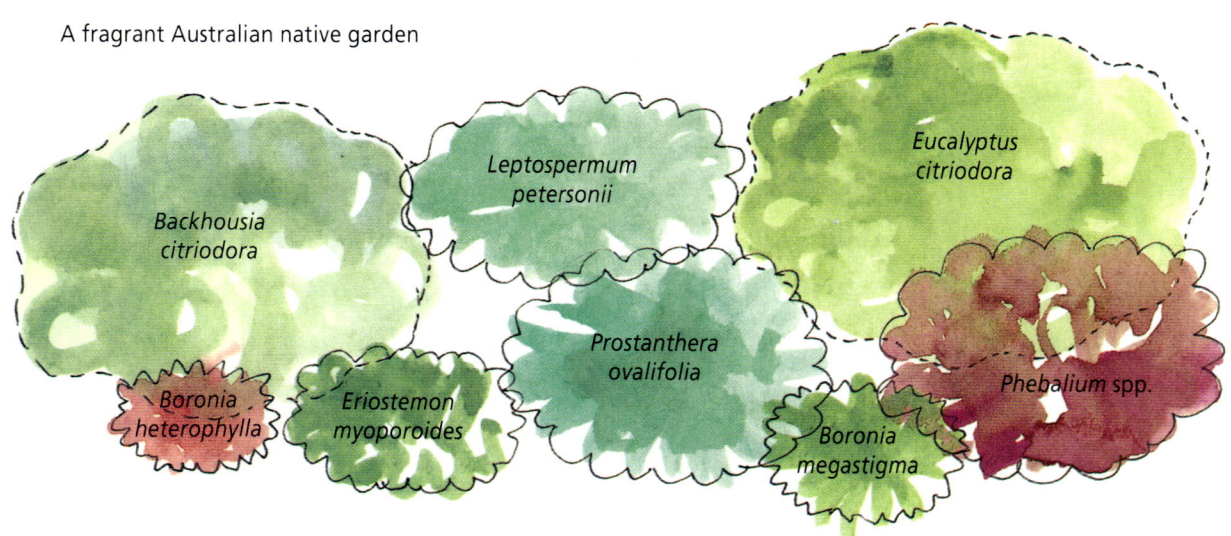

Backhousia citriodora

Leptospermum petersonii

Eucalyptus citriodora

Boronia heterophylla

Eriostemon myoporoides

Prostanthera ovalifolia

Boronia megastigma

Phebalium spp.

CARNATIONS *(Dianthus* spp.*)*

Carnations are prolific flowerers in spring, highly scented, and they come in a wide range of colours, from pink and white to red and other more vibrant colours. There are many species grown and loads of named varieties. Some of my special ones are the famous *Dianthus plumarius* 'Mrs Sinkins', which has been around since the 1860s; the mauve–pink 'Old English'; and the clove-smelling variety, 'Little Jock'. 'Devon' is another with a spectacular fragrance.

Dianthus need full sun to grow successfully, otherwise they become straggly rather than neat and compact. They also grow much better in alkaline soils that are well drained, rather than over-rich manured soils. Cut them back after flowering finishes and add a handful of lime to the patch every few years. They will grow to approximately 20 cm high and can spread out to 90 cm in the right conditions.

Propagation

Dianthus are quite easily grown by cuttings, using the non-flowering side shoots. Take off all lower leaves, and put into pots with propagating mix where they will take root in 6–8 weeks.

CHERRY PIE *(Heliotropium arborescens)*

For me cherry pie or heliotrope has the smell of vanilla, quite sweet and strong. The English gave it its common name because they thought its fragrance similar to that of a freshly baked cherry pie. It is a subdued rather than a showy plant in the garden — its pretty veined leaves are not especially notable and the flowers are clusters of mauve–lilac colours — but it works well in amongst other shrubs and perennials. I once saw it growing in a Mildura garden with the lime green euphorbia and violets growing as a groundcover. It looked and smelt sensational.

It is an easy plant to grow, not needing any fussy conditions apart from the odd watering and mulching. It does get knocked by frost, but if this happens, cut it back and it should reshoot.

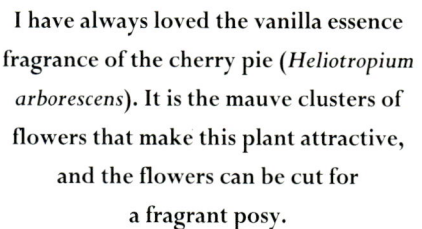

I have always loved the vanilla essence fragrance of the cherry pie (*Heliotropium arborescens*). It is the mauve clusters of flowers that make this plant attractive, and the flowers can be cut for a fragrant posy.

PLANTS WITH FRAGRANT LEAVES

Have you ever been stopped in your tracks by a nose-tingling scent from a eucalypt on a warm day, or the heady rose or peppermint of a patch of pelargoniums after rain? We tend to neglect the variety and deliciousness of scents from foliage when planning our plantings, but many fragrant-leaved plants are easy to grow and offer this bonus.

AUSTRALIAN PLANTS

Crowea (Crowea saligna)
Lemon-scented tea tree
    (Leptospermum petersonii)
Native mint (Prostanthera spp.)
Phebalium (Phebalium spp.)
Wax plant (Eriostemon myoporoides)
Zieria (Zieria spp.)

HERBS

Balm of Gilead (Cedronella canariensis)
    — smells like a lovely antique
    bookshop
Basil — summery and sunny
Lemon verbena — clear and lemony
Mints, apple and Corsican — fresh
Pelargoniums — scented leaf which
    smells like roses or peppermints
Pennyroyal — pepperminty
    and fresh
Rosemary (Rosmarinus officinalis) —
    pine-like

TREE LEAVES

Lemon-scented gum
    (Eucalyptus citriodora)
Lemon-scented myrtle
    (Backhousia citriodora)
Peppermint gum
    (Eucalyptus nicholli)
Pepper tree (Schinus molle)

VIOLETS (Viola spp.)

The old-fashioned violets rank highly as a nostalgic fragrance. A florist once told me that she finds that only elderly folk buy bunches of violets; young people seem to avoid them. Well, they don't know what they are missing!

Violets are beautiful as posies or as cut flowers in a small vase. For the finishing touch, encircle the flowers with a ring of violet leaves to frame the posy. They will last longer if you mist spray the leaves and flowers each day to keep them fresh. And the more you pick violets, the more they will keep flowering. In her Mildura garden my mother has a large patch of violets covering an area 1 m x 10 m; from this she picks about fifty bunches to give away each year, from July to October.

For a groundcover that is fast growing and easy to look after, the sweet violet (V. odorata) is a beauty. It grows about 15 cm high and spreads by stolons along the ground or just under the surface. Don't grow it in too much shade as there will be lots of leaves and few flowers.

Dig in lots of organic matter to help aerate the soil, and after it has flowered throw on a handful of blood and bone to every square metre. Some growers cut the clumps right back in spring, literally taking off all the foliage and leaving bare crowns so the plants come back with new vigour.

Violets can be divided after 2–3 years, by digging them up when flowering finishes and looking for a stolon (or stem) with a few roots and a growing point. Replant in rich soil, leaving the crowns above the soil surface.

There are many varieties, some single flowered, others semi and double flowered, and they vary in colour from white through to pink, mauve and purple. Perhaps none are quite as heavily scented nor as strong growing as V. odorata, but their scent is still remarkable.

WALLFLOWERS (Cheiranthus spp.)

Another perennial worth its weight in scent is the wallflower. Wallflowers are long flowering and incredibly hardy, tolerating cold and frost. They need sun and make excellent rockery or cottage plants. They seem to spring into life in the most awkward spots, living up to their common name, as they grow in the crevices of walls and stone work.

A wallflower (*Cheiranthus* spp.) growing in the most fitting location, a crevice in a wall at Sissinghurst Castle garden, England. It has a singularly beautiful fragrance.

There are many varieties, ranging from orange and yellow to mauve, with plenty of new ones being released as people realise their potential. They grow to approximately 90 cm high and are very free flowering. Once the flower flush ends, cut back the stems so the bush will thicken up with new growth.

Sweet peas
(Lathyrus odoratus)

*O*ld gardener's lore has it that you should plant your sweet pea seeds on St Patrick's Day, 17 March, but any time from March to the end of April will do. Sweet peas are always worth growing. They do well in a pot or in the ground, are simple to grow, children love them, and they are hard to beat as a posy to give to a friend. In Victorian times, sweet peas were amongst the most popular annual plants — every piano in the parlour had a vase of sweet peas on top.

The sad thing is that the fragrance of sweet peas seems to have diminished. Some of the species that specialists grow have a fine fragrance, but most of the seed packets you see in nurseries and supermarkets produce flowers that have nowhere near the strong perfume that even I can remember from years ago. Hopefully, plant breeders in future years will think of our sense of smell and reintroduce their 'real' fragrance.

My favourite sweet pea varieties

L. o. 'Bijou'. A dwarf growing bush which always has masses of flowers in pink, red, white and mauve

L. o. 'Early Sunshine'. One for a trellis, with fragrant pink flowers

L. o. 'Leading Light'. One with darker wing petals than the standard petals, in a lovely mauve

The modern sweet pea makes up for its fainter perfume, however, by being a prolific flowerer, providing masses of colour in late winter and early spring.

HOW TO GROW SWEET PEAS

- Plant them in a sunny position; the more sun, the more flowers you will get.
- The best flowers will grow in well-prepared soil, though sweet peas will grow in any kind of soil. Dig the soil over well and put in loads of animal manure and compost, along with a couple of handfuls of blood and bone to every square metre. A complete fertiliser can also be used. Sweet peas are big feeders.
- Some varieties of sweet peas are tall growing, up to 2 m high, so they need supporting. A wire-netting trellis or plastic mesh will be enough support, or you may like to grow them on a 'wigwam' of bamboo stakes, placing three or four stakes firmly in the ground and a seed at each base so they twine upwards.
- For the smaller growing varieties in a pot, plant them in very well composted and fertilised soil. The pot should be at least 25 cm deep.
- Sow sweet pea seeds in the ground direct into their position, at least 2.5 cm deep. Water sparingly until the seedling appears. When it starts flowering, feed with liquid fertiliser.
- Remove spent flowers and your sweet peas will keep flowering on and on.

FRAGRANT PLANTS BY SEASON

SPRING
Bouvardia longiflora
Citrus
Climbing mandevilla
  (*Mandevilla laxa*)
Jasmine (*Jasminum officinale*
  J. polyanthum)
Mock orange (*Philadelphus 'Virginal'*)
Ornamental grape (*Vitis vinifera*)
White cedar (*Melia azederach*)

SUMMER
Chinese star jasmine
  (*Trachelospermum jasminoides*)
Evergreen magnolia
  (*Magnolia grandiflora*)
Gardenia (*Gardenia florida*)
Stocks (*Matthiola* spp.)
Sweet-scented tobacco
  (*Nicotiana* spp.)
Tuberoses (*Polyanthes tuberosa*)

AUTUMN
Camellia sasanqua
  'Setsugekka'
Ginger lily (*Hedychium gardnerianum*)
Rosemary (*Rosmarinus officinalis*
  'Blue Lagoon'*)
Sweet Alice (*Alyssum* spp.)

WINTER
Acacia floribunda
A. iteaphylla
A. podalyriifolia
A. retinodes
Coast banksia (*B. integrifolia*)
Heath banksia (*B. ericifolia*)

One of the headiest fragrances in autumn is from the ginger lily (*Hedychium* spp.). Neighbours will also love this plant, as the perfume wafts such a long way.

Design of a fragrant herb garden

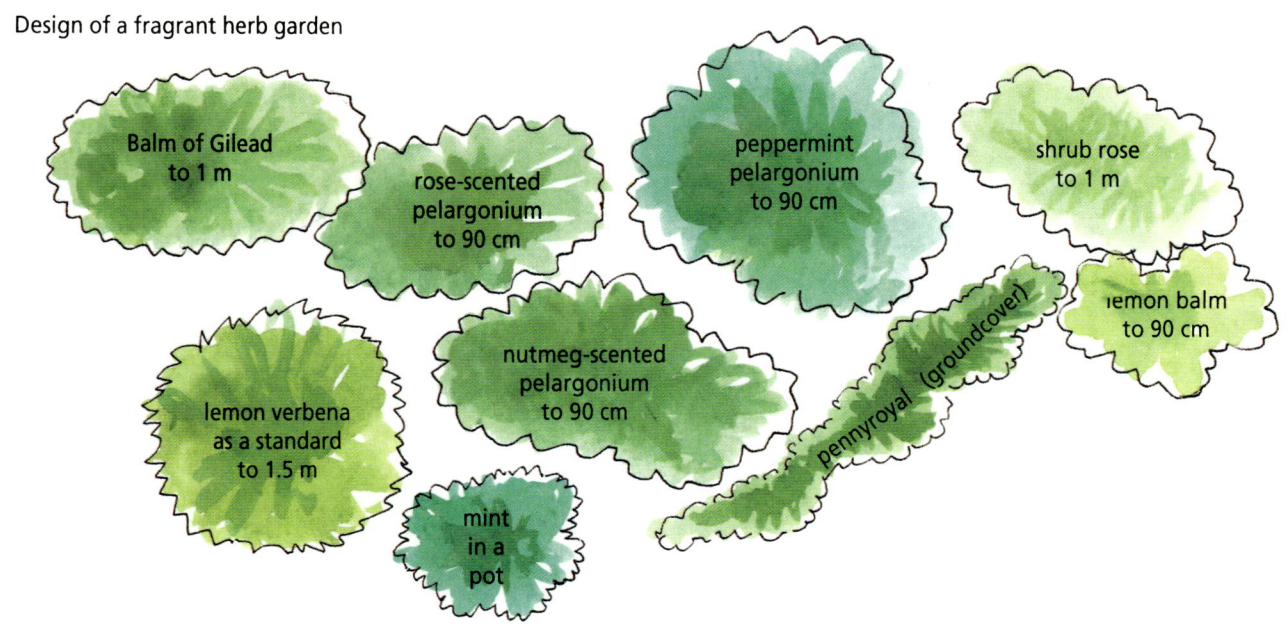

WINTER SCENTS AND CHEERFULNESS

There are plenty of flowering plants that give colour in the rather bleak season of winter, and there are many to grow for fragrance. Winter may not be a time for riotous colour, but all is not boring and flowerless. Rather winter, unlike spring, summer and autumn, is more reserved in its colours, more discreet and less flashy.

However, the scents and perfumes of many winter-flowering plants are not at all reserved, some creep up and overwhelm you!

ALLSPICE (Chimonanthus praecox)

This is wintersweet, sometimes known as 'Carolina allspice'. A few sprigs of this plant in a vase will fill a room with magnificent fragrance. The flowers are waxy yellow with a purplish centre. They are certainly rather strange-looking, but they make up for this with the scent, which reminds some people of violets. This is a deciduous shrub and during winter the flowers appear as if by magic

on the shrub's leafless branches. The flower may not be crowd stopping, but the perfume certainly is! Allspice fits in well in a mixed shrubbery. It is a medium-sized bush growing to approximately 2 m high and 1.5 m wide. It will grow well against a wall where it gets some reflected heat. To keep the bush looking neat and tidy, prune back any long growths after it has finished flowering.

CHINESE WITCH HAZEL
(Hamamelis mollis)

The Chinese witch hazel flowers in late winter or early spring. Another deciduous shrub, it has strange twisted flowers that appear on bare stems. The flowers are bright yellow and very sweetly perfumed. It is an appealing shrub, deciduous and reaching 2–3 m high. Not all nurseries will stock this plant, so you may have to search for it. There is also a pale yellow form called H. mollis pallida.

VIBURNUM (Viburnum spp.)

Viburnums are another genus of plant that are thankfully becoming more popular in gardens. Many varieties are easy to grow, needing little of the gardener's attention, but they have a fragrance to knock you out. One of my favourites is Viburnum × burkwoodii. It has clusters of white flowers that emerge from pink buds earlier than other viburnums, such as V. carlesii. As a medium-sized shrub of 2–3 m high, V. × burkwoodii can be fitted in anywhere in the garden scheme, and it is good for filling a gap. It has dark green leaves, and the flowers appear as large balls or clusters, up to 8 cm across, in winter and into spring. They will grow in full sun or light shade and I have seen them growing as an unusual hedge, planted about 1.5 m apart. They can be cut back by nipping off 10 cm underneath the finished flower. Fertilise with a low-release fertiliser.

Magnificent magnolias

Magnolia × soulangeana **is one of the most popular of all magnolias as it is very free flowering.**

Magnolias are truly magnificent flowering trees for temperate to cold areas. With a certain amount of poetic licence, the flowers remind me of a flock of doves roosting on the leafless branches. Many people know them as 'tulip trees' as the white or soft pink flowers look rather like tulips growing all over the tree.

Growing conditions

If you are looking for a plant to make a statement in your garden, a magnolia will certainly do the trick. They can grow amongst other shrubs or in a spot where the beauty of their form can be fully appreciated. A large magnolia in July is a magic sight, with its flower buds all wrapped in their furry coverings, ready to pop out as spring approaches.

Magnolias are not fussy about where they grow, except that they need a sunny spot and, being frost hardy, they make good plants for southern gardens. They also need some protection from strong winds, which can wreak havoc with the flower petals, and from dry north winds in summer, which can 'burn' the leaf edges. Magnolias will grow in alkaline, neutral or acid soils and are tolerant of pollution, but make sure you dig in plenty of animal manure, compost or leaf mould to lighten up the soil, whatever type it is.

I've often seen magnolias growing in the middle of a lawn, with grass growing right up to the trunk. This makes life pretty hard for the tree, as most water and food is being used by the grass. Keep a circle of at least 1-m diameter around the trunk free of grass.

Magnolias need little pruning, as they grow into a lovely shape naturally. A friend of mine has a very old one, grown to 7 m high, and is lucky enough to be able to cut off long stems at will to bring indoors.

Varieties

My family used to take a Sunday drive up to the Dandenong Ranges, outside Melbourne, specifically to see a giant pink magnolia (*M. campbellii*) in flower in an old nursery there. It will only flower when it reaches maturity at 10–15 years old, but when it does it is magnificent — the flowers can be 25–30 cm across!

On a trip to the Yunnan province of China, I was very excited to come across a very old magnolia in a public garden. This was the 'Yulan' (*Magnolia denudata*), which is often seen in cool and temperate parts of Australia. It will grow to 10 m high, spreads to 4 m and produces masses of fragrant, creamy white, cup-shaped flowers. A friend of mine once said that seeing this tree in full bloom was like being in a dream.

The most commonly grown magnolia is *M. × soulangeana*, with white to rose pink flowers in which the colour deepens a little towards the base of the petals. The flowers are tulip shaped and, again, they look breathtaking on the bare branches. There are many varieties, such as *M. × soulangeana* 'Alba Superba', which flowers early; 'Brazzonii', with large white flowers; and 'Lennei', with deep rose-purple flowers.

A popular, smaller growing variety is the star magnolia (*M. stellata*), a compact bush approximately 4 m high by 2m wide, which suits most small gardens. The flowers are made up of narrow, ribbon-like petals rather than being cup-shaped. They are profuse and fragrant and there are both white and pink forms.

EVERGREENS

There are also evergreen magnolias which grow readily and look equally spectacular. The Bull Bay magnolia (*M. grandiflora*), from the southern states of the USA, flowers in mid-summer in Australia. The fragrant, white, open flowers are huge and contrast beautifully with the glossy green leaves. *Michelia doltsopa* is another lovely evergreen, with pointed white flowers which completely cover the tree (photograph on page 4).

Magnolia denudata will give you immense pleasure when it's in flower as its creamy white flowers are a spectacular sight. It is worth hunting for this variety in specialist nurseries.

PORT-WINE MAGNOLIA
(Michelia figo)

The port-wine magnolia has a fragrance that reminds me of tutti-frutti bubble gum, very sweet indeed and almost fruity. It flowers in late spring and its aroma drifts around in the warm air, unfailingly causing people to stop and sniff. Some say it reminds them of banana-flavoured icecream; others of a glass of port wine.

The flowers will not remind you of its common name, magnolia, although it does look as if it belongs to the family. The flowers are creamy with mauvish edges and quite small, set amongst glossy green leaves. It is an evergreen shrub, growing to 2–3 m high, and can be clipped to keep its shape after flowering.

The gardener's palette: Planting by colour

Being creative with colour in the garden can make for quite different displays of colour in different seasons. Spring is the time to try something different, maybe something flamboyant, which can be enjoyed in the summer months when you entertain or just relax in the garden. Late winter is the time to plan ahead to get the most out of summer.

Pastel colours have been very popular for some years now, but there are also many plants with dramatically coloured flowers that can look very striking. If you look at fashion trends in the interior design industry you will see a move towards stronger colours. Following suit, mauves, violets, tangerines and citrus oranges — all colours that have depth and definition — are beginning to reappear in many gardens.

Red-hot pokers (*Kniphofia uvaria*) live up to their name with their flaming spires of flowers, which make a strong colour statement. They are easy to grow in sunny spots and can look stunning amongst other perennial plants, or you can leave them to naturalise in grassland. Choose them if you want a long-flowering show, and look out for other cultivars in creamy white, yellow and salmon pink. I once saw a clump growing in a country cemetery, where they received no attention but were thriving, so maybe I'll order them in my will!

The native hibiscus (*Alyogyne huegelli*) produces its mauve flowers practically all year round.

The colour wheel

The colour wheel can be used to plan a colour scheme for your garden. Some colours seem to blend better than others, so you can use colours on the same side of the wheel to create visual harmony; or maybe you would prefer a completely different 'look' in your garden by choosing contrasting colours from opposite sides of the wheel.

A selection of some of my favourite plants in the different colour groups can be found on the following pages.

A wreath of living flowers depicting the colour wheel, to show how colours blend, complement or contrast with each other.

Oranges and yellows

For the most cheerful colours in the garden you cannot go past yellows and oranges. They are both strong colours and will always have high impact. If you want to be dramatic, use yellow and orange plants to contrast with intense blues. If you want to tone down these colours you can mix them with some cream, grey or white to soften the picture.

Californian poppy (*Eschscholzia californica*). Easy-to-grow annual that requires a sunny spot, with bright yellow–orange flowers that open in the sunshine. Also in cream.

Chinese lantern (*Abutilon* spp.). An easy-to-grow plant, reaching 2 m in sun or semi-shade. Free flowering, with orange or yellow lantern-shaped flowers, containing nectar that attracts birds.

Coreopsis spp. Easy to grow in a sunny spot, bright yellow flowers.

Cosmos 'Sunny Gold'. An excellent background plant for other low-growing annuals with its double yellow flowers, which also make excellent cut flowers.

Dahlia spp. Easy to grow from tubers, in a well-drained, sunny spot. May need to be staked to protect plants from the wind. Available in many bright colours, including a range of oranges and yellows.

Gazania spp. Easy-to-grow, fast-spreading groundcover with masses of daisy flowers in bright yellow, orange or bi-coloured. Grows well in a sunny spot.

Kangaroo paw (*Anigozanthos* spp.). These days there is a range of yellow–orange varieties available in these unusual flowering shrubs. They form clumps of leaves and long stems with vibrant flowers in clusters. Many are dwarf growers, others grow to 90 cm. All prefer sunny, well-drained soil.

Lion's ear (*Leonotis leonurus*). This is a lovely old-fashioned shrub to 2 m, and is easy to grow. It has bright orange, velvety, tubular flowers that grow in clusters.

Marigolds (*Calendula* spp.). Easy-to-grow annual plants. African marigolds are taller than the more compact French marigolds with large flowers in orange or yellow.

Mexican sunflower (*Tithonia* spp.). An attractive, sun-loving, annual plant with russet–orange flowers.

Jerusalem sage (*Phlomis fruticosa*) thrives in hot, dry conditions and will never disappoint you. It is a perennial shrub growing to 90 cm high, and it flowers for ages with unusually shaped yellow flowers and tough, sage-like leaves. It also withstands frosts.

Nasturtiums (*Tropaeolum* spp.). Very adaptable, colourful annual plants which are easy to grow in sun or partial shade. The flowers are bright and range from yellow to deep orange, and the spicy leaves are delicious in salads.

Red-hot poker (*Kniphofia* spp.). Easy-to-grow, clump-forming plants with strap leaves and tall spikes of flowers. Plants grow well in a sunny spot.

Yarrow (*Achillea* spp.). This is very easy to grow, with lacy, green, mat-forming foliage and yellow flowers on massed flowerheads.

Blues and purples

For cool colours, the blues and purples always look good. You can combine them with pinks, white and grey to give a soft, hazy effect. There are very few 'true' blues in flowers, but the range of mauves and purples is immense. These colours all make for good background as they give the garden depth.

Ageratum spp. For a sunny, well-drained spot, a pretty low-growing, annual plant to 60 cm high with fluffy, bluish flowers

Bee bush (*Echium* spp.). A spectacular flowering plant to 1.5 m high. Grows well in a sunny spot with large spikes of mauve-blue flowers.

Canterbury bells (*Campanula medium*). A fast-growing, easily maintained plant, varieties from groundcover to tall, 1 m high stems, masses of blue–purple flowers shaped like bells.

Catnip (*Nepeta cataria*). This is a good plant for edging and garden beds, growing to 60 cm high, with soft grey leaves and mauve flowers. Hardy and easy to maintain.

Ceanothus spp. A showy shrub to small tree, growing to 2.5 m high, noted for its rich blue, fuzzy flowers in spring.

Columbine or granny's bonnet (*Aquilegia* spp.). A lovely plant, best grown in clumps or drifts for a variety of colours in a herbaceous border. Easy to grow and will self-seed in dappled shaded spots.

Delphinium spp. Tall annuals with spikes of bright blue–mauve flowers.

For a brilliant clear colour, the blue Lechenaultia *(L. biloba)* is a very beautiful perennial plant. It does need perfect drainage, growing best in sandy soil or on a mounded-up bed. Yellow and blue flowers always work well together; the yellow in this case is the tufty *Conostylus* spp.

The blue trumpet vine (*Thunbergia grandiflora*) is suitable for a warm, protected wall. It has one of the most magnificent violet-blue flowers that you will see in summer — it will stop the traffic!

Lasiandra (*Tibouchina* spp.). This is a long-flowering, easy-to-grow shrub 2–3 m high. It has velvety leaves and large, open mauve flowers.

Lavender (*Lavandula* spp.). There are many varieties of lavender with spikes of blue–mauve–purple flowers. The French lavender grows taller than the English variety and there are dwarf varieties such as *L.* 'Munstead'. *L.* 'Sidonie' has a ferny leaf. All have fragrant foliage and flowers over a long period if grown in a sunny spot.

Lobelia spp. Perfect annual for edging along the front of a garden bed, or in a basket, some lovely sky blues and mauves.

Lupins (*Lupinus* spp.). Annuals with spikes of mauve flowers, perfect for the back of a garden bed.

Petunia spp. Easy-to-grow annuals which prefer a sunny spot; plenty of blues, mauves and violets to select from.

Salvia spp. Hardy plants in many colours, including some really good blues and mauves; loves a sunny position.

Pinks and reds

Red is a very intense colour. If you look on the colour wheel you will see that it is directly opposite green, and indeed red and green are complementary colours in nature's own palette. Take advantage of this by making a strong statement with red used in a one-colour garden theme, relying on the fresh green foliage to complement it.

On the colour wheel, pink lies between red and the mauve-blues. Pink is soft and harmonious, a gentle colour to co-ordinate with other pastels, soft blues and whites. These pastel combinations will always have charm, but you may like to go for something a bit stronger.

Begonia spp. Excellent low-growing plants for borders and edgings, flowers in red, white or pink, in single colours or mixed, long flowering.

Cosmos spp. A good background plant with fancy foliage and simple flowers; prefers a sunny spot.

Crepe myrtle (*Lagerstroemia indica*). A lovely tree which grows to 3 m high, or there is a dwarf variety which grows to 1 m. The flowers have a crepe-like appearance, in deep red or pink, and flower best in a sunny spot.

Diascia spp. Pretty, small-growing plants that look good in the front of a garden bed; soft apricot–pink flowers and very free flowering.

English daisy (*Bellis perennis*). Dainty, low-growing plant with red, pink or white flowers massed on short stems, fast growing and easy to maintain.

Foxgloves (*Digitalis* spp.). Tall spikes of flowers, usually in pastel shades, easy to grow, feed well with animal manure, prefers dappled shade.

Fuchsia spp. In pots or garden beds in dappled shade, fuchsias will perform well. There is a huge range of colours, some soft and pastel, others deeper colours such as magenta. In summer all fuchsias should be watered daily, especially on hot, windy days.

Geraniums (*Pelargonium* spp.). Excellent plants for the hottest, sunniest position. They look good in pots as well as in the garden and there are many pinks and reds to choose from.

Grevillea 'Robyn Gordon'. An outstanding plant, growing to 1.5 m high, with ferny foliage and bright red flowers that attract birds.

Impatiens spp. Very popular plants for dappled, shady spots, long flowering in a variety of colours — look for intense red with deep green leaves, a perfect flower for Christmas.

Lavatera spp. Tall-growing to 2 m with soft pink flowers for background colour in the garden, easy to grow in a sunny position.

Petunia spp. Always a summer favourite, easy-to-grow annual which likes a sunny spot, there is a variety of colours from pastel pinks to deep, vibrant colours.

Perennial petunia. A ground-hugging plant with variety of colours; red is a new strain. It needs feeding and a sunny spot.

Roses (*Rosa* spp.). There are masses of roses in a wide range of reds and pinks, so the choice is really up to you. You may want a fragrant rose, a climber or a shrub. For better flowers, make sure your rose is given an open, sunny spot and is well fed and watered.

Salvia spp. This is easy to grow in a sunny spot. It grows between 1–2 m high and there are varieties with pink and red flowers.

Spider flower (*Cleome* spp.). A tall, spiky annual plant with spidery pink flowers. It looks good at the back of a garden bed.

Sweet Alice (*Alyssum* spp.). There are many colours of this annual, low-growing edging plant. All are easy to grow from seed.

The striking flowers of deep red, blotched with intense black, of the Shirley poppy (*Papaver rhoeas*). (This plant is sometimes called the Flanders poppy as they were the first flowers to bloom on the Flanders battlefield in World War I.) They are annual plants and need a sunny position. They look their best when grown in an informal way, left to self-seed amongst perennial plants.

Greens, greys and whites

Greens and greys (foliage) and whites (flowers) can be used as complementary colours and as a foil to stronger colours. They allow your eye to 'rest' from the vivid tones of reds, oranges and yellows. Plants of those colours will stand alone, but they also sit well amongst any of the other colours.

Feverfew (*Chrysanthemum parthenium*). An easy-to-grow annual plant up to 60 cm high, with simple, open white flowers with yellow centres, prefers a sunny spot.

Gardenia spp. Either a shrub or low-growing plant with creamy white flowers that are highly fragrant, best grown in a warm, sheltered spot with good drainage, or in a pot beside an entrance door so the fragrance is highlighted.

Gypsophila spp. Grey foliage with white flowers, very pretty in the garden or as cut flowers.

Lobelia spp. There are many colour varieties, but the white ones always look good on the fresh green leaves; easy-to-grow annual, up to 30 cm high.

Marguerite daisy (*Chrysanthemum* spp.). Wonderful free-flowering plants that will grow just about anywhere. The old-fashioned Marguerite daisy grows to about 1 m high, but for people wanting a more compact plant, there are two recent releases in the Federation series, which grow from 45–60 cm high: *C.* 'Sugar Baby' and *C.* 'Summer Angel'. Both have white flowers.

May bush (*Spiraea* spp.). A 1-m high shrub with masses of white flowers in clusters, rather like tiny roses, hardy and easy to grow.

Mexican orange blossom (*Choisya* spp.). An evergreen shrub growing to a little over 1 m high, with masses of fragrant white flowers which look like orange blossoms. It is a hardy plant, and useful in a garden bed, or it can be clipped to make a hedge.

Native daisy bush (*Olearia* spp.). Another native plant that should be grown more often for the masses of white daisy flowers that grow in loose trusses.

Paper daisies (*Helipterum* spp.) are annual plants with deep to pale pink or white flowers and grey–green leaves. In full flower they complement the other subtle tones of Australian native plants.

Paper daisy or paper cascade (*Helipterum* spp.). Low-growing to 20 cm high, with grey–green leaves and masses of papery white flowers; loves a sunny spot.

Petunia spp. An annual which loves the sun. The white varieties are always popular.

Queen Anne's Lace (*Ammi majus*). A tall-growing plant 1–2 m high, with frothy, light flowers in clusters at the top of the plant. It is easy to grow and good for cut flowers.

Sweet Alice (*Alyssum* spp.). The white alyssum is a good, annual, ground-covering plant with masses of flowers. It loves well-drained soil and a sunny position and is easy to grow.

Thryptomene spp. A group of the hardiest native shrubs, to 1 m high with masses of tiny white flowers along the stems. Good for cut flowers.

Verbascum spp. An unusual plant with grey leaves and tall spikes of white flowers. It loves a hot, dry sunny spot.

When in flower, all euphorbias are eye-catching. Pictured here is *Euphorbia wulfenii*, which grows to 1 m high and has bluish-green leaves and lime-yellow clusters of flowers on the end of the stems. Euphorbias are remarkably hardy perennial plants which grow in most positions, but prefer a sunny or partly shaded spot. When flowering finishes, trim the stems back as hard as you like so that fresh new growth will ensue. Be wary of the milky sap in their stems as it can cause skin irritations.

The pleasures of a picking garden

Flowers have a wonderful quality — bringing just a few inside immediately makes a house friendlier, and a bunch of flowers says so much as a gift or for a special occasion. There are ways of caring for your flowers so they last much longer in a vase, and these hints will be most helpful to those who want to extend the life of a flower arrangement. When choosing your flowers at a florist or market, always look carefully for the freshest ones and avoid bunches with any withered-looking flowers or leaves. Choose those with plenty of buds ready to open, rather than shrivelled brown buds. Steer clear of bunches of flowers with slimy stems or yellowing foliage as they are 'over the hill'.

Flowers bought from shops or picked from your garden should be placed in a bucket of clean water immediately. Don't leave them standing in the sun, in the back of the car or exposed to car fumes.

When you are ready to arrange the flowers, cut off 2 cm from the bottom of each stem with secateurs or a sharp knife. It will help if you do this with the stems under water in the sink, so that air cannot block the stem and prevent water flowing freely up it. Even though flowers have been cut, they are still living things, so they need basic requirements like water! Remove any leaves that will be below the waterline in the vase so they cannot foul the water.

Imagine being able to pick naturalised daffodils like these to your heart's content! When most of the garden is dormant in winter and early spring, these brilliant clumps of *Narcissus* spp. will cheer you up, and remind you that this is only the beginning of plenty of pretty spring flowerings to come.

In past years people used to hammer stems with secateurs or a hammer to flatten them, but most florists and cut-flower growers no longer advocate this. They say that the stem should be free to take up as much water as possible.

Getting the best from your cut flowers

- To support long-stemmed flowers in an upright arrangement in a glass vase, use something in the water to support the stems. A variety of 'collectables' are suitable for this; for example marbles, seashells or small lemons can complement many arrangements.
- To finish off a little posy beautifully, select enough leaves of a plant such as a violet or small-leaved geranium to surround the posy to give it a pretty, uniform appearance.
- Float flowers such as camellias, fuchsias or hibiscus in a beautiful shallow bowl or a bird bath. Add small floating candles, available at florists or gift shops, for a warm, welcoming touch when entertaining.
- To prolong the life of cut flowers, wash and clean out the vase regularly as the bacteria in stale water will shorten their life. Fresh water daily does wonders.
- A bowl of capsicums, red peppers, gourds, pomegranates and small pumpkins make a fine table decoration, with autumn tones predominating. Look around your local green-grocer or market for interesting or unusual fruits and vegetables as an alternative to cut flowers.
- If there is not a lot of flower colour in the garden, pick a small bunch of leaves, especially of herbs such as thyme, oregano and lemon verbena and fragrant-leaved plants such as some of the pelargoniums. One of my favourites is a 'touching posy', which you have to pat or gently squeeze to make the leaves give up their fragrance.
- To enjoy autumn and all its colour, buy a small circle or wreath of florist's foam and collect a basket of autumn leaves such as liquidambar. Pierce the foam with the stems of the leaves and push the leaves in to cover the top and sides of the wreath.

PICKING FLOWERS

ANNUALS

Aster (*Aster* spp.). Similar to chrysanthemums, pinks, purples and whites

Bells of Ireland (*Moluccella*). Tall spikes of green calyces

Cornflower (*Centaurea*). Bright blue flowers, or pink and white

Cosmos. Single daisy-like flowers in pink, maroon or white

English daisy (*Bellis perennis*). Pink or white pom-pom flowers with short stems, ideal for posies

Iceland poppy (*Papaver nudicaule*). With their long stems, beautiful crepe petals in a variety of colours or single cream-white, opening from lovely buds

Nasturtium (*Tropaeolum* spp.). Hardy plants in yellow, red, orange or deep russet, good for posies

Pansies (*Viola* spp.). Short stemmed, with lovely 'faces', either a clear colour or with markings, in pastels, ivory, vibrant oranges, yellows, blues and mauves

Summer forget-me-not (*Anchusa capensis*). Tiny blue flowers

Snapdragon (*Antirrhinum* spp.). 'Faces' like a dragon, excellent cut flowers in shades ranging from yellows and reds to pastels

PERENNIALS

Baby's Breath (*Gypsophila*). Soft sprays of white flowers

Carnation (*Dianthus* spp.). Mixed colours, those with short stems are good for posies

Columbine or granny's bonnet (*Aquilegia* spp.). For informal posies

Larkspur (*Delphinium* spp.). Tall spikes of mauve-blue flowers

Salvia spp. Tall spikes of flowers ranging from white to blue and mauve

Statice (*Limonium* spp.). An everlasting papery flower in mauve, pink or white

Yarrow (*Achillea* spp.). Mixed colours in pinks, reds and yellows

Hang it on the front door or use it as a centrepiece to welcome family or guests.

- To extend the vase life of carnations, you can re-cut their stems every so often — best done with a sharp knife, cutting between the joints.
- Daffodils emit a slimy sap from their stalks which contains a chemical that can be deadly to other plants in the same container. Cut 1 cm off the stalks and place them in a vase by themselves for a day. The stalks will be sealed then, and you can rinse them off and put them into new water with other flowers.
- Daisies and stocks make the water smelly fairly quickly, so you need to change the water daily.

Foliage for picking

- Eucalyptus leaves are distinctive in an arrangement — gungurru (*E. caesia*) has a silver-grey bloom; *E. cinerea* has blue-grey leaves; cider gum (*E. gunnii*) silvery, round leaves in its juvenile growth; and book-leaf mallee (*E. kruseana*) also has round, silvery leaves.
- Fragrant-leaved pelargoniums such as rose and peppermint geraniums
- Ivy. About the only time ivy is useful, as it is such an invasive plant in the garden, is in flower decorations. For instance, a simple arrangement of a trail of ivy with honesty and a couple of pears looks very effective as a table centrepiece.
- Fern leaves. Some ferns, such as maidenhair (*Adiantum* spp.) and asparagus fern (*Asparagus* spp.) provide very delicate foliage amongst flowers.
- Lemon-scented Verbena (*Aloysia triphylla*) is always useful for its lime–green leaves with a strong lemon fragrance.

Yarrow (*Achillea millefolium*) has ferny foliage and yellow flowers and will spread to cover the ground in a very short time.

Crab apples (*Malus* spp.) are tough plants, tolerating plenty of sun and most soil types. Their beautiful little apples hang on the tree over autumn and winter. The variety featured here, *Malus* 'Jack Humm', is one of my 'picks' as its large, orange-red apples stay on the branches for three months. The fruit is large, up to 7 cm in diameter, and it makes a lovely jam or jelly.

Something different

*B*e adventurous — use different natural materials for indoor decoration. The following plants are colourful and interesting and last for ages.

- Bells of Ireland (*Moluccella laevis*) has tall spikes of bell-shaped, lime-green calyces which turn white after 5–6 weeks. They last for months.
- Crab apples (*Malus* spp.), yellow and red ones such as 'Golden Hornet' (yellow fruit), 'John Downie' (orange-red), 'Jack Humm' (red), 'Gorgeous' (deep red), 'Ballerina Maypole' (red)
- Grasses of all kinds
- Hawthorns (*Crataegus* spp.), especially the Mexican hawthorn with its large, bright yellow fruit. *C.* × *smithiana* is the red one and is most decorative, with branches hanging with fruit
- Honesty (*Lunaria annua*) has flat, round, green seed pods (we used them for play money as children) that turn transparent white. These look great mixed with other flowers.
- Hop bush (*Dodonaea* spp.) has attractive, long-lasting red seed pods and ferny, lacy leaves.
- Lemons, individually packed into a glass cylinder (a spaghetti jar) or left hanging from branches, where they will hang for six weeks or more, especially in winter
- Medlar (*Mespilus germanica*) has beautiful autumn foliage and unusual brown fruits
- Nuts, pine cones, banksia cones, eucalypt seed pods
- Persimmons and pomegranates, left on their branches in a big vase, or the individual fruit in a dish
- Poppy (*Papaver* spp.) seed pods
- Quince (*Cydonia oblonga*), with its large lime-yellow fruit with a soft powdery brown fuzz on the skins
- White cedar (*Melia azederach*) has small yellow fruits in clusters that stay on the branch for weeks (these berries are poisonous).

Wreaths

*W*reaths are a pretty way to decorate a door or a window at festive times. You can buy them ready-made from craft shops, but they are simple and very cheap to make from materials gathered from your garden.

Collect wisteria or grapevine canes and twist or plait into a circle. Tie with raffia or florist's wire. This makes a strong wreath that can be easily decorated. Willow or grass can also be used for a more slender wreath.

To decorate the wreath base, you can use fresh flowers, dried flowers, grass heads, foliage, herbs, pine cones, gumnuts or seed pods from other native plants. Cover the wreath with plenty of plant material so that it looks generous. For a complete circle wreath, start at any point and work round in one direction so that there are no bare spots. The flower or foliage material can be wired or glued onto the wreath using fast, clear-drying glue. A little backing of dried sphagnum moss or air fern (*Tillandsia* spp.) will help the flowers attach firmly.

Have an overall design in your mind, with colour and scent uppermost. All sorts of natural materials can be used — leaves, especially small ones of olive green or silvery colours; nuts; pine cones; grass seeds; wheat sheaths; and interesting seed pods.

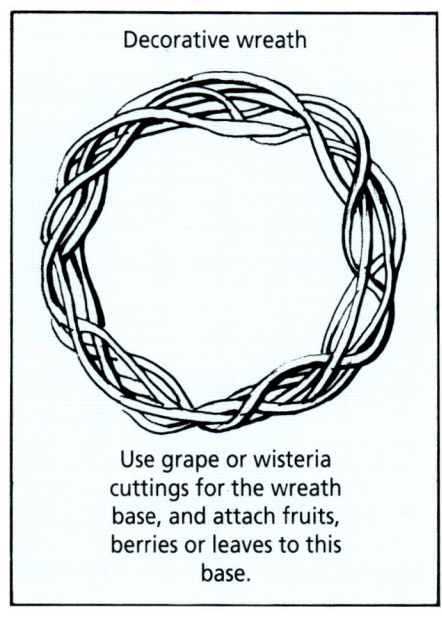

Decorative wreath

Use grape or wisteria cuttings for the wreath base, and attach fruits, berries or leaves to this base.

Dried flowers

PERENNIALS GOOD FOR DRYING

- Baby's breath (*Gypsophila* spp.). Tiny white flowers in masses
- Cornflower (*Centaurea* spp.). Blue, pink and white flowers
- Everlasting daisy (*Helichrysum* spp.). Straw-like flowers in yellow, pink and white
- Hollyhock (*Althaea* spp.). Tall spikes in many colours, and can be dried whole
- Honesty (*Lunaria* spp.). Round, transparent seed pods that many will know as the money plant
- Larkspur (*Delphinium* spp.). Tall spikes of pink, white or blue flowers up the stems
- Love-in-a-mist (*Nigella* spp.). Seed pods like straw balloons

PLANTS WITH INTERESTING SEED HEADS

Poppies, leeks and other members of the allium family, such as garlic, dill, fennel and many grasses, have decorative seed heads which will add interest to a dried arrangement.

- Marigold (*Calendula* spp.). Masses of orange flowers for drying, potpourri
- Sea holly (*Eryngium* spp.). Blue flower like a thistle
- Statice (*Limonium* spp.). Several varieties and colours
- Yarrow (*Achillea* spp.). Flat heads of cream, pink or yellow flowers

SHRUBS FOR DRIED FLOWERS OR FOLIAGE

- English box (*Buxus sempervirens*). Small leaves that dry well and excellent as a 'filler' in arrangements
- Gum (*Eucalyptus* spp.). Many and varied grey-green leaves and, of course, unusually shaped nuts
- *Hydrangea macrophylla*. The entire flower head will dry well, or each small floret can be dried separately
- Lavender (*Lavandula* spp.). Sweet-smelling purple spikes, lasts well.

Pressed flowers

*E*very time I receive a letter from my aunt, I know it is going to have a little 'signature' of hers to make it personal. My aunt takes great pleasure in making gift cards of pressed flowers —simple flowers that are pressed flat in books all over her lounge room floor. She uses plants like the sweet-faced Johnny-jump-up or a fern leaf gently glued to a piece of paper. It is a fabulous idea for anyone of any age who loves flowers.

HOW TO GO ABOUT IT

If you collect flowers for pressing, make sure you do it in the morning before the sun hits them and bleaches out the colour. Most people start collecting and pressing flowers by the simplest method — a thick book and a few sheets of tissue paper or blotting paper to put between the flowers and paper to absorb excess moisture from the plant material.

You can use any thick book — an old telephone book will do. (I can remember pressing flowers in our family's encyclopaedia when I was young!) For a really professional result or for the fleshier flowers, however, you may need to use a proper flower

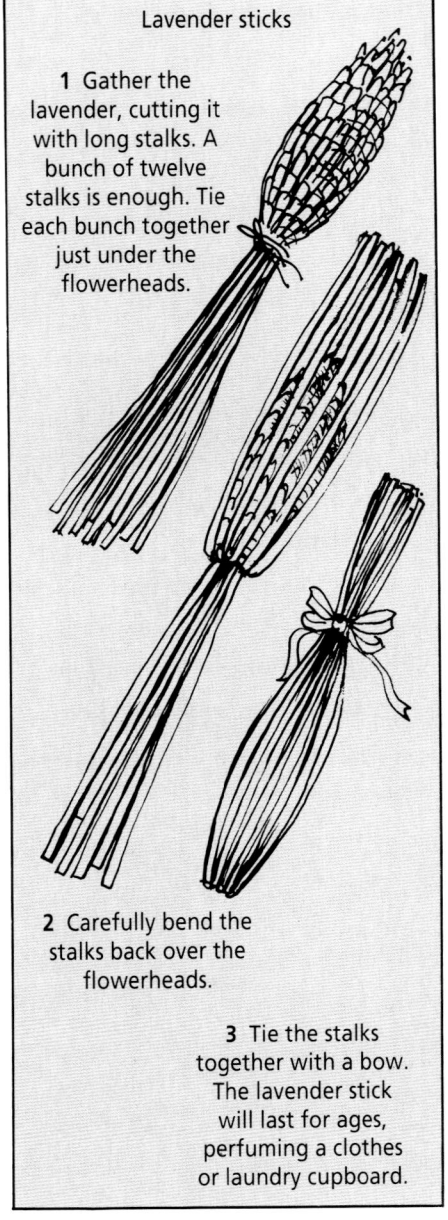

Lavender sticks

1 Gather the lavender, cutting it with long stalks. A bunch of twelve stalks is enough. Tie each bunch together just under the flowerheads.

2 Carefully bend the stalks back over the flowerheads.

3 Tie the stalks together with a bow. The lavender stick will last for ages, perfuming a clothes or laundry cupboard.

SOME FLOWERS THAT PRESS EASILY

Acacias (wattle flowers and ferny foliage)
Californian poppies
Dianthus, carnations
Ferns
Fuchsias (small-flowered varieties)
Grasses
Larkspurs
Lobelia
Native violet
Potentilla
Violas, pansies

press. They come in sizes from about 12 cm square and are made of chipboard or plywood with screws in each corner which can be tightened or loosened as required. As the flowers dry you may have to tighten the screws slightly.

Generally, large flowers such as daisies will take 6–8 weeks to press, though tiny flowers like forget-me-nots only take two weeks. You will need to cut larger flowers that are also thick into separate petals or, as with a rose, in half, then reconstitute them when they have been pressed.

Posies: the language of flowers

*M*any flowers have, through history, been given to people for their special meanings — they have a language all of their own.

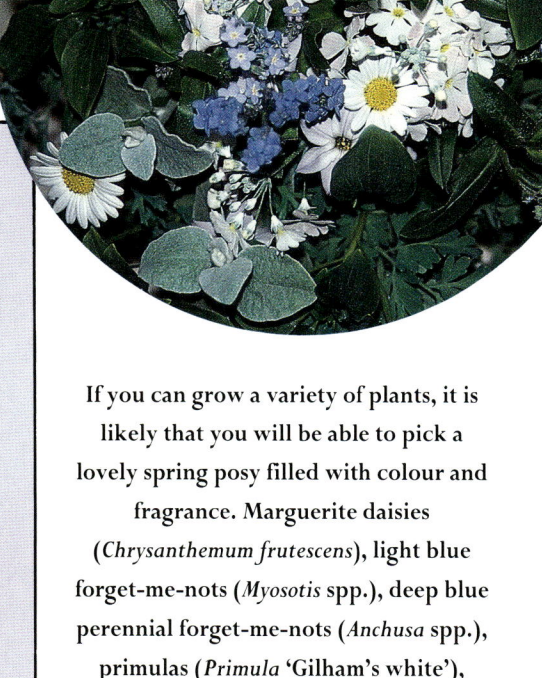

Friendship posy

Dock • *Patience*
Geranium (oak leaf) • *Everlasting friendship*
Ivy • *Friendship, fidelity*
Larkspur • *Lightness, purity*
Pansy • *You occupy my thoughts*
Zinnia • *Thoughts of absent friends*

A Posy to say 'I love you'

Camellia (white) • *Perfect loveliness*
Clover (four-leaf) • *Be mine*
Forget-me-not • *True love*
Heliotrope • *Devotion*
Honeysuckle • *Sweet bonds of love*
Myrtle Rose • *Love*

A get-well posy

Pansy • *You occupy my thoughts*
Peppermint • *Warmth of feeling*
Rosemary • *Remembrance*
Salvia (blue) • *I think of you*
Sweet basil • *Good wishes*

A good luck posy
(for exams, hospitalisation)

Almond blossom • *Hope*
Bay • *Glory*
Hawthorn • *Hope*
Iris • *Message*
Pansy • *You occupy my thoughts*
Sweet basil • *Good wishes*

If you can grow a variety of plants, it is likely that you will be able to pick a lovely spring posy filled with colour and fragrance. Marguerite daisies (*Chrysanthemum frutescens*), light blue forget-me-nots (*Myosotis* spp.), deep blue perennial forget-me-nots (*Anchusa* spp.), primulas (*Primula* 'Gilham's white'), creamy freesias (*Freesia refracta alba*) and pale blue spring star flowers (*Tritelia* spp.) make up this delightful posy. Try to pick some leaves to arrange as a ruff around the flowers, as their freshness and greenness gives a lovely contrast.

Design for a picking garden of native plants

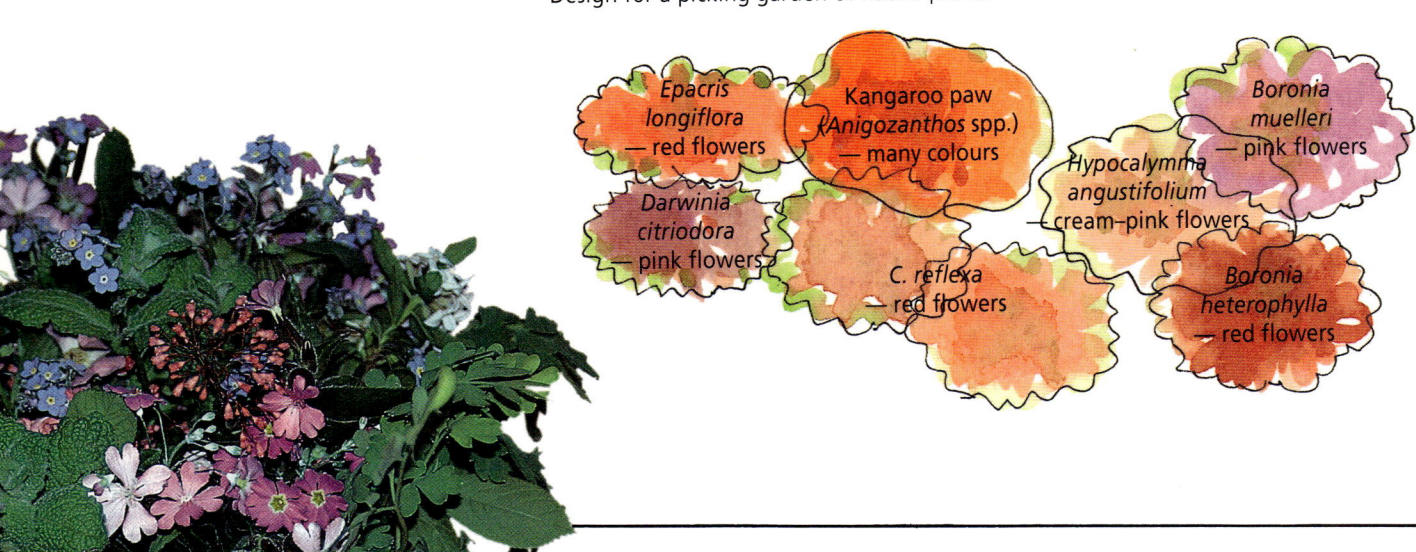

Forget-me-nots (*Myosotis* spp.), primulas
(*Primula malacoides*) and fragrant white
jasmine (*Jasminum officinale*) are mixed in
with the aromatic foliage of apple mint
(*Mentha suaveolens*) to make a posy of
spring joy.

A PERFECT POSY OF NATIVE PLANTS

Boronia heterophylla. The lovely red
boronia is my pick of the bunch
for cut flowers, followed closely
by the brown and the yellow
varieties.

Boronia muelleri 'Sunset Serenade'.
A soft pink, starry boronia,
delightful flowers but without a
fragrance

Brachyscome spp. Lovely small daisies
in pink, white and yellow, as well
as the usual mauve

Correa spp. especially *C. glabra*,
C. 'Mannii' and *C. reflexa.* All
native fuchsias are very valuable
to add to a posy.

Darwinia citriodora. This and other
species of the Darwinia have
hanging flowers like miniature
lanterns.

Hypocalymma angustifolium.
Tiny pink-white flowers massed
all the way up graceful stems,
very delicate in appearance

Kangaroo paws (*Anigozanthos spp.*).
A growing number of dwarf and
medium-sized kangaroo paws are
being bred for more disease
resistance.

Melaleuca spp. Especially
M. armillaris, which has cream
flowers with a pleasant honey
smell; *M. laterita* (robin red-
breast bush), with startling red
flowers; and *M. thymifolia,* with
small mauve flowers

Native Heath (*Epacris* spp.).
Tubular flowers in colours varying
from white, pink to red

Straw flowers, or paper daisies.
The 'everlasting' daisies.
'Paper Cascade' and 'Paper
Daisy' have white flowers and are
dainty in a posy.

Wax plant (*Chamelaucium uncinatum*).
Lovely soft-looking flowers and
fine foliage

Roses as cut flowers

Most gardeners who grow roses love to pick them to bring inside for a flower arrangement in a vase. Roses, like all flowers, will last much better if they are picked in the early morning or late evening, out of the heat of the sun. Carry a bucket of water out into the garden with you so you can put the stems immediately into water. If possible, leave them dunked in this bucket for a couple of hours. If you have bought roses from a florist or market, re-cut the stems under water: a few centimetres is enough.

The freshest water in the cleanest container is the principle — as with all cut flowers. Change the water every few days, remembering again to cut the base of the stems back. Add a preservative to the water to prolong flower life. A slurp of household bleach or a little lemonade will act as a disinfectant to prevent the growth of algae.

CRAB APPLES

One of the most beautiful spring-flowering plants is the crab apple, a member of the *Malus* family. Some species have beautiful flowers as well as fruits, and others present wonderful buds. Small branches or stems with buds just opening will look spectacular in a vase indoors. One of my favourites is the single-flowering Bechtel's crab apple (*M. ioensis 'Plena'*) which has perfect clusters of tiny pink buds, opening to lovely white blossoms. This tree is covered with spring blossom, and it grows to a manageable size of 5 m high by 3 m wide. This is a good choice for people looking for a shapely deciduous tree that is not going to get out of hand, and suits a cottagey atmosphere.

Other varieties of crab apple worth noting are *M. spectabilis*, a really showy tree. It has red buds that open to single pink flowers. The purple variety, *M. purpureus*, has reddish leaves, matching coloured flowers and small purplish fruits. For a taller tree, *M. floribunda* is very attractive, with pale pink flowers followed by small yellow apples that hang on from autumn through to winter. This type grows to 8 m high by 5 m wide.

SOME ROSES TO BRING INDOORS

R. 'Apricot Nectar'. Lovely buds opening to a full, wide, soft apricot flower with a gold centre with masses of stamens

R. 'Catherine McCauley'. A plant that has numerous flowers most of the season, clear yellow and long stems, ideal for putting in a vase

R. 'Iceberg'. Always a favourite as there are usually two or three to pick even after the season for most roses has finished

R. 'Mr Lincoln'. For anyone who enjoys a rich red rose, this is a must for its velvety appearance and large flowers

R. 'Ophelia'. A beautiful soft pink

R. 'Queen Elizabeth'. Always bears prolific amounts of soft pink, cupped flowers

R. 'Young at Heart'. A very free-flowering rose in soft, peachy pink

Many of the banksias originating in Western Australia make excellent cut flowers. A large number are air-freighted around the world as interest in Australian plants as cut flowers grows.

The big bold banksias

Everyone remembers May Gibbs' children's stories of Snugglepot, Cuddlepie and the big, bad, banksia men. I was never really frightened of these creatures as a child — I was fascinated by their shapes — and I think May Gibbs deserves a lot of credit for introducing very young people to these beautiful plants.

Banksias are spectacular plants for their diversity of form and colour, particularly the Western Australian forms, but it is the flower development that I love. It is fascinating to see the stages of the flower forming, from tiny spiral 'rods' to the uniform rows of 'hair pins' that make up the intriguingly symmetrical flower cones. The strange, hard seed pods which follow the flowers are very ornamental in their own way, and wonderful to use in fresh or dried flower arrangements.

Celia Rosser's name is always associated with banksias, and she has spent many years recording the genus in botanical paintings which are renowned throughout the world.

Some special varieties

There are over sixty species of banksias, and more are being discovered all the time. Some are indigenous to the heathlands of eastern Australia and a large range originates in Western Australia. Plants from the east coast such as the heath banksia (*Banksia ericifolia*) and the coast banksia (*B. integrifolia*) are very readily grown in home gardens. They are attractive in flower and give plenty of nectar for honeyeaters. Many of the Western Australian species are spectacular, but they may be difficult to grow because they are subject to root rot caused by the fungus *Phytophthora*, and need perfect drainage to avoid it.

A Western Australian banksia which I love for flower arrangements, although it is subject to root rot, is the scarlet banksia (*B. coccinea*), with its neatly lined-up rows of bright red styles on a cylindrical flower up to 8 cm long. It is enough to have a few as dried flowers to mix with other native plants, fresh or dried, if you find this plant too hard to grow.

The heath banksia (*B. ericifolia*) is a good reliable plant for the eastern states. It grows into a dense shrub or screening plant about 3–5 m high and 2 m wide. In autumn and winter it is covered with orange spikes which encourage birds into the garden. There are various cultivars, such as 'Giant Candles', with flower spikes which can reach 40 cm long.

Another Western Australian which is breathtaking, though hard to grow in home gardens, is bull banksia (*B. grandis*), a large shrub with very strong-looking, toothed leaves and large yellow flower spikes which can grow to 25 cm long by 8 cm wide. It is certainly worth trying if you can provide it with very good drainage.

For shrubby growth, attractive serrated leaves and fine, orange-white flowers, *B. hookeriana* is another outstanding plant.

B. prionotes will grow well in an open, sunny position with well-drained soil. It is a tall shrub, growing to 5–7 m high, with orange flower spikes up to 15 cm long. I first saw it growing in a beautiful native garden in the Warby Ranges near Wangaratta, Victoria, where the orange cones looked wonderful set against the blue sky.

And banksias don't only grow as trees and shrubs. There are various prostrate species such as *B. prostrata*, which has an extraordinary growth habit. Its stems grow horizontally, hugging the ground, while the beautiful flower cones sit straight up from the ground.

The bull banksia (*Banksia grandis*) is a pretty 'macho' looking plant with long flower spikes and very agressive looking leaves, but what a beauty!

Daffodils

It is a good rule to get your daffodils in early — they will do better! Plant them in February or March, either in bands (though nature never has regimented rows so why should we gardeners grow them like this?), or in clumps, as I prefer them, around other shrubs or at the base of trees, where they look natural. Space the bulbs no more than 7–10 centimetres apart, so that they give a massed effect rather than looking too sparse. It is a good idea, too, to plant daffodils amongst perennial or annual plants so that when the bulbs finish flowering there is other garden interest to take their place. Then the yellowing leaves of the daffodils will not look so tatty. Do be sure to leave this untidy foliage for at least six weeks so that the bulbs can store up the full complement of nourishment ready for next year's flowering. It is essential that the withering, yellowing leaves are left to do their 'thing' of photosynthesis, pushing more food down into the bulb over the six or seven weeks after flowering has finished. This means that your daffodil patch, or those naturalising in the lawn, will look a bit messy, but this is the price that has to be paid.

Just be careful of summer watering if daffodils are planted amongst other plants, as poor drainage could rot the bulbs.

DAFFODILS FOR ADVENTUROUS GARDENERS

Daffodils come in white, pink and bi-colours, and in some spectacular double forms, not just the usual large yellow trumpets. There is such a variety to choose from, in colour, form, height and time of flowering, that I love to visit the many bulb farms that are open while the daffodils are in full bloom, usually from early September to early October, and to pore over their enticing catalogues. Whether you are a traditionalist or an adventurous gardener, here are some pointers!

• There is a huge range of traditional yellow daffodils, larger flowering and taller growing, and it is possible to have different daffodils flowering from late July to late September.

• Of the daffodils which have orange-red cups contrasting with yellow petals, 'Jago' is a beauty, with deep yellow petals and an intense red-orange cup.

• There are also sulphur-coloured varieties with petals in shades of soft lime yellow, lemon or sulphur. The cup of the late-flowering 'St Patricks Day' goes from a clear lemon yellow to soft white with a frilled yellow edge.

An early spring-flowering daffodil is *Narcissus* 'Ice Follies', with creamy white petals and large, primrose yellow cups.

• The many white daffodils are elegant, ranging from rich cream to brilliant white. And for a complete change from these, look out for the pinks — there are bright apricot–pinks, bright pinks and mauve–pink.

• I particularly like the double daffodils with their full flowerheads of layer upon layer of petals. Last year I grew 'Dick Wilden', which has a mass of rich golden inner petals. It flowered prolifically and the large flowerheads nodded on for ages.

Some gardeners make the common mistake of thinking that daffodils grow in the shade, but they will never flower at their best there. Daffodils need full sun, or just a *little* dappled shade from overhead trees in hot inland places. Too much shade is one of the most common causes of failure to flower in daffodils.

Daffodils do not need lifting each year, though some energetic gardeners lift their bulbs after four or five years to get increased vigour and flower size by replanting and fertilising. If you are growing daffodils in pots, lift them each year once flowering has finished and leaves have died down, and replant in the ground to rejuvenate.

Daffodils will do much better if they are given fertiliser as their leaves pop up through the soil. A fertiliser high in potash, rather than the other nutrients of nitrogen or phosphorus, will generally benefit them. Too much nitrogen will lead to plenty of foliage but fewer flowers.

GARRYA ELLIPTICA

There is a magnificent picking plant that excels in its male form, in fact it beats the female plant hands-down.

It is the *Garrya elliptica*, or catkin bush, with lime-greenish, pendulous flowers hanging all over it (in winter and early spring). The male plant produces these elegant tassels of catkins which hang down about 20–25 cms. A well-grown bush will grow 2–3 m high by 2 m across. The female plant produces much smaller catkins, so nurseries generally sell the more outstanding versions. The garrya will grow well in cool to temperate climates, originating from parts of America like New Mexico and California. The leaves are tough, a greyish green colour and oval in shape and, provided it is grown in a well-drained spot, it is a very hardy plant. Once the catkins have finished, the bush can be pruned

lightly just to shape it. Older style gardens often have a garrya amongst other mixed plants, and it always has a very distinctive beauty in a garden. Another way to grow it is against a wall, where its branches can be fanned out and pinned against the wall support to make an espalier. And with its graceful catkins, it makes a very special presentation in a vase.

An unusual, attractive flower, *Garrya elliptica*, with its long catkins (up to 12 cm) hanging from the branches, is stunning when arranged in a large vase. It is a hardy plant which prefers a sheltered, sunny position. It can be trained against a wall so that its branches fan out and display the catkins, which are always larger and more attractive on the male plant. Cut branches will last for a long period indoors.

My all-time favourite roses

A lovely Bourbon rose, R. 'La Reine Victoria' has masses of globe-shaped flowers in a true rose pink.

I believe every garden deserves at least one rose, but there is such a variety that choosing one is difficult. There are modern hybrid tea roses that are bold, beautiful and always cheerful. And then there are the roses from the past: those with a history, rich textures and intoxicating perfumes. There are literally hundreds of roses to choose from, and every year several new hybrids appear.

Some people associate roses only with the modern hybrid tea types, but for me there is a world of enchantment in the roses of yesteryear. Some of these old-fashioned roses are amongst the earliest of all cultivated plants, and many give you a great sense of history as they have been around in large and small gardens for centuries. Think of the Empress Josephine, who is probably as well known for growing heritage roses as for her association with Napoleon, or of the red rose of Lancaster and the white rose of York, the symbols of the War of the Roses in English history.

Some old roses are simple, single flowers, as is *Rosa bracteata* 'Mermaid'; others, like the old-fashioned cabbage rose, *Rosa centifolia*, have a mass of petals. Their shapes range from flat, open singles and quartered roses to the brandy balloon shapes of the Bourbon roses. Colours come in all shades of red, white, pink, yellow and mauve and some are striped. Unlike most of the modern hybrids, fragrance is a main characteristic, as is the beautiful green foliage and the elegant arching stems.

(See Glossary of rose terms on page 57.)

You will often see these old-fashioned varieties growing neglected around old farmhouses and cemeteries. They seem to be able to cope with drought, poor soil and diseases such as black spot. But of course, like any other plant, they will do much better with feeding and watering. They will respond to a heavy feed of old manure or a complete rose food. Mulching with a layer of well-rotted grass clippings or other organic mulch around the root area will help to retard weed growth and keep moisture around the roots.

Modern roses need to be pruned hard every year to encourage new wood on which the flowers bloom. The old-fashioned roses do not need this type of hard pruning. See pages 52–4 for detailed pruning guidance for each rose type.

A few of these lovely old roses may only bloom once in a season, but there are many varieties which are 'repeat' or 'continuous' flowerers. Many are perfumed — lovely to have floating in a bowl and soft and romantic in any garden. My favourites are predominantly in shades of pink — 'La Reine Victoria', a Bourbon rose, has masses of globe-shaped flowers in real rose pink, and it is a wonderful shrub rose. Closely related to it is the 'Mme Pierre Oger' rose — a lovely ball of overlapping petals in translucent, silvery pink.

Make sure you do not crowd out these shrub roses; they need plenty of room to spread out to perform well. You can plant annuals or perennials to match their colours underneath them, but make sure you feed and water the plants so that they will cope.

Of the white old roses it is hard to beat the Bourbon rose 'Boule de Neige' with its pink-tinged buds opening to silky white flowers shaped in a ball. It has a rich perfume and is a good performer.

It is hard to choose my very favourite climbing rose as the choice is wide and quite bewildering. There are the blush white balls of 'Madame Alfred Carrière' or the fragrant pink 'Zéphirine Drouhin', and there is 'Gloire de Dijon', which has a lovely scent and buff yellow petals.

One of the most popular in recent times has been the China rose 'Cécile Brunner', both the climbing and shrub forms, and it really is a wonder with its exquisite buds shaped exactly like tiny hybrid tea roses. In any place the superb rambler 'Albertine' is

DAVID AUSTIN ROSES

R. 'Jayne Austin'. Soft yellow–apricot

R. 'Lilian Austin'. Wavy petals in salmon pink

R. 'Prospero'. Deep crimson ageing to purple

R. 'The Nun'. White flowers, cupped petals

R. 'Wise Portia'. With many petals, free flowering pink

Rosa 'Boule de Neige' is a rose that for me typifies the old-fashioned types, with many petals shaped into soft balls, and a luscious fragrance. Its name means snowball, and you can see why when you see the mass of blossoms set against the dark green leaves.

hard to beat with its coppery pink blooms and wonderful scent.

In recent times there has been much breeding and hybridising of these old roses with the modern hybrid tea roses. David Austin, the English breeder, has created roses that have all the charm and fragrance of traditional old roses together with the more compact growth, longer flowering and extended colour range of modern roses. It is clever indeed to combine the best characteristics of the old and new roses.

David Austin roses are available in many varieties. One of my favourites is the English rose 'Graham Thomas' which has cupped yellow blooms and a tea rose scent. 'Charles Austin' is another yellow–apricot rose with a beautiful fragrance. It is best grown as a feature over a small arbour or pergola. There are many more varieties, some large, and others, such as 'Chaucer', which are smaller shrubs.

In recent years the lovely floribunda rose 'Apricot Nectar' has been a prime choice for its soft colour tones. Many of the small patio roses are winners too — 'Parfum', as its name suggests, has a beautiful fragrance from double yellow blooms with a slight flush of pink. In a pot on the verandah or in the garden it grows to 60 cm high and flowers for a very long time.

Then there are the 'new' groundcover roses such as 'Flower Carpet'. It performs well as a landscaping plant, spreading over an area of a metre or so with abundant pink flowers, though it does need a lot of feeding (especially if it develops yellow leaves). If you are growing these roses in a pot or hanging basket you should certainly feed them, but only once a year if using a proprietary slow-release formula for roses.

Yellow is always a sought-after colour in roses and this David Austin rose, *Rosa* 'Graham Thomas', is one of the best. It has a delicious fragrance, is multi-petalled with a cup shape and grows into a shrub about 1 m high. I have seen it grow higher, sending up vigorous long shoots, but these can easily be cut back.

The white 'Flower Carpet' has lustrous green leaves and larger white flowers compared with the pink, and they have a slight fragrance. White is a good colour for contrast in the garden and this plant has been bred to bloom for twelve months of the year.

The carpet roses do need chopping back. Even though they are 'easy-care', they produce strong shoots which inevitably grow upwards to the sky. To keep the bushes lower and more compact cut them back (with the hedge or garden shears, not the secateurs — just clip, clip anywhere) in early spring. Trimming off finished flowers will promote more flowering.

There is a large range of 'easy-care' roses in the Meilland group, bred by one of the world's leading rose breeders. They are also landscape roses — some are used as groundcovers to mass plant over slopes or banks — and grow 60–90 cm high with a 1–1·5 m spread. They come in white, coral, blush pink or red. There are other Meilland roses which grow a bit higher, to about 1.5 m, and make a great hedge, massed with colour. Of these, 'Bonica' has semi-double clusters of pink flowers and would suit a cottage garden, while other varieties of pinks and reds are dazzling when in full flower.

Using old roses in the garden

There are plenty of ways that old-fashioned roses can be used when landscaping but, like any other rose, they do best in full sun in a well-prepared bed.

Although many people leave roses to grow with no competition from plants growing beneath, I prefer a living carpet to soften the whole effect. There are some very attractive annual plants such as sweet Alice (the white alyssum) whose shallow roots will not compete too much with the roses for water and food. An edging of lavender, rosemary or grey-leaved lamb's ears will always look good. All roses need plenty of sunlight (at least four or five hours a day), otherwise growth will be long and lanky and you will get few flowers. Lack of sun will make the plant more susceptible to fungal diseases such as black spot as well. The more air movement and sun, the better your chances of a healthy, vigorous plant.

TEN FAVOURITE OLD ROSES

R. × *centifolia*
'De Meaux' has small, pink, fragrant flowers massed on a bush that only grows 1 m high.

R. 'Fantin-Latour' dates back to the 1850s. It has masses of fragrant pink flowers, heavy with petals and a 'button eye' in the centre. It forms a round bush about 1.5 m high.

R. 'La Reine Victoria' has clusters of double pink flowers, gently rounded in shape. It grows to 1.5 m high and is an erect bush.

R. 'Madame Ernst Calvat' can be grown as a shrub, or up a pillar, and performs excellently with masses of blooms in clear pink with a strong perfume.

R. 'Mme Isaac Pereire' has large, deep pink flowers with a strong fragrance, lots of petals and a quartered centre.

R. 'Reine des Violettes' is a large-growing shrub, with wonderful

purple-mauve flowers, as befits its name, 'Queen of the Violets'.

- R. 'Roseraie de l'Hay' is a rugosa type rose, with magnificent, rich wine-red flowers in clusters. It grows in a dense shrub to 2.5 m high and is a quality rose for its fragrance.

- R. *rugosa alba* has large, pure white flowers with golden stamens. A very hardy rose, it will grow in dry or sandy soils, and I've seen it growing in salt-laden winds by the beach. It performs well as a hedge or a barrier, growing thick enough to keep most things out.

- R. *rugosa* 'Sarah van Fleet' has cup-shaped, clear pink flowers massed over a tall shrub. Give it room to spread or use it as a hedge, and prune it back to 1.5 m every spring.

- R. 'Variegata di Bologna' has cupped flowers with mainly white petals with a dash of crimson purple to provide the variegation of its name.

Roses can be grown amongst other shrubs as long as they are not cooped up and cramped. Select a rose of an appropriate size for your position, and give the arching canes plenty of room to spread. There are some roses that can be grown up a pillar, to twine their way up and over a pergola or even up into the branches of a tree.

Planting roses

Winter is the best planting time for roses, when they are available in bare-rooted form, that is, not in pots. Roses are adaptable to many types of soils — clay soils are fine; in fact I have seen the best blooms on plants growing in very heavy soils.

PLANTING A BARE-ROOTED ROSE

First, dig a hole deeper and wider than the spread of the roots. Whether in clay or sandy soils, it is always a good idea to incorporate compost into the planting hole. Mix up as much home-grown compost as you can, and add several handfuls of animal manure into the soil. Form a little mound of soil in the bottom of the hole and place the rose on top of this mound with its roots spreading around it. Cut off any long or damaged roots. This can be done with impunity at this time of the year as the roses are dormant.

Make sure the part of the stem where the grafting or budding has been done is at least 3–5 cm above the soil level. Don't ever allow this bud union to be buried, as there is always a chance that the root stock, rather than the selected top section, will grow.

I'll never forget seeing a beautiful vase filled to the brim with this lovely old rose, *Rosa* 'Fantin-Latour'. It has all the characteristics to make it one of the best roses; heavy fragrance, a mass of beautiful, soft pink flowers in the height of the rose season, which make the branches arch over with their weight. R. 'Fantin-Latour's' historical background also interests me, as it is named after a great 19th-century French flower painter.

Hold the plant in position and fill the hole, firming it with your hands and pressing down hard to get rid of any air pockets. Water the rose in well with at least a full bucket of water to settle it into the soil. In about three weeks time, give the rose a good feed with pelletised, organic fertiliser or a small amount of slow-release fertiliser sprinkled around the base of the plant.

Pruning roses

*E*nglish gardeners say you should treat a rose bush as your own worst enemy! It is hard to believe, but this 'bon mot' refers to pruning roses, and this is what they do in England: cut them right down practically to ground level. You can cut, snip and prune most roses as hard as you like and they will still bounce back — they really are tough.

Of course, they will reward you much more if you prune them correctly, but even if you make a total botch of pruning they will still give you a reasonable number of flowers. So, take courage and your secateurs and set forth.

Each type of rose has different growth and habits and should be pruned slightly differently. Always use good quality, clean, sharp secateurs as it makes the job so much easier. The best time to do this is in the dormant season, mid-winter, when the bushes have lost all their leaves. The exceptions to this rule are the evergreen roses such as 'Lorraine Lee' and the banksia roses, which can be pruned after flowering.

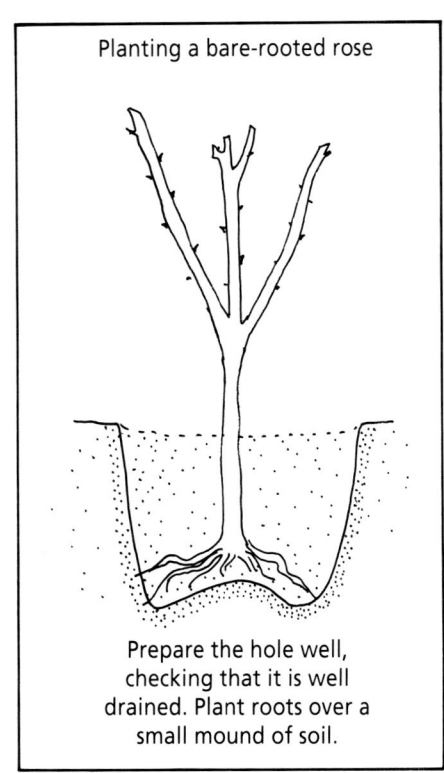

Planting a bare-rooted rose

Prepare the hole well, checking that it is well drained. Plant roots over a small mound of soil.

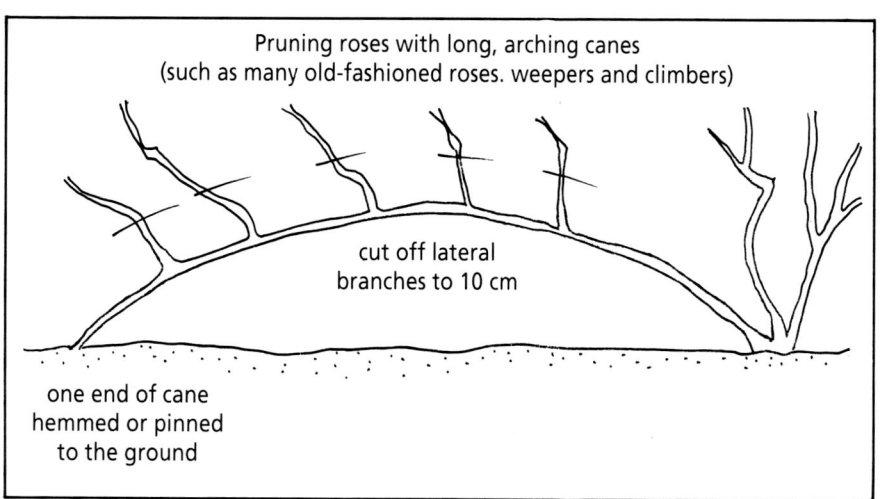

Pruning roses with long, arching canes
(such as many old-fashioned roses. weepers and climbers)

cut off lateral branches to 10 cm

one end of cane hemmed or pinned to the ground

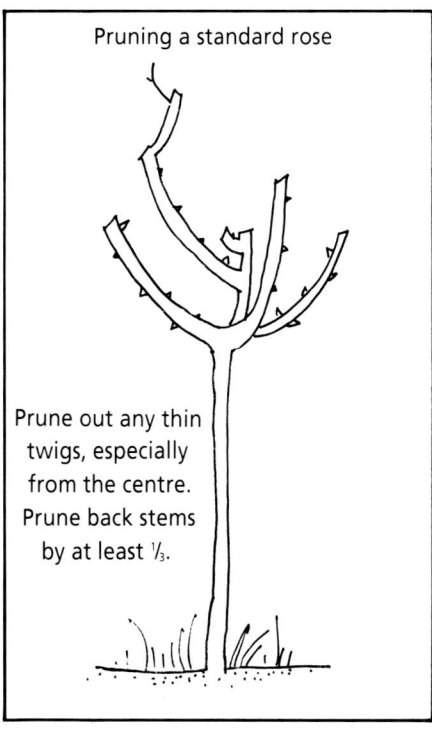

Pruning a standard rose

Prune out any thin twigs, especially from the centre. Prune back stems by at least ⅓.

MINIATURE ROSES

These are the easiest roses to prune. Simply chop them off, virtually in one fell swoop, down to about 10 cm above soil level. They will then grow again in a small clump, giving masses of miniature leaves and flowers. These miniatures are wonderful plants for the veranda in pots, and they can be brought indoors for 2 or 3 days at the height of their flowering. They must be taken out again to freshen up.

HYBRID TEA AND FLORIBUNDA ROSES

These are one of the most commonly grown roses, generally grown as bushes. First, cut away any diseased, dead or really spindly wood, snipping it down to healthy green growth. These thin, spindly growths are virtually useless, so have no fear about cutting them off flush with the branch they grow from.

Now look for the main stems, about the diameter of your thumb, and cut them back by at least a third or even harder. Aim for an outward-facing bud so that the new growth will grow outwards rather than into the middle of the bush.

Some older rose bushes may have developed long water-shoots. These are the new canes which will form the structure for future flowering and should be encouraged. Don't confuse watershoots with suckers. Suckers come from underneath the graft union, and should be removed immediately you spot them. Watershoots, on the other hand, are long canes that shoot up from above the graft, usually with a cluster of flowers at the top and no branches. Watershoots need not be pruned hard; just tip prune them and they will flower well next season.

WEEPING ROSES

These are roses pruned to grow on a single 1–2 m stem, with a weeping rose, usually quite a vigorous rambling rose, grafted onto the top. Look for the oldest canes or stems — that is, the thickest or woodiest — and cut these back to their base. This will leave a lot of young, more vigorous canes which you can cut back about one-third from the end to an outward-facing bud.

OLD-FASHIONED HERITAGE ROSES

Remove any old canes at the base, so leaving the newer, younger stems to flower. You can tip prune these canes back by a

MODERN HYBRID TEAS

These recent releases are very worthwhile:

R. 'Belle of Berlin'. Soft pink flowers and a delicious fragrance, excellent as a cut flower

R. 'City of Adelaide'. Shapely coral pink flowers

R. 'Delicious'. A miniature growing to approximately 80 cm with rich, clear pink blooms, free flowering and strongly perfumed

R. 'Golden Friendship'. Buff–yellow buds; tall, erect habit

R. 'Many Happy Returns'. Masses of soft pink flowers on deep green foliage; a beautiful spreading rose

R. 'Simplicity'. Soft pink flowers

R. 'Wagga Wagga'. Yellow flowers on strong stems

R. 'White Simplicity'. Masses of white, semi-double flowers

ROSES FOR MAKING A HEDGE

R. 'Albertine'. Apricot pink

R. bracteata 'Mermaid'. Cream-yellow, single

R. brunonii. Cream

Rugosa roses; for example, 'Frau Dagmar Hastrup',

R. rugosa alba, R. rugosa 'Scabrosa'

HERITAGE ROSES

R. 'Buff Beauty'. Lovely apricot–yellow flowers

R. 'Crépuscule'. Masses of semi-double flowers, the colour a mix of apricot and tanned gold

R. 'Gloire de Dijon'. Warm yellow with slight pink–apricot colourings

R. 'Mme Grégoire Staechelin'. Pink

R. 'New Dawn'. Delicate pale pink, clusters of small flowers

R. 'Penelope'. Large swags of creamy flowers

R. 'Raubritter'. Clusters of small cupped flowers, masses of pink petals, perfect for a small posy

Abundant is how I would describe *Rosa* 'Penelope'. It is a rose that is shell pink to cream in colour, and the yellow stamens featured in the centre of the petals always attract me. *R*. 'Penelope' is bred from *R*. 'Ophelia', another wonderful shrub rose, and has good-looking dark green foliage which sets off the flower clusters.

third. Make sure that the canes are arching over in a hoop shape and peg the end in the ground. By hooping the canes over you will find that flower buds will develop all along the stem.

CLIMBING ROSES

Prune roses that climb on an archway or over a fence by removing some of the older stems, right back to the ground, and pull them away from the rest of the plant.

The butterscotch yellow banksia rose can grow into a huge mass of canes, all arching over each other. If left too long this rose can become unruly, so thin the canes out regularly, cutting out any thick, old branches, and pegging back or tying down any canes that waft in the breeze.

Pests and diseases

*A*phids are one of the most common insect pests of roses. They damage new shoots by feeding on the sap. They breed very quickly, but can be controlled by squashing them with your fingers or dislodging them with a forceful jet of water. If they are very numerous and you want to spray, use a low toxic spray such as pyrethrum with garlic.

Some seasons are very bad for thrip damage. These are tiny black insects which come in plague numbers and feed on the petals, more commonly on pale or white flowers. Sometimes you notice them on damp sheets on the washing line where they gather for the moisture. Heavy rain kills many of them, so try hosing, but you may need to spray in a bad thrip season.

Some all-time favourites

DAVID AUSTIN ROSES

One of the good David Austin roses is 'Wildflower' which regularly repeat flowers if chopped back immediately after one flush finishes. As promptly as can be it will flower again eight weeks later! 'Wildflower' is a lovely single cream with prominent stamens and it grows in a way which my mother describes as 'loose'. By that she means the graceful, relaxed form of the stems. This rose is a great 'doer' and seems not to be susceptible to the usual diseases.

R. 'LORRAINE LEE'

This rose is of great interest to me because it was bred by the great Australian rose breeder, Alister Clark, in Bulla, Victoria. It was released in 1924 and became very common in home gardens, especially as a front hedge, during the next two decades. It is now making a comeback as new gardeners recognise the beauty of its rich fragrance and strong pink colour, with apricot at its heart. 'Lorraine Lee' also has the big advantage of flowering from autumn into winter when there are few flowers around.

R. 'PENELOPE'

This rose is typical of the hybrid musk group of roses which have long canes that grow in arches, forming a luxuriant bush. 'Penelope' has masses of lovely, fragrant, creamy white flowers which open from blush pink buds in early summer, and again in another flush in autumn.

All the hybrid musk roses make fine flowering shrubs as they form large bushes which are completely smothered in flowers, often with a lovely fragrance. They look best when planted among perennials and climbing plants such as clematis.

Either in climbing form, or as a bush rose, *Rosa* 'Lorraine Lee' has rich green leaves and fragrant, coral pink flowers. It was bred by Australian rosarian, Alister Clark, and has been popular since the 1920s when it was released.

MY FAVOURITE SINGLE ROSES

R. 'Autumn Delight'. Crisp cream, very recurrent

R. 'Carabella'. Blossom-like pink flowers, very recurrent

R. 'Dainty Bess'. Delicate pink with beautiful stamens

R. 'Jessie Clarke'. Beautiful single pink

R. *bracteata* 'Mermaid'. Cream–yellow, very vigorous climber

R. 'Nancy Hayward'. Large, winter flowering, single red

R. 'Souvenir de St Anne's'. Pale pink, very recurrent

R. 'Sparrieshoop'. Strong bush, apricot–pink flowers in large clusters

R. 'Wildflower', loose growth, single cream, very recurrent

The fashion for roses comes and goes. This rose, *Rosa* 'Albertine' was very popular in the 1920s and is now making a comeback — and so it should, as it is quite spectacular with its masses of salmon pink flowers in spring.

LARGE SPREADING SHRUB ROSES

These are best pinned down so their laterals can flower. Let them grow over an area of 2–3 square metres.

R. 'Conrad F. Meyer'. Pink, cupped flowers
R. 'Frühlingsmorgen'. Cream–pink single flowers
R. 'Graham Thomas'. Yellow flowers
R. 'Lordly Oberon'. Pink
R. 'Mme Hardy'. Full, flat, white flowers
R. 'Shropshire Lass'. Pink flowers

POPULAR CLIMBING ROSES

R. 'Albertine'. Noted for its deep pink buds that open to a lovely pink flower, very vigorous, hardy and quick growing
R. 'Altissimo'. Bright red, single blooms, long and repeated flowering, very showy, matt green foliage
R. 'Cécile Brunner'. The climbing form of a popular bush rose often known as the sweetheart rose for its pale pink buds, which make lovely posies. Flowers abundantly in spring
R. 'Clair Matin'. Semi-double, pastel pink flowers, fragrant, recurrent flowering, dark foliage giving good contrast with the flowers
R. 'Gloire de Dijon'. A lovely buff-yellow to apricot flower and a deep rich perfume
R. 'Iceberg'. Free flowering, recurrent, white flowers, one of the most popular of roses in recent times
R. laevigata (Cherokee rose). A very vigorous grower, single, pure white petals, can grow to 6–7 m high
R. 'Mermaid'. A very vigorous grower, dark glossy leaves, single sulphur yellow flowers with lovely stamens
R. 'Sombreuil'. A climbing tea rose, quartered, cream–white flowers, fragrant
R. 'Souvenir de la Malmaison'. Old-fashioned, quartered, pink blooms, fragrant, vigorous grower, flowers tend to go mushy in the rain

ROSES FOR HIPS

Hips or 'heps' are the seed pods that develop from the finished rose flower. Some roses set hips well, others do not; some are really attractive on the bush or in a vase. Rugosas, such as the large, red 'Frau Dagmar Hastrup', and the single white R. rugosa alba, have the best hips.

R. brunonii. Long pale orange–apricot hips
R. 'Daydream'. Red hips
R. 'Fritz Nobis'. Beautiful orangey hips which last for ages in a vase.
R. 'Geraldii'. Clusters of small hips
R. longicuspis. Very dark red, small hips, with plenty in a bunch. The hips stay on the bush for ages, and last much longer if you pick them.
R. moyesii 'Geranium'. Bright red hips
R. 'Wedding Day'. Clusters of small orange hips

Another virtue of roses, is that many varieties have these lovely hips, or seed capsules, that remain on the bush after flowering. *Rosa moyesii* is an excellent one for its hips.

RECURRENT ROSES

These roses have a flush of flowers in spring and then, if you cut them back and feed them, they will have another flush about eight weeks later.

R. 'Bonica'. Pink
R. 'Carabella'. Pink in clusters
R. 'Duchesse de Brabant'. Pink
R. 'Edelweiss'. Cream
R. 'Gold Bunny'. Yellow

R. 'Grüss an Aachen'. Pinky apricot
R. 'Limelight'. Strong grower, good for picking
R. 'Mary Rose'. David Austin rose, pink
R. 'Penelope'. Creamy apricot
R. 'Stanwell Perpetual'. Lovely growth, pale pink–white flowers
R. 'Tamora'. A David Austin rose, soft apricot
R. 'Wildflower'. Cream with lovely yellow stamens

HAPPY COMBINATIONS OF ROSES AND OTHER PLANTS

R. 'Gloire de Dijon' (apricot) with cherry pie (mauve)
R. 'Grüss an Aachen' (pinky apricot) with orange salvia
R. 'Jessie Clarke' (single pink) with wisteria (purple)
R. 'Sunny South' (pink) with larkspurs (blue)
R. 'Tamora' (pale apricot) with honeysuckle (cream–yellow)

GLOSSARY OF ROSE TERMS

Bourbon: these plants arrived in Europe from the Isle of Bourbon in the early 1800s. They are characterised by neat whorls of rounded petals forming a cup-shaped flower. They generally flower only once, in early summer.

Cabbage: these are often seen in 17th century Dutch flower paintings, and are recognisable by their globular shape and massed petals. The Latin name for these roses is much more evocative: *Rosa centifolia* or 'rose of a hundred petals'. Cabbage rose bushes spread to approximately 1.8 m high by 1.2 wide and the flowers are generally very fragrant.

Floribunda: cluster-flowered roses bred early this century from smaller and less significant clustered roses. Beginning in the 1920s, the Danish breeder Svend Poulsen raised many varieties of cluster-flowered roses with larger blooms which remain important floribunda types today. These include 'Iceberg', 'Irish Wonder', 'Queen Elizabeth' and 'Fragrant Delight'.

Hybrid tea: these are often described as 'large-flowered roses' and their history began when the gardening public started to demand new roses in a greater range of colours. They are often more repeat flowering than old-fashioned roses, and their blooms are characterised by being high-peaked rather than round and flat. They were bred to last, and to keep their scent longer. There are many improved varieties of hybrid tea roses.

Musk: this group of roses is noted for lingering perfume and (usually) multi-petalled flowers.

Perpetual: continuous flowering over a season.

Quartered: many Heritage roses are 'quartered'; that is, they have an abundance of petals which form distinct whorls, usually four in number, with one in each quarter of the generally cup-shaped flower. This is a most attractive feature of these old roses, giving them a quite different charm from the highly peaked flowers of modern roses.

Recurrent: this word is often used in rose catalogues and books, and it refers to the plant's ability to flower in more than one flush. This characteristic is also referred to as 'remontant'.

Rugosa: these roses originated in China and Japan and are noted for their attractive foliage, which is a light lime green and stongly veined. Rugosas also form hips of lovely colours in autumn, so leave the spent flowers on the plant so the hips can develop.

A culinary garden

There are plenty of people who would rather grow plants to eat than to admire: they feel the relaxation and achievement of producing wholesome vegetables for the table is all they need. And I must say this is an approach I sympathise with. What more could one possibly ask of a plant when it is both beautiful and useful?

Apart from having food on your table that is as fresh and flavoursome as you can get, the other advantage is the control you have over chemicals and fertilisers. You can choose, and many people do, not to use chemical sprays to control pests and diseases, and you can dig all the organic material you like into the soil.

Vegetables

STARTING A VEGETABLE GARDEN

For a vegetable garden to be successful it should be sited in full sun, that is, with at least five hours of direct sun each day and away from the shade of buildings and trees. There is no reason to put the vegetable patch way down the back of the garden. Having the plot close to the kitchen will probably encourage you to use it more. Why not grow your vegetables amongst the flowers and shrubs? Many vegetables and herbs such as capsicums, eggplant, tomatoes, basil and parsley are colourful and decorative plants. With little effort all sorts of vegetables can be grown from seed or seedlings so that all through the year you will be picking a wonderful home-grown harvest.

Before planting either seeds or seedlings, spend some time digging over the garden bed, removing weeds and rubbish and breaking up any clods of soil. If you have a compost heap, and no gardener should be without one, fork in a shovelful of compost per square metre to help improve the soil. You should also dig in plenty of animal manure and blood and bone, natural nutrients high in nitrogen. These are particularly good for leafy vegetables. As the vegetables grow they will need more of a complete, all-purpose fertiliser with potash (K), phosphorus (P) as well as nitrogen (N). The N:P:K ratio is always stated on the back of the pack.

If you want to retain fertilisers in the soil rather than having them wash out, so plants can use them over longer periods, try adding a natural mineral call zeolite to the soil. Add a few handfuls to the compost heap, too, to cut back on the smell of rotting vegetation.

Vegetables need watering regularly as they grow. Have a tap close by and a hose long enough to reach the whole garden. A soaker hose winding its way through the bed will get water efficiently to where it is most needed: right to the plants' roots. One soaker hose available is made of recycled tyres so it is sturdy yet weeps water from its pores. This method uses up to 70 per cent less water than a conventional hose. You only need a quarter turn of the tap, letting it trickle for 20 minutes every couple of days, for effective watering. For busy people this is a really efficient method of watering any garden bed.

Mulch is good for keeping moisture in the soil, as well as for restricting weeds, so use a layer of rotted grass clippings, compost, straw, pea straw or lucerne hay. All you need to do is shift the mulch aside to plant into the soil and then tuck it back around your seedling.

Many vegetable growers like to mound up their beds for better drainage, too.

Silver beet is commonly grown, as it is easy and tasty. This is the red-stemmed variety (*B. vulgaris* 'Ruby Chard'), with Italian parsley growing as a border.

TWO VEGIES TO GROW INDOORS

I start this section on vegetables with two favourites of mine, both included because anyone at all can grow them, for they grow indoors. So even if you live in a bedsitter at the top of a highrise, there's little excuse not to try growing these delicious and nutritious vegies.

Mushrooms

I love mushrooms, eaten raw, stewed in a little butter or wine, popped into a casserole or stuffed. They make a great meal on their

PICKLED CHAMPIGNONS

For a lovely pre-dinner snack, nibble on pickled champignons (or button mushrooms). They are easy to make! Slice up some onions into rings, just cover them with vinegar and cook until clear.

own, but I can think of few savoury dishes they wouldn't enhance. Mushrooms are always a wonder to find in the paddocks or down by the creek, where they pop up after a patch of autumn or early winter rain followed by sun. However, you can grow them in a specially prepared box available from nurseries and garden centres, in a kit form, so you don't even have to venture outside.

These kits consist of a polystyrene box filled with special compost that contains the thread-like fungus which will develop into mushrooms. A small bag of humus, made up of lime and peat moss, is included for spreading over the top of the compost. If kept moist, this top layer will encourage the mushrooms to grow up into it. Keep enough moisture in the top layer to make it look black in colour and to enable you to squeeze a drop of water from it.

Hot and dry conditions are *not* what mushrooms need to be happy. A comfortable room temperature will be fine, but anything over 30°C or below 12°C will stunt their growth. They will grow in a position that gets indirect sunlight, but they do not need sun at all. Don't try to grow them in a cupboard, though, as they do need fresh air. A cellar, if you have one, is a good place for mushroom growing.

Mushrooms will develop in different flushes 10–14 days apart. They will keep producing for up to three months, depending on the conditions. You can pick them as they grow — the first tiny ones, the unopened button ones, are good to add to soups or sauces. The slightly larger ones have a beautiful taste, I think, and are the best for many types of cooking. If you leave the mushrooms to grow larger so they become open and flat, they have a very rich flavour, good for stews and casseroles. However you like to use them, mushrooms are rich in protein and vitamins, especially Vitamin B, and a good thing to know is that they are great for weight watchers as they contain little carbohydrate.

Sprouts

Another nutritious vegetable that you can easily grow indoors at any time of the year is sprouts. These are the green, vitamin-full shoots (or sprouts) that emerge from seeds that are quick to germinate in a moist environment. You can buy sprouts such as mung beans, alfalfa and many others, from supermarkets or greengrocers in plastic containers, but why not have the fun of growing them in your own home?

Sprouts are a beaut idea for those who may not have the room

Add vinegar, salt and ground pepper, and then the little champignon mushrooms. Just bring to the boil (don't over-cook them) and put into jars with 1/3 vinegar and 2/3 water to cover. They will last in the fridge for months.

for a vegetable garden or for anyone who wants the pleasure of cutting a fresh green salad vegetable at any time of the year. They do not need to grow in soil, and need very little sun. All they need is to be washed out every day and picked when they are about 3 cm high. They are easy and instant — some, such as alfalfa and radish, are ready to eat four days after sowing!

Seed for sprouts is cheap to buy in packets and available all year round. All you need is a jar in which to grow them. Cover the top with a nylon stocking so you can drain the water away, or you can buy a special seed-sprouting plastic container with three levels: two for two different seed varieties, the lowest level for the water to drain into.

Spread the seed evenly and water with clean, fresh water daily, making sure the water drains away so the seeds are not sitting in it. Once the seeds have sprouted, pick them and use whole in salads or sandwiches.

GARLIC (Allium sativum)

Many people know the value of garlic, both for improving the flavour of many food dishes and as an antiseptic and general tonic. It is widely used in cooking and has been shown to reduce blood pressure, help with colds, flu (in fact it is being sold as a cold and flu herb), sinus and congestion. It is also a disinfectant (and was used for that purpose in the First World War). If you can cope with the distinctive garlic breath, you will find immense pleasure in growing it.

You can grow garlic for the bulb or for its green shoots, which can be used as a herb. It will grow from fresh cloves, or you can buy tubers ready for planting. Garlic bulbs bought from supermarkets are usually imported so have been fumigated and are unlikely to shoot. Make sure the cloves you buy for planting are locally grown and fresh.

Individual cloves can be planted 3–5 cm deep in full sun with well-drained soil. They are best planted from May to August.

Before planting dig in some fertiliser which has a high potash content. Animal manures should not be dug in too close to the bulb; in fact it is better to dig the manure in three months before planting.

When you harvest your garlic depends on you. The shoots can be used as they grow, but if you wait until late summer when the tops have dried off and withered, you can lift the bulb with tops

HOME-MADE GARLIC SPRAY

You can make your own garlic spray by pounding up several cloves and mixing them with water and a handful of pure soap. Dilute this mixture to spray over plants to kill insects on contact. Some sucking insects may need three sprays to be knocked out.

still attached so it can be hung and dried off. Shake the soil off the bulbs. Using the dried foliage, knot or plait the bulbs together and hang them in a dry, airy spot. They are a decorative addition to the kitchen and convenient for the cook. Shallots and onions can be stored in the same way. Save some cloves or a bulb to replant next season.

Garlic is a lovely ornamental plant with long stems that can grow to a metre or so high and mauve balls of flowers in summer. Try a giant form, the Russian or elephant garlic, which has cloves the size of a small fist. It has the distinctive garlic taste but is not as strong as the smaller one.

Rose growers often grow several garlic plants amongst their fancied shrubs as a repellent against aphids, and many natural deterrent sprays for chewing and sap-sucking insects in the garden are based on garlic.

FRENCH SORREL (Rumex scutatus)

This perennial plant looks like a weed, but it is great to use in soups and salads and is full of goodness. The leaves are high in iron, so this is a useful herb to add to your diet. It is an accommodating plant to grow, needing only a shovelful of compost in its hole at planting time. French sorrel looks like dock weed, grows into a clump 90 cm square and needs partial to full sun. A bunch of French sorrel leaves is the basis of a delicious soup.

Every couple of years dig up the entire sorrel clump so you can separate it and start off with fresh pieces taken from the older, 'worn-out' plant. Using a garden fork or spade, dig up the clump and cut through the roots with a knife. Separate the outer shoots and roots, these being younger and more vigorous, discard the older part and replant the new pieces.

The bright lilac flowers of elephant garlic (*Allium giganteum*) grow on stems up to 1.2 m high. The large bulb has a milder flavour and odour than common garlic (*Allium sativum*) so it might suit less adventurous cooks. All garlic varieties require good drainage in fertile, slightly alkaline soil that has been well dug over. Cloves should be planted in late autumn to winter as they need a period of chilling to develop well.

MY MOTHER'S RECIPE FOR SORREL SOUP

Chop up 3 potatoes, 2 onions and boil in chicken stock until soft. Take the stalks off 20 French sorrel leaves and add leaves to the pot. Boil for one minute and put the whole lot through a food processor or strainer. Serve with a dob of cream.

OTHER VEGETABLES TO GROW

Name	Variety	Seed	Seedling	Planting time	When to harvest	Can be grown in pots
Beans	Broadbeans, climbing	✓		Autumn–winter	Late winter–spring	✓
	(Blue lake Stringless)			Spring–summer	Summer–autumn	
Carrots	Dwarf (Gourmet Delight)	✓		Spring–summer	Summer–autumn	✓
	Baby			Spring–summer–autumn	Spring–summer–autumn	✓
Lettuce	Brown & green mignonette	✓	✓	Spring–summer	Summer–autumn	✓
Peas	Snow peas	✓	✓	Winter–spring	Spring–summer	✓
	Sugar Snap	✓	✓	Winter–spring	Spring–summer	✓
Pumpkins	Golden Nugget	✓		Late spring	Late summer	
Radishes	All varieties	✓		All year	All year	✓
Rhubarb	Sydney	✓	crowns	Winter–	All year	✓
Senposai	Japanese greens	✓		Winter–spring	All year	✓
Silverbeet	Fordhook Giant	✓	✓	All year	All year	✓
Sweetcorn		✓	✓	Spring–summer	Summer	

Fruit

BLUEBERRIES

Blueberries are now a very popular berry fruit, especially if you are a keen muffin maker. They grow best in cool areas in soils rich in organic matter and high in acidity, much like the best conditions for azaleas, of which they are relatives. But don't despair if you can't provide these ideal conditions; blueberries are quite versatile, though they don't like sticky clay soils. They should grow in most cool/temperate areas of Australia.

Not only is the fruit good to eat but the bushes are very ornamental, with lots of tiny flowers and masses of blueberries. I have seen them growing amongst shrubs in a garden border, looking very striking, especially with bright autumn foliage.

CURRANTS

For people with small spaces or maybe a fence to grow something against, currants are a good investment. Red and white currants can be grown on wire supports or left free standing in a sunny position. Black currants are grown as free-standing bushes. They respond well to blood and bone and well-rotted manure.

RASPBERRIES

Of all the berries, this is the one I love best for taste. Raspberries grow well in temperate to cool climates. They are planted into well-drained soil as bare-rooted plants. Mix organic matter like compost into the soil, and you will need to provide wire supports about 1.5 m high, as the fruit grows on long canes. After harvesting, prune the raspberries by removing the old canes. Tie the new young canes to the wire support. Raspberries need plenty of water in summer when the fruit is developing.

STRAWBERRIES

Strawberries are one of the most enjoyable fruits that a gardener can grow — they are so delicious. There is nothing quite like them if picked fresh off one of your own plants. All the soft fruits deteriorate quickly in shops, so are best grown where they can be picked and eaten instantly. Unfortunately they are also attractive to birds and, although you can be generous to a certain

extent, it is worthwhile protecting the fruit as it ripens with bird netting.

Strawberries grow on the ground, or in pots, as long as the soil is well drained with plenty of organic matter incorporated to retain moisture over summer. Most people grow strawberries on a raised mound for drainage. They do need a sunny spot. Mix some blood and bone into the soil before planting. As strawberries grow close to the ground, the fruit can be prey to slugs or spoiled by dirt, so mulching is particularly important, not only to keep weeds down and moisture in, but also to protect the fruit. Straw is a good mulch as this raises the fruit off the ground as well as retaining water. Black plastic, usually so unsightly around the garden, is also ideal. Spread the plastic (or you can use weedmat) over the bed, and cut holes for each plant. The fruit stays clean and is easily picked with this convenient technique.

Always buy reputable varieties of strawberries guaranteed to be virus-free.

FRUIT TREES

Growing citrus trees

Being Sunraysia born, I can say sincerely that one of the best fruiting trees to have in any garden is a citrus tree. A lemon tree is the most commonly grown, but others such as orange, cumquat, grapefruit or mandarin are very worthwhile in any garden. They look very attractive at most times of year — glossy dark green leaves, fragrant white flowers, cheering bright fruit that can hang decoratively on the tree for many months or supply enough fruit to be enjoyed by your family and given away. If you haven't the room, citrus make very good container plants, too, given a large enough pot.

What a splendid summer sight — strawberries (*Fragaria* spp.) in their punnets at an outdoor market in Nice, France. Their taste was of 'real' strawberries, not too watery and insipid. This is the way they will grow in your own garden.

RASPBERRY MOUSSE

My neighbour, Lois Wake, makes this fabulous raspberry mousse when raspberries are in season, so I inevitably hover round her door at that time!

250 ml whipped fresh cream
500 ml custard
300 ml raspberry puree
2 tablespoons sugar
25–30 g gelatin dissolved in
2–3 tablespoons water.

Mix custard, raspberry puree and sugar together. Fold in whipped cream and stir in dissolved gelatine. Pour into mould to set. Decorate with extra raspberries.

General requirements for citrus

Although citrus trees, especially cumquats and oranges, will withstand moderate frosts, they may look a bit yellowish in winter cold. They really prefer warmth and sunshine, so try to position the tree in the sunniest spot in the garden and provide some wind protection when the tree is young.

Citrus trees grow best in light, sandy loam soil that drains freely. If their roots are subjected to long periods in water they can develop root rot. Definitely check the drainage before planting. If you have heavy soils, install some type of drainage system or dig in plenty of organic matter and coarse sand to make the clay more open and aerated. Alternatively, plant the tree in a raised garden bed or mound up the area about 30 cm higher than the surrounding garden.

Mulching any tree is always beneficial as the material will help conserve moisture and keep the roots cool over summer. Always keep the mulch well away (about 30 cm) from the tree trunk, as it can cause collar rot.

Feeding

Spring is the best time to plant out a new tree, when the danger of frosts is over. Leave a newly planted tree about six weeks before fertilising so its roots can become established and you can see new growth shoots. In early spring feed with a handful of complete fertiliser, citrus food that is high in nitrogen or a matchboxful of ammonium nitrate to every square metre, from the trunk out to the outer branches of the tree. Whatever you do, give the ground a good soaking before you apply fertiliser and then water it in well so the roots are not burnt. Feed again in autumn. Well-established citrus trees will need a lot of fertiliser for good growth.

Varieties of citrus trees

Lemons are easily the best bet in the citrus field as they are used practically every day. The 'Lisbon' lemon is a very prolific bearer of fruit, especially in spring, and is a strong-growing tree that will stand up to cold and frost better than other varieties. 'Eureka' is a variety with few thorns which does better in warmer areas and will bear well in summer. The 'Meyer' lemon is less sour than other lemons, and smaller growing, so is quite suitable to grow in pots.

Especially in the colder areas of Australia, the Meyer lemon (*Citrus limon* 'Meyer') is a hardy citrus tree which produces fruit constantly. It doesn't have the typical taste of the 'fish and chippy' Lisbon lemon (*Citrus limon* 'Lisbon'), as it is less acidic and more like a combination of orange and lemon. It is a small-growing tree, preferring a sunny, well-drained position.

WENDY'S ORANGE AND LEMON PUDDING

A dear friend and great family cook, Wendy Bus always makes sure her visitors are treated to taste-tempting food. This is one of my favourites.

3 eggs
1 cup sugar
2 tablespoons gelatin
juice of 2 lemons
juice of 1 orange
1 cup hot water
Beat egg yolks with sugar, add orange and lemon juice. Dissolve gelatine in hot water and add to mixture. Beat egg whites stiffly and fold into mixture. Refrigerate until set.

Oranges will bear their best fruit in milder climates that are dry rather than humid. 'Valencia' oranges are full of flavour with lots of juice, and are good value in summer. 'Navel' oranges are beautiful for eating in winter and there are some early varieties such as the 'Leng' navel. The 'Seville' variety is not seen much these days, more's the pity, as it makes such beautiful marmalade.

Grapefruit trees prefer a long warm period, but will produce good eating fruit in most areas. The most popular one is 'Marsh's Seedless', probably because it is virtually seedless. For more cold tolerance 'Wheeny' will probably do better, but it has more seeds.

Mandarins love a warmer climate than most other citrus, but they taste terrific so are worth trying to grow. 'Ellendale' and 'Emperor' varieties are both very juicy. 'Imperial' is the most popular and produces fruit which is easy to peel and has a good taste. It can be grown in most parts of Australia.

Limes really need a warmer climate, preferably frost-free, but many people want to grow them in cooler areas as the fruit is so useful. The Tahitian lime is more suitable for cold climates; the Mexican or West Indian one is cold sensitive and only suitable for the subtropics and tropics, although it can be grown in southern Australia in a very protected position.

Cumquats are more frost tolerant than any other citrus. They are grown for their fruits, which make excellent marmalade and brandied liqueur, but are also good ornamental trees in containers. Varieties to choose from are 'Marumi' and 'Nagami'.

SOME COMMON PROBLEMS WITH CITRUS TREES

• *Yellowing leaves. A bit of yellowing of the leaves is natural, especially in the winter cold. If you fertilise the tree in early spring, leaves will become green. In heavy clay soils you may notice the leaves going yellow between the green veins; this indicates an iron deficiency. Apply iron chelates to the leaves and into the soil.*

• *Very thick rind. Excessively thick skin can be due to over-use of nitrogenous fertilisers, so use a complete fertiliser. Also make sure the tree is not drying out.*

• *Lack of fruit on young trees. Even though a newly planted tree may have a few fruit on it, it is preferable for the tree to establish itself over another two or three years without fruit. In fact if you see small fruit developing you would do*

The summer orange, *Citrus sinensis* 'Valencia', is always a sweet, juicy one.

best to pick them off until the tree is more mature and settled into the ground. Be patient — a lemon will produce a crop in 4–5 years.

• Poor growth and lack of fruit on an established tree. This is often the case if the tree's roots are suffering, perhaps from poor aeration and too much water. Try to improve the soil's condition by working in plenty of organic matter and do not over-fertilise the tree.

• Leaves falling off. Check the drainage; the cause is most likely to be waterlogging around the roots. Other possibilities are that the tree has been allowed to dry out, or fertiliser burn. Make sure you soak the root area before applying any feed.

• Fruit fly is essentially a problem of warmer areas. It should be treated by experts, such as departments of agriculture, and must be reported immediately so traps can be laid.

FEIJOA JAM

Peel and slice 2 kg fruit.
Place in a pan with 300 ml water.
Bring to the boil and simmer until fruit is tender.
Add grated rind and juice of two lemons.
Add 2 kg of sugar. Dissolve and boil hard for 10 minutes.
Test for set on a saucer.

FEIJOA

It is not uncommon to find the fruits of the feijoa (*Feijoa sellowiana*), sometimes called the pineapple guava, left scattered on the ground underneath the tree. It's my guess that the owners of these trees do not realise the potential of this wonderful fruit, and just leave it to rot. What a waste!

The fruit forms over autumn, looking like large green eggs. When ripe, and that is usually when they fall onto the ground, they go soft inside, though the outer skin is still firm. Cut open the fruit and scoop out the yellowish flesh — it may not look particularly attractive but it tastes wonderful! I find it a sort of a mixture of banana, passionfruit and fruit salad, topped off with a lovely fruity fragrance.

More people should consider growing a feijoa. It is an evergreen tree with dark green leaves, grey underneath, and will reach around 4 m high. It is not fussy about the soil it grows in, but needs a sunny spot. The flowers are attractive, with numerous crimson stamens, rather like a bottlebrush or melaleuca flower.

It will grow fairly quickly, especially if given a small handful of slow-release fertiliser at planting time and stacks of compost or mulch around the roots' surface. Make sure that you keep the water up to the feijoa over summer when the fruit is forming. In spring, give the tree a good feed with a fertiliser high in potash and you will be greatly rewarded by the number and size of your feijoas.

You can eat the feijoa fruit straight from the tree or make jams or jellies. The colour of feijoa jam is a perfect red; it simply makes my mouth water every time I see it. Here's a recipe for feijoa jam from noted food and gardening writer, Gail Thomas.

FIGS

Nearly every old house that I have lived in has had a fig (*Ficus carica*) in the backyard. A loquat was also pretty common in old houses as they are very hardy trees, surviving through tough times.

Fig trees are resolute; they will just keep on growing no matter how hot, dry or cold the spot. The only problem is birds which peck holes in the fruit just as it ripens, so bird netting at the appropriate time is necessary. You can let the tree get quite large as a summer shade tree, or keep it pruned to 4 m high. The variety 'Brown Turkey', with nearly black skin, is a beauty, and for fig jam the greenish-brown-skinned 'White Adriatic' is excellent. The black and white Genoa fig is delicious eaten fresh. You should take care to look out for fruit fly in figs in the warmer areas of Australia. Always destroy any infested fruit.

Figs (*Ficus carica*) are a wonderful taste, either fresh or as a jam (add a little bit of ginger). Fig trees are very hardy, growing in most climates and situations. These are the black and white Genoa fig (F. *carica* 'White Genoa', F. *carica* 'Black Genoa').

GUAVAS

Apart from the oranges of the Sunraysia district, one of my early memories in the fruit line is of guavas and feijoas. Big shrubs of these two similar fruits encroached over the fence from the neighbour's garden, leaving enough fruit to be gobbled up by us children. It was a real treat to be the first to find a ripe guava and eat it straight off the tree.

When I talk about guavas what I am remembering is the strawberry guava (*Psidium littorale*), with round, purplish red fruit which has a distinctive strawberry taste. People lucky enough to live in subtropical and tropical areas can grow the large yellow guava (*P. guavaja*), the true guava. It is a messy tree, and prone to fruit fly, but a delicious fruit nevertheless. The strawberry guava is a small shrubby tree, about 3 m high, which will grow just about anywhere as long as frosts are not too harsh. It has lovely glossy leaves.

Both the guava and the feijoa have places in the garden on ornamental grounds alone. Both are tough plants withstanding frosts and droughts. Both will benefit from a small amount of potash in late spring and mulch around the tree's roots in summer.

Mulberry trees are exceptionally
hardy and are grown for their foliage,
which turns yellow in autumn, and their
edible fruit. Just take care when you
pick the fruit as it stains hands and
clothes (rubbing your hands with a green
berry will remove any stains). Both the
white mulberry (*Morus alba*) and the
black mulberry above (*Morus nigra*)
form beautiful trees, with gnarled,
character-filled trunks.

MULBERRIES

My brother has a very old mulberry in his garden. It is a virtually neglected tree, though full of character with its gnarled trunk, yet every year it produces buckets of fruit. Of course everyone has to wear their 'mulberry-picking' clothes especially for the inevitable stains from the juice.

Mulberries are great trees for ornamental and shade value, and they are very hardy, as evidenced by those still remaining in old farm gardens. The fruit of the black mulberry (*Morus nigra*) resembles a blackberry and is large and juicy, as long as the tree is well-watered. And silkworm lovers, as we were when young, treasure the white mulberry (*Morus alba*) for its leaves.

PERSIMMON

Another fruit that fools some people who have never been introduced to its taste or appearance is the persimmon. Over autumn you may have noticed a tree poking its head over someone's fence, covered with round fruit that resemble a cross between a large tomato and an orange. You will see many persimmon trees (*Diospyros kaki*) growing in homes owned by Italian gardeners.

The ripe fruit is heaven. Well, some people find it an acquired taste, but for me there is nothing like a squishy persimmon to ooze down your chin. The taste is nothing like any other fruit. It must be eaten when the flesh is very squashy and squelchy — in fact some people say it should only be eaten in the bath so you can make a real mess of it!

Apart from being edible, the persimmon is a lovely ornamental tree. Over autumn, the foliage turns orange-red then falls off to reveal the large, round, orange fruit which hangs on the tree for some weeks.

They are adaptable trees, growing to 3 m high, but they do need the chill of a cold snap to produce a good crop and for the fruit to colour up well. Pick the fruit while it is firm and leave it to ripen to the squishy stage before eating it. This is essential for the astringent varieties such as 'Dai Dai Maru' and 'Hyakumi'. Don't try to eat a firm fruit or your mouth will immediately react and become unpleasantly furry and dry. There are some non-astringent varieties, such as 'Fuyu', but even these are more delicious when a bit squishy.

POMEGRANATES

For a fruit tree with a difference, the pomegranate (*Punica granatum*) is a most decorative one, with flowers that last for ages, followed by a magnificent fruit that can grow as large as an orange, with tangerine skin that splits open to reveal masses of small red juicy seeds. Whether you leave it on the tree to beautify the garden, bring branches indoors for decoration or eat it, a pomegranate is a valuable asset to any garden. It is a tough customer, too. It originated in the Middle East, Iran and Afghanistan, so can put up with heat and drought. It will grow to 4–5 metres high.

QUINCE

The quince (*Cydonia oblonga*) has plenty of memories for me: a lovely painting of green-golden fruit hanging in the lounge room and a very old tree in the back yard, with clusters of fruit to be made into jelly or stewed for a dessert. Quinces are such a pretty colour, whether on the tree, bottled, made into jam or jelly or hanging on branches picked for indoor decoration. The trees, which grow between 2 and 4 m high, are very hardy and extremely productive. And it has a fragrant, rose-like flower, since the quince is part of the Rosaceae family.

Quinces are easy to grow and, like pears, will reach a grand old age with little maintenance. Watch out for fruit fly as the fruit ripens, and in areas where this is a declared pest you won't be able to leave the fruit long on the tree and must destroy any dropped fruit. In New South Wales, for example, the fruit must be picked in April.

TAMARILLO

For a frost-free spot, the tamarillo (*Cyphomandra betacea*) is a beauty. Commonly called the tree tomato, it grows to 3 m high in a warm, sheltered spot, and has longish oval fruits with a dark reddish skin and a taste that is rather like passionfruit with a suggestion of tomato. The trees should be staked, as they are prone to wind damage, and planted in a well-drained spot with lots of organic matter mixed into the soil. The fruit, which sets from autumn on, can be eaten fresh (scoop out the flesh), stewed or made into tamarillo jam or preserve.

To stew tamarillos: Simmer tamarillos gently in water with a little sugar for 10 minutes, cool, peel and serve with a lemon custard.

As children, we practically fought over the first ripe pomegranate fruit (*Punica* spp.). As the orange-red fruit splits open on warm autumn days, the small red seeds are revealed in neat rows. Actually the taste is not overwhelming, but quite sweet enough to tempt a child. Nowadays I grow them for their ornamental value as the fruit hangs on the tree, or in a vase, for ages.

Herbs

*M*ore and more people are becoming aware of herbs and appreciating the pleasure these plants give in the garden, kitchen and for cosmetics, medicines and repellents around the house. I couldn't live without my herb garden. Whether you are thinking of renovating an existing herb garden or just introducing this wonderful group of plants into your life as a new gardener, you will find them amongst the easiest and most pleasurable of plants to grow.

Herbs will do best in full sun and need only well-drained soil because their roots do not like to be water-logged. For convenience a herb garden, or even a simple herb pot if space is tight, near the kitchen is the way to go if you are always looking for a flavouring or garnish for cooking.

If you grow them indoors, choose a north-facing windowsill with at least six hours of sun and use a good quality potting mix rather than garden soil

They are one of the few plants that do not need to be fed. With too much fertiliser they will grow far too rapidly, outgrowing their space and producing weak flavour and fragrance; all leaf and little of the volatile oil which is the essential ingredient to give flavour to your sauces and spice to your curries.

Many herbs naturally repel insects — wormwood and pennyroyal, for instance. Some herbs, like any other plant, attract insects, but if they are edible herbs I do not recommend spraying them with pesticides. Try a home-made spray. A couple of crushed garlic cloves mixed with tabasco sauce is a very simple one, and I've given another recipe on page 62.

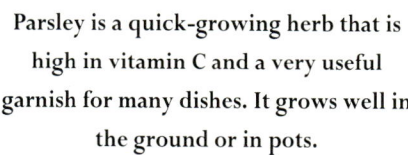

Parsley is a quick-growing herb that is high in vitamin C and a very useful garnish for many dishes. It grows well in the ground or in pots.

Over summer all herbs grow very rapidly and should be cut back constantly. Either use the leaves fresh or dry them by hanging bunches up in a cool, airy spot. Small amounts can be wrapped in brown paper and put in the crisper of the fridge.

Herbs always taste better if used fresh or dried rather than in jars where they really lose their flavour. They can be easily hung to dry and used for flavourings in cooking or as infusions for interesting herbal teas. To dry herbs, pick them in the early morning with no moisture on them, tie into small bunches and hang them upside down in a dimly lit part of the house or garage. If you hang them in the kitchen. avoid anywhere where steam might interfere with their drying.

Herbs can also be frozen into ice-blocks. Chop into small pieces or select small flowers and leaves, and place them in ice-block containers; fill with water and freeze until required for cooking or your favourite iced teas, fruit punches or cocktails. The endless variety of mints available is especially good for teas and edible flowers such as borage, nasturtium or geranium would add a decorative touch to long summer drinks.

Chopped herbs mashed into butter make great toppings for meat, chicken and fish, and you can freeze rolls of this herb butter to use when required.

The favourites are parsley, sage, rosemary and thyme, and these are all very useful. Parsley needs to grow quickly and does best in soil with plenty of organic matter added. Unlike most herbs, it will benefit from regular (every two weeks) doses of a liquid fertiliser to keep it green and lush. Pick it in bunches for salads, tabouleh and garnishes.

Sage is a grey-leafed herb, very hardy, loves the sun and is pleasant to grow amongst other shrubs and perennials. A leaf or two (don't overdo this pungent herb) of chopped sage used in stuffing for chickens will add piquancy and a wonderful flavour.

The prostrate rosemary and thyme grow well as edging plants hanging over a garden border, where their fragrance can be appreciated. Both herbs have wide uses in cooking, especially if a casserole needs added zest, or just a little nip of rosemary or thyme on a rack of lamb makes a delicious roast dinner. Try growing rosemary near the barbecue so you can easily break off a twig to throw on the coals or the meat as it cooks.

HERBAL TEAS

Most herbs can establish themselves well through autumn and can be used for various purposes throughout winter in the kitchen, but I want to entice you to try herbal teas. Most of us enjoy or need a cup of tea or coffee at regular intervals during each day, but with a herb garden within easy reach of the kitchen it is a very good reason to vary the flavours of the cuppa! As well as being enjoyable, herbal teas are an aid to good health.

There is an art to making a good cup of tea and patience is number one on the list. Herbal tea making is not a quick jiggle – the brew must be allowed to steep for a few minutes. When you have selected the variety of tea you would like to make — for example, mint, chamomile or sage — the freshly picked leaves need to be crushed or bruised gently to release the aroma. Most herbal teas take on the appearance of weak tea, generally golden or light green, depending on the strength. Now to some herbs suitable for making a special brew.

An all-time favourite is chamomile (*Chamaemelum nobile*). The small daisy-like flowers need to be collected and dried to use in tea making.

lemon and the herbs lemon balm, lemon grass or lemon verbena can all be used for a deliciously flavoured tea. Lemon balm (*Melissa officinalis*) is a hardy perennial that will form a large clump in the garden. Beware, it can spread under ideal conditions. Lemon grass (*Cymbopogon citratus*) is more suited to the tropics and subtropics. Any further south and the plant may need protection and a little tender loving care, especially through the winter. It is a perennial plant and needs a sunny spot and plenty of moisture. It grows in clumps. Use its leaves for tea and its root or bulb for the delicious and characteristic lemony flavour in Thai curries and soups.

Lemon verbena (*Aloysia triphylla*) can grow into quite a large shrub, but it will take radical cutting back in winter. If you do not feel there is enough room in the garden or you are worried about keeping it under control, why not try growing it as a standard in a large terracotta pot? It does require a sunny position and a regular prune.

For an extra strong flavour, peppermint (*Mentha piperata*) is usually a successful choice. This ground-hugging creeper with purple flower stems needs to be kept contained as it can get out of hand. Keep it well pruned and enjoy your tea breaks!

A cup of sage tea will do you the world of good. Sage is part of the Salvia family and the meaning of the Latin word *salvia* is 'health'. This herb has long been recommended by herbalists as helpful in enhancing memory, retarding the ageing process and improving eyesight. Sage tea can also help to relieve a sore throat if you use it as a gargle.

Herb-flavoured oils and vinegars

Pick herbs. Put twigs of fresh herbs into clean bottles. Fill with a good quality olive oil or vinegar. Add cloves of garlic, peppercorns or red chillies for taste. Seal the bottles.

HERBS

Name	Annual or perrenial	Seed	Cutting/ slip	Seedling	Height harvest	Planting time	Uses
Basil	Sweet basil/annual	✓	✓	✓	40cm	Spring–summer	fresh/ dried tomato & pasta
Chives	Perennial	✓		✓	30cm	Spring–summer–	Salads soups, egg dishes
Coriander	Annual	✓			40cm	Spring–summer	spicy food
Marjoram	Perennial	✓	✓		40cm	All year	fresh/ dried
Parsley	Biennial	✓		✓	30cm	Spring–summer–autumn	fresh/ dried Flavour & garnish meat & salads
Rosemary	Perennial	✓	✓		90 – 150cm	All Year	Meat dishes
Thyme	Perennial	✓	✓		60 – 90cm	All Year	Salads, egg dishes

Oriental vegetables and herbs

*O*ver recent years there has been a big change in our eating habits, evidenced by the popularity of Asian, Italian, Greek, Chinese, Middle Eastern and other wonderful 'ethnic' restaurants. As a result, gardeners throughout the country want to grow a greater range of vegetables at home. I love the simplicity of stir-fry and steam cooking methods and have tried a great range of oriental vegetables. Some of the flavours of Asian vegetables and herbs are already well known — garlic, coriander, Chinese chives, lemon grass and bok choi (the Chinese cabbage), for instance. I've spotted others in the markets without knowing their names, let alone how to grow and cook them. But the process of learning and experimenting has given a new direction to my vegie patch and is great fun.

The following crops can be successfully grown in many parts of Australia, and most are just as easy to grow as our familiar broccoli, cabbage and carrots. They are also great to cook with, because their preparation is so simple.

Chinese cabbage, wong bok, doesn't form a head as other cabbages do. It has distinctive white stems and light-green leaves, all of which can be stir-fried.

LEAFY VEGETABLES

There are various types of celery cabbage (also known as 'wong bok'). Some have loose flowery heads; others have elongated leaves wrapped over each other; still others are oval-shaped with leaves curling over each other.

Chinese broccoli or Chinese kale is another in the cabbage family, with oval leaves and fleshy stems which can both be eaten boiled, steamed or stir-fried.

Chinese white cabbage or bok choi (or 'pak choi') has spoon-shaped green leaves, white mid-ribs and short stems. Both the stems and leaves are succulent and crispy, and both can be eaten fresh when young or cut up in soups or stir-fries. It grows as a neat, upright plant, whereas the Chinese flat cabbage, another in the Brassica family, has its leaves spread out into a flat saucer-shaped plant. The Chinese cabbage is a good source of vitamin C and adds fibre to your diet.

Bok choi is a tasty vegetable which is delicious in stir-fries or when steamed. Perilla is a herb with purple-coloured leaves. Use it as a garnish in a vegetable stir-fry mix.

Chop suey green ('shungiku') This is an unusual plant as it is an edible type of chrysanthemum. The young growth can be stir-fried or steamed with other vegetables. Even the chrysanthemum flowers can be added as decoration as they, too, are edible.

Japanese perilla (shiso) is an annual plant with green or purple leaves which can be used to garnish dishes to add colour.

Spinach mustard (or Japanese spinach, 'komatsuna') has grey-green, roundish leaves on long stems, rather like spinach. It is high in vitamins and can be cooked as greens or used raw in salads and sandwiches.

LEAFY HERBS

Amaranth spinach is not really a spinach but has leaves with tinges of red which can be used in soups or stir-fry dishes.

Asian basil or lemon basil has a lemon flavour and fragrant leaves and, like any basil, is good in fish dishes. The lemon basil is very strong and you can dry the leaves and use them in potpourri.

Chinese parsley or coriander is an annual plant and quite short-lived. The leaves have a very distinctive flavour, strongly aromatic. Use them in salads or soups, or for flavour in Chinese or Indian dishes. Coriander needs a rich fertile soil with good drainage and plenty of organic matter dug in.

Vietnamese mint ('kesom'), also known as 'hot mint' as its flavour is very spicy, is very popular in Asian cuisine, in soups or

stir-fries (just a little leaf will do). It grows as a perennial plant spreading over the ground and is best grown in a container as in warmer areas it can become a nuisance.

ROOT VEGETABLES

Chinese chives (*Allium* spp.) or 'gow choy' is a perennial plant growing in clumps to about 30 cm high. It has flat leaves rather than the rounded leaves of the common chives. The leaves have a mild garlic taste, a little stronger than ordinary chives. They do not die back over winter, are very hardy in full sun and should be used fresh in egg dishes, salads and other dishes.

Chinese/Japanese radish ('loh paak') is grown for its white root, which reaches 30 cm long and can be eaten cooked or raw. It has a crunchy texture and mild flavour. It is very different in colour, size, shape and flavour from the usual red radish. It will grow in all types of soils, but is best in light, sandy soil and when temperatures are higher, as in cold times it can bolt into seed too early.

Japanese bunching onion, sometimes known as the 'Welsh onion', never forms a fat bulb like the common onion. Instead it has small bulbs and cylindrical, hollow leaves, both of which can be used in soups, omelettes and seafood dishes.

Taro (wo tau) is a perennial plant with large brown underground tubers. It really needs warm tropical or semi-tropical conditions. Use chopped for stews or stir-fries.

Potatoes

*P*otatoes are high on the list of commonly eaten vegetables, and it is pleasing nowadays to have a good range of potatoes available from markets. Even better from the gardener's point of view is the recent availability of different types of potatoes suitable for growing in the garden or in containers.

Each variety has its own colour, texture and special cooking and eating qualities. There's the baking potato ('Pontiac'), the gourmet potato ('Desirée'), the chip potato ('Kennebec'), the potato salad one ('Bintje'), and the all-purpose spud ('Sebago'). Others are 'Patrones' (for salad), 'Toolangi Delight' (an excellent all-rounder with purple skin) and 'Kipfler' (with a yellow skin, good for baking).

METHODS OF CULTIVATION

Potatoes are very susceptible to frosts, growing best in the warm season with at least 120 frost-free days. Young shoots will be badly affected by cold weather so, in highland or southern areas, the tubers are best sprouted indoors and planted out when frosts are over. Generally this means sowing from August into the warmer months, depending on where you live.

Leave the tubers exposed to the light for a week or so until sprouts shoot from their eyes. Choose strong-growing sprouts to plant, and generally it is not a good idea to cut the seed potatoes in half before planting. Open wounds on a cut potato encourage disease and 'bleeding', so your harvest will be reduced. It is important that you use certified seed potatoes, rather than sowing from the previous year's crop, which can lead to a build-up of diseases such as root-rot. Disease-free seed potatoes mean better yields.

Potatoes will grow in any well-drained soil, and if you add organic matter to the soil they will grow well. They will do best of all in acidic soils with a pH level of 5.0 to 6.0. Alkaline soils with any lime added will raise the pH level to above 6.5, so good crops are not produced, and there is a chance of potato scab disease. It is best not to grow potatoes in the same ground in which tomatoes or other root vegetables have just finished their season, so rotate your crops. Test your soil, add organic matter and practise crop rotation, to ensure that your potato patch is not too alkaline.

Trenching

Dig trenches 15–20 cm deep and 60–75 cm apart and form a small hill at the bottom, only 5 cm high. Spread a complete vegetable fertiliser or animal manure along the bottom, and space the tubers 25–30 cm apart. Cover them with soil so the fertiliser does not come in contact with the new shoots, then fill in the trench.

As the new shoots emerge after two to three weeks (depending on the soil temperature), keep them well watered — regular moisture is vital until harvesting. By now the new growth will be about 15 cm high. Mound up the soil, leaving only about 5 cm of the shoot uncovered, so supporting the plant. Your new crop of potatoes will form above the seed potatoes in the newly dug soil of the trench and mound, not below.

You can grow potatoes even if you have a small garden — in containers, large garbage bins, 44-gallon drums or a high-rise pile of tyres. Place a tyre in a sunny spot and fill it with well-rotted manure and compost, adding a handful of complete fertiliser and a light layer of soil. Put 5 to 6 seed potatoes in the container, about 15 cm from the outer edges, and cover them with 10 cm of potting mix or soil. In cold climates where there is a danger of frosts, cover with newspaper or polythene.

As the stems grow keep adding layers of compost to the top 5 cm of each stem, plus another tyre to hold the soil. As the plant grows you can add up to three or four tyres so you can harvest a crop all along the stolons.

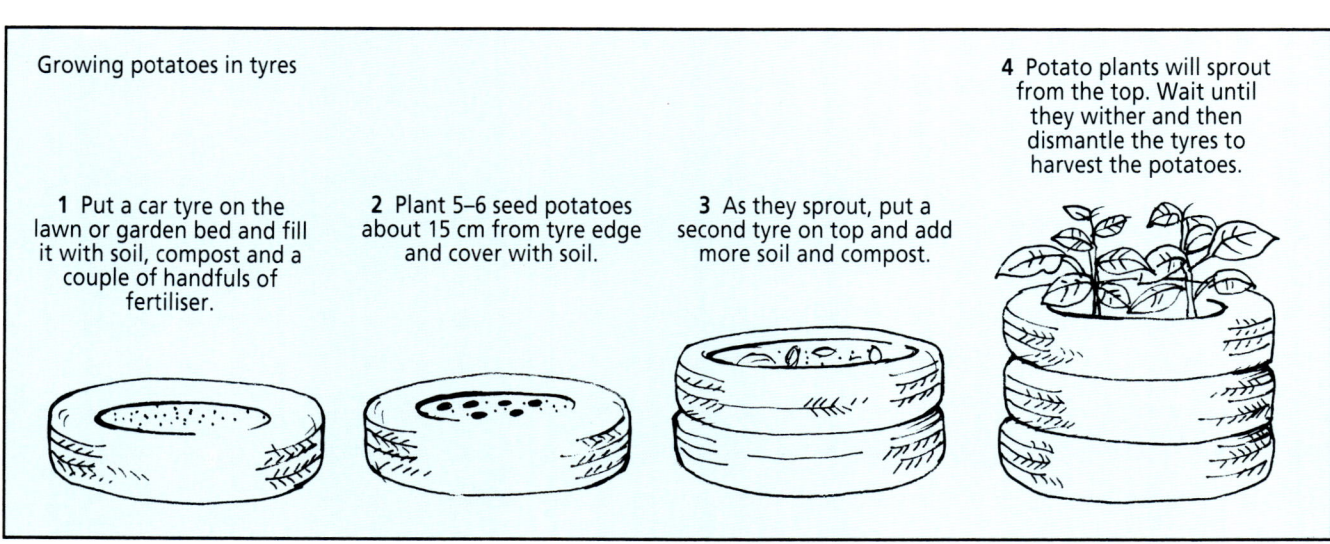

Growing potatoes in tyres

1 Put a car tyre on the lawn or garden bed and fill it with soil, compost and a couple of handfuls of fertiliser.

2 Plant 5–6 seed potatoes about 15 cm from tyre edge and cover with soil.

3 As they sprout, put a second tyre on top and add more soil and compost.

4 Potato plants will sprout from the top. Wait until they wither and then dismantle the tyres to harvest the potatoes.

A non-dig method

Place the potatoes about 30 cm apart, directly on the ground where you plan to grow them (even onto the lawn or weedy patch), remembering that they take up a fair bit of room. Cover them with a layer of straw, 40–50 cm deep, and water it well. Now spread animal manure and blood and bone over the top of the straw. Your potatoes will grow up through the straw. It's important to keep adding straw as it rots down and the potatoes form, to keep them covered. Exposure to light turns potatoes green and poisonous.

HARVESTING YOUR CROP

If you want to eat small and delicious 'new' potatoes, dig the plant up a month after it has flowered, just when the lower leaves are turning yellow. For larger potatoes, or if you want to store them for a time, wait until the whole plant has died down before digging. Use any damaged ones immediately; 'new' potatoes with their higher moisture content and thin skins should also be used immediately. Store others in a dark cupboard or any cool, dry, dark place, remembering that unwashed potatoes will keep longer. Remember, too, potatoes must be kept in the dark to prevent them greening.

Tomatoes

A home-grown tomato always tastes so much better than a bought one, and there is now a huge variety to choose from for whatever suits your taste. They can be grown by seed or seedlings, and any tomato needs a couple of shovelfuls of compost in the planting hole so it gets a good start. When you have transplanted a tomato seedling into the ground, cover it for a few days with a plastic bag or a used soft-drink bottle or milk carton until any cold or frosty weather has gone, and then remove it once the weather is warm and settled. A couple of weeks after transplanting, give your tomato a dose of fertiliser, especially a tomato food high in potash (potassium). This is especially important when the first flowers appear, as potash will help the flowers set and form fruit.

Tomatoes are one of the many heirloom vegetables that are coming back into favour. They also have great flavours — pictured here is 'Green Zebra', which certainly tastes as good as it looks!

As soon as the weather warms up, it is important to keep water up to the plant. Water regularly, especially as the plants are growing, and then decrease after the fruit has set. A drip irrigation system installed around the plants is a simple way to ensure regular waterings, so fruit development is healthy.

Controlling the weeds around the plants is another important part of growing a good tomato. Weeds will rob the plant of water and nutrients, so pull them out early. A thin carpet of mulch — such as rotted lawn clippings, compost, rotted leaves, organic straw, pea straw or lucerne hay — over the soil and around the plants will help to retard weed growth, reduce moisture loss and add nutrients to the soil.

The taller growing varieties of tomato need some kind of staking, with the stems trained and tied to the stakes. This will allow more air and sun to get in and around the plant for better health. Pruning is easy — simply pinch out the tiny lateral branches which grow at the point where the leaves meet the stem. Leave 3–4 growing branches to bear the fruit and fix the main stem to a stake with a flexible tie.

In fruit fly areas you will need to bag fruit as it ripens, keep a sharp eye out for the pest and destroy any rotting fruit on the ground.

Whether you choose to grow from seeds or seedlings, the number of tomato varieties is huge. There are the old, tall favourites like 'Burnley Surecrop', 'Grosse Lisse', 'Ox Heart' and 'Rouge de Marmande' which are always reliable fruiters.

Some people like to grow 'Sweet Bites', a tall variety with large bunches of cherry-sized fruit, sweet to taste and good to put whole in salads. One of the old heirloom tomatoes that has been voted by some as the best tasting is 'Tommy Toe'. It sets fruit from January through to May, setting a good crop. Give it a go and see if it lives up to your taste. Children seem to like cherry tomatoes particularly — my nephew James likes the way the seeds shoot into his mouth when he bites into one.

Not all tomatoes are red. Other heirloom varieties that are becoming more popular are 'Black Russian', with a dark black skin and tasty flesh, and 'Green Zebra' with a green-and-yellow striped skin. The 'Yellow Pear' is a small yellow one.

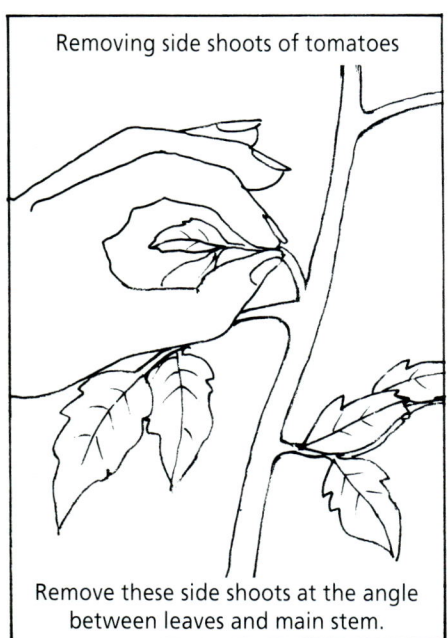

Removing side shoots of tomatoes

Remove these side shoots at the angle between leaves and main stem.

Home-grown tomatoes have a taste all of their own, far surpassing bought ones. 'Mighty Red' tastes spectacular when picked and eaten straight from the bush.

SUN-DRIED TOMATOES

Sun-dried tomatoes have become a fashionable favourite with many cooks and home gardeners. It is not unusual to see trays of tomatoes spread in the sun beside the vegetable patch.

'Roma' or 'Mama Mia' varieties are the best to use, but any tomato is worth a go. Cut your tomato in half, sprinkle with some salt and put on a wire rack with the fleshy side up. Leave them for three or four days in a hot, sunny spot such as a sunny veranda, until they become quite dry and leathery. A piece of wire mesh or fine cotton fabric laid over the top will deter bugs and birds.

Once dry the tomatoes can be washed, but make sure they dry off again before you store in jars. Cover with oil and you have a variety of taste sensations in store. They taste dramatically different with different oils (olive oil is by far the best), garlic (as much as you like, chopped up) and sprigs of fresh herbs such as basil, marjoram or thyme.

Tomatoes can also be slowly dried in the oven or microwave or by using specially designed food-drying equipment.

Climbers, creepers, groundcovers, screeners . . .

There is something very satisfactory about growing most climbing plants. Once the plant is established it can take off — some plants will grow several centimetres each week; some several metres in a season. Your irregular inspection of the garden can reap great rewards — you really seem to be making progress.

There is something very good, too, about the way a climbing plant can bring heavily scented flowers or delicious fruit to tantalise the garden wanderer, dangling just at head height or just out of reach, unless heavy rain has weighed down the foliage and caused the flowerheads to droop down to brush your shoulder or hair as you pass. All in all, I do encourage any gardener to cover a wall, pergola or old fence with some of these interesting and productive vines and climbers. I have listed some unusual ones, as well as my old favourites.

Strictly speaking, a climbing plant is one that can make its own way upwards without extra help, by attaching itself to a wall or fence by means of aerial roots, such as ivy or the creeping fig, (*Ficus pumila*) or by adhesive pads on the stems, such as Virginian creeper (*Parthenocissus quinquefolia*). Other climbing plants, such as the passionfruit and kiwifruit, have tendrils and twining stems that hook on to supports to hoist their way upwards. They need the branches of other plants, wire or trellis to get started, and then up they go.

The autumn colour of the Virginian creeper (*Parthenocissus quinquefolia*) is one of the best you'll see in any plant. It is a creeper that clings by tendrils to a wall and can cover a large area, giving a garden 'old-world' charm.

Planted on or around St Patrick's Day in March, sweet peas (*Lathyrus odoratus*) will reward you each year with a magnificent fragrance. They take up little space and look wonderful planted along a driveway or covering a fence.

Sweet peas will grow up a wire support against a fence, or will look good in a garden bed growing up a few bamboo poles tied together at the top, wigwam style. There are plenty of plants to choose from to cover a large pergola — Kiwifruit to give you plenty of fruit (see page 95) or, for beautiful flowers, the native bower of beauty (*Pandorea jasminoides*) with its pink and white trumpet flowers, or wisteria with its hanging mauve racemes of flowers which look best from below.

The thorns and prickles with which roses seem intent on grabbing you as you go by actually help the plant scramble up a wall. Some roses (the yellow banksia rose for example) have long canes instead of thorns, with which they climb on themselves by arching the stems over one another, but they do need a vertical support such as a wall.

Some climbing plants will twine their way up different kinds of supports — some of the less vigorous roses look really good on a pillar, for example. The white rose 'Iceberg' is very popular for this purpose, whereas an extremely strong rose like the banksia rose looks better growing over a larger structure such as a shed. A beautiful climber can become a real highlight of the garden when grown over a gateway or arch, and climbing plants can look really effective planted at the base of trees, so that they twine their way up amongst the branches. Clematis (*Clematis* spp.), with its large pink or mauve flowers, looks good planted at the bottom of a tree such as an apple, and allowed to grow freely through the tree. A gardening couple I know were so attached to their lemon tree, which died after 45 years of faithful service, that they decided not to pull it out but instead planted an ivy geranium that twines its way up the old branches and flowers profusely. The ivy geranium (*Pelargonium peltatum*) is a very hardy plant that takes full sun.

A popular native climber is the sarsaparilla (*Hardenbergia violacea*), which grows thickly, flowering with purple pea flowers in spring. Or, for a climber that flowers for most of the year, try a potato vine (*Solanum jasminoides*). It has masses of white flowers and will grow in any sunny position.

One of the brightest climbing plants is the black-eyed Susan (*Thunbergia alata*) which has cheery bright orange flowers with black centres, hence the common name. It fairly jingles with colour in autumn. Plant this in a warm, sheltered spot if you live in a frost-prone area. Otherwise it simply needs a bed prepared with compost and complete fertiliser to grow well.

Privacy seems to be a 'must' in many people's minds. That is why so many houses have high fences or brick walls surrounding them. High barriers may help keep street noise down and unwelcome visitors out, and they make your garden space a little more peaceful, but a bare wall is very boring to look at. It's a great idea to clothe it with a living green and even better with a plant that flowers as well as climbs. Sometimes a fence may be so low that peeping eyes can watch your activities in the garden. One solution is to attach lengths of lattice securely to the top of the fence to give extra height, then cover the lattice as quickly as possible with a fast-growing climbing plant.

There are climbing plants to suit any situation. If you are intrepid you may like to grow the spectacular cup of gold or chalice vine (*Solandra maxima*). It is a rapidly growing evergreen vine on long arching stems that can grow to 8 m high up a tree. In summer and autumn it has huge, yellow, trumpet-shaped flowers up to 20 cm across, with a purply stripe down each petal. The flowers are shaped like a cup or chalice, hence the name, and have a very strong fragrance. Be sure it has room to grow and a strong support. This very attractive vine grows best in hot areas.

A WORD OF WARNING

As a climbing plant ivy is particularly aggressive. It can take over, eventually growing too strong for its support unless you constantly clip it back. I prefer to keep ivy contained in a pot where it cannot spread. Otherwise, be prepared to clip it back about three times a year.

Plants to clothe a wall

Walls and fences are often forgotten as places where wonderful plants can grow. There is no reason why ugly buildings and outhouses cannot be softened with a lovely climbing plant, or an unflattering view of your neighbour's house hidden by a trellis smothered with something special. Two of the most common and reliable climbers to cover a wall are:

• Creeping fig (*Ficus pumila*). Evergreen, grown for its foliage, needs to be kept clipped as its leaves can grow too big in older age, regular clipping keeps leaves neat and small.

• Boston ivy (*Parthenocissus tricuspidata*). Deciduous. It will cling to a wall, and can grow to cover a two-storey house completely. Its leaves turn beautiful shades of red and copper in autumn.

Unusual climbers

CLIMBING HYDRANGEA (*Hydrangea petiolaris*)

Hydrangeas are very familiar plants, especially the large-leaved ones with colourful round flowerheads, called the hortensias. There is a species of hydrangea, not commonly grown, called *H. petiolaris* which grows either as a roundish shrub or as a climbing plant. I have seen it growing exceptionally well on shady walls in many gardens in England, and it is certainly becoming more available from garden centres here.

After a slow start it will grow vigorously, flowering with creamy white lacecup flowers in summer. It self-clings to a wall or up a tree trunk with its aerial roots, and will easily cover a space 4 m wide by 10 m high. Grow it in dappled shade or in a little more sun. Like other hydrangeas it prefers a moist, well-composted soil.

FREMONTIA or FLANNEL BUSH
(*Fremontodendron californicum*)

This is a vibrant plant with large, bright yellow flowers, 8–10 cm across, which cover the plant profusely from summer to autumn. It needs full sun and a well-drained soil to grow into a spreading shrub. Given a start close to a wall, it will grow 5 or 6 m high, so the fremontia is really a wall plant rather than one that climbs. It may be difficult to obtain from general nurseries, but those dealing in rare or specialist plants may have it. Once again, visitors to English gardens will have brought word back about how spectacular these wall plants are, so I hope nurseries will jump to and grow more of them.

HOP (*Humulus lupulus*)

It is the lime green female flowers of this scrambling and climbing plant, which grow in drooping clusters, that are used to make beer. You may not want to get into beverage making, but the hop makes a terrific, vigorous plant to hide an ugly wall or to cover a pergola. It will grow up to 5 m in either full sun or partial shade in well-drained soil. It is a herbaceous plant that dies back in winter and then grows back quickly in spring.

The hops creeper (*Humulus lupulus*) is a fast-growing creeper and the female plant has hanging clusters of hops. It will cover a large area up to 5 square metres, and dies back in autumn to sprout again in spring.

NOT-TOO-VIGOROUS CLIMBING PLANTS

Blackeyed Susan *(Thunbergia alata).* Cheery bright orange flowers.

Love creeper *(Comesperma volubile).* With sprays of blue, pea-shaped flowers, this is a beautifully delicate native evergreen creeper, not often seen in gardens but highly recommended.

Madagascar stephanotis *(Stephanotis floribunda).* I think this has one of the loveliest perfumes of all flowers. It needs warmth, protection and well-drained soil to do well.

Mandevilla 'Alice du Pont'. Rose-pink cultivar of the white mandevilla, needs a warm, frost-free position

Manettia bicolor. Red, tubular flowers with yellow ends. This evergreen climber will need frost protection, but worth growing as it is unusual.

Purple apple-berry *(Billardiera longiflora).* A native evergreen with greenish-yellow tubular flowers followed by purple berries that hang on for ages.

JAPANESE WISTERIA *(Wisteria floribunda)*

Most gardeners would be familiar with the most popular wisteria, *W. sinensis,* the Chinese variety of this wonderful spring-flowering climber. Less common but far more spectacular is the Japanese wisteria *(W. floribunda).* It has a form called 'Macrobotrys' with drapes of purplish flowers that can hang down to 1 m, quite magnificent if grown where the flowers can be seen from below. There is a white form *(W. floribunda* 'Alba') with long racemes up to 60 cm long.

All wisterias are deciduous and need to grow in the sun to flower at their best. They do need to be controlled, as their growth can take over. I have seen one growing 20 m up in a tree, a spectacular sight, but against a house it could mean trouble. You can best keep it under control on a verandah if you train the tendrils around a sturdy wire frame rather than the framework of your house.

Climbing plants for dappled shade

CHINESE BELL FLOWER *(Lapageria rosea)*

This plant really needs to be grown in a cool area, with good, deep, loamy soils. Originating in Chile, it grows especially well in mountainous areas. It has long, deep pink and white, tubular flowers (up to 10 cm long) with a waxy appearance. It does not have a dense covering of leaves although it is evergreen, but it is the flowers that are worth waiting for. There are several hybrids that make up a lovely collection. Lapagerias do well with their roots in moist but well-drained soils, and look spectacular trained up a 2-m pillar.

CLEMATIS SPECIES AND HYBRIDS *(Clematis* spp.)

Clematis grows in a variety of situations, climbing over a pergola, up a trellis, against a wall or to cover a tree stump. The plants need to have their roots in cool, moist and well-drained soil, but their flowers need to be in the sun; in other words give them a cool root run, protected by mulch or even slate or other paving materials.

C. *aristata* is the native Australian clematis. Like most native plants and unlike most clematis, it is evergreen. It has creamy white flowers like stars and is sometimes called 'old man's beard' for the fluffy seeds that follow the flowers and hang attractively on the plant for a long time. It will cover a fence or grow up a pillar or old stump to 2 m.

Of the deciduous clematis there are the large-flowered 'Jackmanii' hybrids with spectacular flowers. These large-flowering clematis never fail to raise a comment, with flowers the size of small dinner plates in a variety of colours. They are a deciduous climbing plant and there are varieties which flower in spring, summer or autumn. They flower best if grown in an easterly facing spot; that is, not too much hot afternoon sun and with their root system in a cool place.

One of my favourites is *C. napaulensis*, which has unusual cup-shaped, creamy yellow flowers and will grow to 5 m high. *C. tangutica* has yellow, lantern-like flowers and when it finishes flowering it is covered by a mass of silky seed heads. It will cover a wall quite densely.

There is also the Chinese evergreen clematis, *C. armandii*, with creamy white flowers, a very strong-growing plant.

DUTCHMAN'S PIPE (*Aristolochia elegans*)

This unusual plant has peculiar flowers that give rise to its common name — they are like a trumpet with a flared opening, spotted purplish and red. The flowers hang amongst masses of evergreen, heart-shaped leaves. It needs a warm, protected spot, out of danger of frosts, and will cover a large area, so needs trellis or wire for support.

HONEYSUCKLE (*Lonicera* spp.)

There are many varieties of this fragrant-flowered, evergreen creeper. All will grow in most spots as they are quite tough; in fact *L. japonica* grows so vigorously that it can run wild and become a problem in the garden.

The giant honeysuckle (*L. hildebrandiana*) is a spectacular climbing plant which reaches great heights in its native Burma and

This plant is named the old man's beard (*Clematis aristata*) for the fluffy white seeds that follow the starry flowers. It is a wanderer, and will scramble through other plants for support. It will happily grow up a pillar or trellis.

With the smell of a cottage garden, honeysuckle (*Lonicera japonica*) is a fragrant plant with woody stems, which scrambles its way up and over whatever it happens to lean on. It is good for hiding an ugly wall, an outdoor shed or the old backyard dunny!

south-west China. In summer it has huge, creamy flowers, 10–15 cm long, which age to deeper gold then red. It is a very strong-growing, evergreen climber or wall-covering plant with large leaves — a beauty if you can track it down. It needs a warm, frost-free position.

NATIVE SARSAPARILLA
(Hardenbergia violacea)

The purple pea flowers of hardenbergia always put on a good show in late winter and spring. It is a strong, evergreen climber, needing support to grow to approximately 3 m high. There are pink and white forms, too, and all look best in a garden where they can romp casually over tree stumps, rocks and other plants as well as a fence.

Western Australian bluebell creeper (*Sollya heterophylla*) does well in filtered sun and has attractive, evergreen foliage and dainty, bell-shaped, blue flowers. Watch this plant as it can be a pest in areas where it can invade indigenous vegetation.

Climbers for a sunny position

BOUGAINVILLEA (*Bougainvillea spp.*)

Bougainvillea is a summer and autumn flowerer. It is really a tropical plant, so in southern climates make sure it is in a really warm position. Although it is evergreen, it may lose its leaves in the cooler southern areas. It comes in many shades of reds, pinks and purples. Bougainvilleas will grow in well-drained, moist soil, but will not do well in heavy soils. They also make good container plants provided the container is large enough.

CHILEAN JASMINE (*Mandevilla laxa*)

This lovely climber has pure white, fragrant, trumpet flowers which contrast well with the green leaves in summer. It is quite a strong climber, twisting its way up post or pergola, and will cover a fence or archway quickly. It does best, in southern climates, where it may lose some leaves in the cold season, in a sheltered spot.

COMMON JASMINE (*Jasminum officinale*)

This popular evergreen climber flowers in spring with starry white, highly perfumed flowers. It needs to be kept under control as it can get away from you, so cut it back hard after flowering.

CUP AND SAUCER PLANT (*Cobaea scandens*)

The flowers of this unusual evergreen climbing plant look like mauve and green cups and saucers, hence the common name. It needs a frost-free position or a warm, sheltered fence where it will take off in a vigorous manner. The young flowers are light green, gradually changing to light then deep purple — they make a very attractive addition to a posy.

KENNEDIA SPP.

Some of the kennedias are very strong growers and will cover a fence in a season or two. *K. coccinea* has a twining or scrambling

BOUGAINVILLEAS WORTH TRYING

Bougainvillea × buttiana 'Mrs Butt'. Crimson red

B. glabra 'Magnifica Traillii'. Deep purple bracts

B. 'Klong Fire'. A popular double red cultivar

B. 'Pagoda Pink'. Double pink

B. 'Raspberry Ice'. Red bracts, variegated cream margins on leaves

B. 'Thai Gold'. Double burnt orange fading to carmine pink

habit and is best when it is allowed to grow where it wants rather than 'forced' on a fence. It has spectacular red flowers in spring. Most kennedias have red flowers but there is also a black-flowered variety called *K. nigricans*

SNAKE VINE (*Hibbertia scandens*)

This has quite large bright yellow flowers which appear for most of the year. It is not a particularly vigorous grower, but will climb up a pole or clothe a fence, spreading to a metre or so wide.

Climbers with a bonus

GRAPEVINE (*Vitis vinifera*)

A grapevine is very fast growing and covers a spot quickly once it is established, so make sure you provide enough support for it. Grapevines make excellent cover for a pergola in summer while, being deciduous, they let in winter sun. If you select a good bearing cultivar, you can pick your own grapes for the table or for wine making and, even though the flowers are rather inconspicuous, few people realise they have a beautiful fragrance.

Jasmine (*Jasminum officinale*) is one of the plants that novice gardeners first learn about, and it should not be disregarded as it grows easily as a climbing plant and its fragrance is a knockout in spring. The small flower shoots can be cut to use indoors in a vase.

Preferring some shade, the twining plant *Pandorea pandorana* is an attractive plant to grow on a wall or fence. It is a hardy plant, preferring a well-mulched soil, and it will quickly cover an area of approximately 2 m. It has masses of creamy yellow flowers in spring and summer.

VIGOROUS CLIMBING PLANTS

Bower of Beauty (*Pandorea jasminoides*). Pink trumpet flowers

Climbing roses: 'Wedding Day', *'Albertine',* R.laevigata and many more

Dusky coral pea (*Kennedia rubicunda*). Coral red flowers in spring and summer

Jasmine (*Jasminum officinale, J. polyanthum*). Highly fragrant, white flowers

Wisteria. Chinese wisteria (*Wisteria sinensis*) and Japanese wisteria (*W. floribunda*) are always breathtaking for their pendulous racemes of flowers, purple, pink or white. A very long-lived plant.

Wonga vine (*Pandorea pandorana*). Clusters of creamy flowers, masses of them set against glossy green leaves

KIWIFRUIT (*Actinidia chinensis*)

A kiwifruit is a good screen plant to hide the sun and it gives wonderful amounts of fruit. It is a very vigorous climber, best trained over a pergola at least 3 m x 2 m in area. Each year the stems can shoot out several metres in length, so this deciduous plant will give good shade in summer while letting in winter sun. The bonus is the edible fruit that forms in bunches and ripens on the vine from autumn. Formerly known as Chinese gooseberries, since that's where they originated, they are now more commonly called kiwifruit as a result of a clever marketing coup by New Zealand growers and exporters. Australian growers are just catching up. They will grow very successfully in our home gardens, so why not have a go?

The most critical thing about kiwifruit is to make sure you buy both a male and a female plant to begin with. Kiwifruit are not self-pollinating, hence you will need one male and preferably two females to train on either side — then you will have oodles of fruit.

Being such a vigorous grower, your kiwifruit will need a strong support to grow on. Space the vines about 3–4 m apart in an open, sunny spot so the fruit will ripen. Kiwifruit will grow in most soils, but prefer good drainage. When you plant your vines, train the main trunks up onto a trellis and then, as the fruiting arms develop, branch them out over an area of about 3 square metres.

Every year in spring fertilise the vines with well-rotted animal manure or pelletised manure. Over summer make sure they get plenty of water — without it, the fruit will be small and bullet hard.

Mulching around the surface of the roots will help retain moisture in the soil. Use old straw, well-rotted lawn clippings or compost about 5 cm thick, and spread some blood and bone over the soil before mulching. Keep the mulch away from the base of the trunk to avoid collar rot.

Pruning a kiwifruit is important. Cut back any really long arms once in summer to keep it under control, and in winter, no later than July, cut the arms back to three or four buds from a main branch. This will be the point from which flowering and fruiting takes place.

There are several varieties of kiwifruit available. The commonly available one is 'Hayward', small in fruit size (about 8 cm long) but a good keeper, which is why you see this variety in shops. Another delicious one is 'Bruno', a longer fruit (up to 10 cm long) with browner hairs on the skin.

Once the brown skin is peeled off, kiwifruit are very decorative — the flesh is translucent lime green with tiny black seeds delicately arranged. All the pulp is edible as well as ornamental, so they are perfect for decorating pavlovas and cheese cakes.

PASSIONFRUIT (*Passiflora edulis*)

This remarkable evergreen vine will cover a fence or wire partition in a very short time. With the bonus of mouth-watering passionfruit from late summer onwards, it makes a great climbing plant. Given a well-drained sunny spot, with plenty of old animal manure worked into the soil, it will repay you endlessly.

Passionfruit are a favoured fruit, great for using in desserts, juice drinks or topping for icecream. Myself, I like to eat the pulp scooped straight from the shell.

Although they are originally sub-tropical plants they grow very well in a sunny spot in cooler climates, so much so that they must be one of the most popular fruiting vines around Australian gardens. Perhaps the passionfruit's quick rate of growth will enthuse you, too — it will cover an area of 3–4 square metres in double quick time. In fact if the vine really takes off you may have to prune it back to keep it under control.

To plant, fork in three buckets of animal manure over an area of 3 square metres — the roots will spread out and, as passionfruits are very heavy feeders, make sure you fertilise them well.

Prune from October on, after the frosts have finished. It is not essential, but if you cut any long twiny bits back to the main branch, it will help new flowers and fruits to form. In early spring, feed the vine with half a bucket of animal manure or several handfuls of pelletised fowl manure. A passionfruit vine needs plenty of water over summer to keep the fruit juicy. If the vine is slow in setting fruit, don't worry. This is usually due to the weather and temperature conditions upsetting them, so be patient. The passionfruit vine is usually a great 'doer', giving plenty of delicious fruit in no time at all.

You may find that after some years the fruit goes hard and

CLIMBING ROSES FOR WALLS OR FENCES

R. 'Blossomtime'. Repeat flowering, dark pink

R. 'Cécile Brunner'. Pink buds, perfect for posies

R. 'Céline Forestier'. Fantastic scent, full blooms, cream

R. 'Clair Matin'. Recurrent single pink in clusters (one of the best)

R. 'Crépuscule'. Beautiful orange-buff colour, plenty of flowers

R. 'Jeanne la joie'. Small, covered in perfect little pink buds

R. 'Lorraine Lee' (climbing). Winter flowering, coral pink, soft scent

R. 'Mme Alfred Carrière'. Delicate soft pink to white

R. 'Penelope'. Cream-pink clusters, recurrent, a sight to behold in spring

R. 'Sombreuil'. For the shape of its pure white flowers and scent

If you have a large space to fill, either a wall or an old tree, plant this beautiful rose, *Rosa laevigata*. It flowers earlier than most other roses, so it heralds the beginning of the rose season.

The symbolism of the passionfruit flower

Native to South America, the passionfruit was noticed by early Jesuit missionaries for the flower's symbolism of the crucifixion. They saw the flower colours of white and mauve as symbols of purity and heaven. The fruit stamens symbolised the five wounds; the three stigma the three nails; the pistil's style the whipping column; the tendrils the flogging cords; the five sepals and five petals the ten disciples (Peter and Judas being omitted); the 'fingered' leaves the hands of the persecutors; and the corona the crown of thorns.

CLIMBING ROSES TO RAMBLE UP A TREE

R. brunonii. Beautiful cream clusters, followed by soft apricot hips

R. 'Duchesse de Brabant' (climbing) Nodding pink flowers that can be seen from below

R. 'Lady Hillingdon'. Soft yellow–orange, flowers over a long period

R. laevigata. Single white, needs a strong tree or other support

R. longicuspis. Single white flowers, small, deep red hips which will last inside as a cut decoration for 12 months, great value

R. 'Paul Transon'. Small apricot flowers, repeat flowering

R. 'Stanwell Perpetual'. Lots of small, double, blush pink flowers

R. 'Wedding Day'. Single white, very vigorous climber, needs a large support

woody with no pulp in the middle. This is a viral disease, and eventually the leaves will go a mottled yellow. Unfortunately there is no cure. All you can do is to remove the affected plant and plant a new one, taking solace in the fact that they are very fast growing.

TURQUOISE BERRY
(*Ampelopsis brevipedunculata* var. *maximowiczii*)

Despite its mouthful of a botanical name, this is a beautiful climbing plant, not commonly grown but very worthwhile. Its common name, turquoise berry or porcelain grape, refers to the fruit that forms in clusters and turns the most beautiful colours, ranging from cream to china blue, mauve and turquoise. Though not edible it is a relative of the grapevine, with similar leaves and twining habit. It is also deciduous and a quick grower, covering an area of 3–4 square metres.

Perfumed climbers

Carolina jasmine (*Gelsemium sempervirens*). Yellow flowers with a fragrance nowhere near as strong as the common jasmine, yet delicate

Chinese star jasmine (*Trachelospermum jasminoides*). Not nearly as rampant as the common jasmine but much prettier, with starry white flowers and a delicate fragrance

Grapevine (*Vitis vinifera*). Perfumed flowers

Honeysuckle (*Lonicera* spp.). Curious, spidery flowers with heady fragrance

Japanese wisteria (*Wisteria floribunda*). An all-round fragrance as it hovers in the air, beautiful pendulous flowers in mauve, the most usual colour, but pink and white forms available

Jasmine (*Jasminum* spp.). Most have strong fragrances, especially *J. officinale*, a real spring fragrance, and *J. polyanthus*, with a more subtle touch.

Mandevilla (*Mandevilla laxa*). White flowers and lovely fragrance

Stephanotis (*Stephanotis floribunda*) White flowers with a delightful fragrance

Wax flower (*Hoya carnosa*). Waxy, white to pink flowers in clusters with a heavy scent

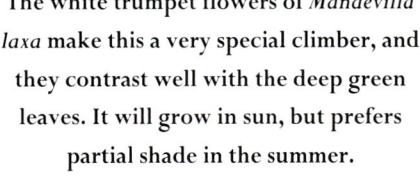

The white trumpet flowers of *Mandevilla laxa* make this a very special climber, and they contrast well with the deep green leaves. It will grow in sun, but prefers partial shade in the summer.

OTHER WAYS OF PRESENTING CLIMBERS

TO GROW UP A TREE

Chalice vine (*Solandra maxima*)

Climbing rose; for example *Rosa* 'Wedding Day' and *R. laevigata*

Potato creeper (*Solanum jasminoides*)

Wisteria spp.

TO TRAIL FROM A HANGING BASKET

Kangaroo vine (*Cissus antarctica*)

Trailing fuchsia (*Fuchsia procumbens*)

Wax plant (*Hoya carnosa*)

TO GROW OVER A RETAINING WALL OR EMBANKMENT

Black-eyed Susan (*Thunbergia alata*)

Kennedia (*Kennedia* spp.)

Native sarsaparilla (*Hardenbergia violacea*)

Western Australian bluebell creeper (*Sollya heterophylla*)

TO GROW IN CONTAINERS WITH SUPPORT

Climbers can be grown in containers, given a support of pre-formed wire cones, timber forms or wooden obelisks. The climbing plant can be kept clipped in a very formal manner as a substitute topiary.

Carolina jasmine (*Gelsemium sempervirens*)

Chinese star jasmine (*Trachelospermum jasminoides*)

Clematis montana 'Rubens'

Snail creeper (*Phaseolus caracalla*)

Sweet pea (*Lathyrus* spp.)

Groundcovers

*I*t may seem odd to group carpeting plants with climbers — I'm keen, as you will have gathered, to cover the ground as well as the walls and overhead with as many plants as possible. If carpeting plants are close planted and grow densely, they can be a very low-maintenance approach to gardening, and how much more visually interesting than a vast expanse of high-upkeep, water-wasting lawn, a heat-retaining slab of paving or, worse, boring concrete. Groundcovering will soften the edges of your garden beds, provide visual links between the bulkier plantings, fill any gaps and cover retaining walls and embankments.

Any plant that covers the soil, especially if it has dense foliage, will help reduce weed growth, as weeds are much more likely to establish themselves on bare ground where there is no competition. Most plants in the garden will look more attractive and better settled into their spot with a groundcover at their base.

Many groundcover plants need good drainage; for example the many species which originated in the sandy soils of Western Australia. You can provide good drainage in heavy soils by mounding, or by providing a rockery for these plants to grow in. You can also put them in pots or hanging baskets where you can make sure of adequate drainage with readily available potting mixes to the Australian standard.

PLANTING

At the time of planting your groundcovers, mix a small amount of slow-release fertiliser granules into the soil before backfilling the hole. With native plants, especially banksias, grevilleas and hakeas, which are phosphorus sensitive, it is preferable to use a fertiliser with low or no phosphorus. In areas with heavy soil that is likely to get water-logged, you can improve the soil with gypsum and organic matter, or mound it up in the planting spot.

PRUNING

The nature of groundcovering plants means that they will often grow out of their bounds, but there is no problem about pruning them back. When the plants are young, it is a good idea to nip out the tips, just cutting off a few centimetres, because this will make the plant much bushier in the long term. Generally it is best to prune when the plants have finished flowering, which is usually by late spring to summer. In frosty districts, don't be tempted to tidy up any frost-burnt plants until you are quite sure the danger of frosts is over.

The so-called groundcover roses, for example, the 'Flower Carpet' pink and white roses, will quickly spread and fill a gap, especially if mass planted at 1-m intervals. They grow between 60 and 90 cm high. Feed them with complete fertiliser and they will retain glossy green leaves and have heavy flushes of flowers. Sometimes a rogue stem will want to grow straight up; cut this off. These plants can take rough handling and pruning whenever necessary. For more on groundcover roses, see page 49.

Few groundcovers will take too much walking on — if you need to get amongst them, put down a few stepping stones or slabs of timber so you can step between the plants.

You will save time and labour if you get rid of all existing weeds before you plant your groundcover. Hand digging or cultivating is the only method if you do not like to spray with weedicides, and unfortunately weeds always seem to grow more quickly than other plants, so you must keep at it. Groundcover plants may not be able to compete with quick and actively growing weeds, so try to get rid of them first. A weeding knife is handy so you dig out the weed's roots before they grow too big and smother plants. If your garden bed is infested with weeds you may find it easier to spray with a weedicide with a chemical base of glyphosate which will take a week or so to kill the weeds if they are actively growing. The chemical is absorbed by the plant's stems and leaves and taken down to its roots. Take care when spraying as spray may drift onto wanted plants.

Once you have planted out your groundcovers, mulch around the plants so that the mulch and plants work together to suppress new weed growth. Organic mulches will decompose over time, but the ground plants should have covered the area to blanket the weeds by then. You can keep replenishing the mulch if necessary.

SOME FAVOURITE GROUNDCOVERS

Most of these groundcovering plants are tough and reliable. They will benefit from a good watering at time of planting and a

Gazania **hybrids may be commonly grown but they are always cheery and ramble around the garden as a ground cover. Originally from South Africa, they are fast growing and tolerant of wind, salt and sun. They have bright daisy-like flowers over a long time in spring and summer.**

teaspoonful of slow-release fertiliser in springtime. They will grow quite quickly, but do remember to keep weeds at bay until they are established.

Bugle (*Ajuga* spp.)

This is a low-growing, spreading mat with foliage in bronze or variegated cream and mauve. All ajugas have spikes of mauve blue flowers in spring which grow up to 40 cm high from the mat. They will grow in full sun or semi-shade, and will take a dry spot, but will do best in moist spots. Take off the runners that grow from the central plant and plant them in other parts of the soil as they will take root. *Ajuga* 'Jungle Beauty' is a particularly good one with taller flower spikes.

Coastal or seaside daisy (*Erigeron karvinskianus*)

So-called because it often grows well on coastal sites (and most other places it is planted) this groundcover has masses of tiny, pink-to-white, daisy-like flowers that flower for a very long time in full sun or part shade. When the plant begins to look tatty cut it right back so it can regenerate.

Creeping Jenny or loosestrife (*Lysimachia* spp.)

This is a good groundcover for dampish spots in semi-shade. It is grown for its light green-yellow foliage rather than its flowers. It spreads by layering itself over the ground.

Creeping lasiandra (*Heeria* or *Heterocentron elegans*)

This is really a low-growing, carpeting plant with small leaves and masses of bright mauve flowers in summer. It grows well over an embankment or a spot where the flowers can be seen, and if you haven't a spot for it in the garden, try planting it in a hanging basket where the flowers can trail down.

Gazania (*Gazania* spp.)

These are really reliable plants for spreading over the soil in the sunniest of spots. They take salty sprays by the coast; will stand up to drought; and will spread over rock, slopes or wasteland. One plant can completely cover an area of several square metres. The flowers are large and daisy-like and come in a range of colours from yellow and orange to russet, contrasting well with the attractive grey or green foliage. Gazanias look their best in spring. They are easy to grow from cuttings, about 10 cm long, taken from the parent plant.

Lawn chamomile (Chamaemelum nobile)

This is grown simply for its foliage which is a lovely lime green and very finely divided. It has a delicious fragrance and I like it most when it grows between stepping stones or bricks in a path, so that when you step on it the fragrance rises up to you. It is a very attractive groundcover, but not foolproof in combating weeds, so you will have to be very diligent.

AUSTRALIAN GROUNDCOVERS

Brachyscome spp.

A lovely native plant that flowers for ages in pink and mauve colours, on a rounded clump of growth. The mauve *B. multifida* and pink *B. angustifolia* are quick growing and always have plenty of flowers. There are white and yellow forms as well, and many new introductions to this genus as a result of constant breeding work to improve colour, vigour and size of flower.

Grevillea spp.

Several of these native plants grow low to the ground and make excellent groundcovers. *Grevillea × gaudichaudii* spreads out to half a metre and has excellent red flowers. *G. curviloba* (sometimes wrongly called *biternata*) spreads out to more than 2 m. It has finely divided light green leaves and grows quite thick. The white, spidery flowers have a strong honey scent. Trim off spent flowers and the occasional shoot that grows up vertically rather than horizontally.

Hibbertia (Hibbertia spp.)

Many hibbertias are spreading or low growing, with golden yellow or orange flowers. They require good drainage and a sunny spot. The snake vine or climbing guinea flower (*Hibbertia scandens*), with large yellow flowers, will climb up with support or scramble on the ground. *H. obtusifolia* is a handy plant, a bit more of a loose shrub, perhaps, than a groundcover, growing to a height of about 50 cm, with distinctive yellow flowers.

Kennedia spp.

These are always eye-catching plants, and many grow as climbers over some kind of support or trail if left unsupported. They need full sun. *Kennedia microphylla* spreads to 1 m, covering

GROUNDCOVERING GREVILLEAS

G. 'Bronze Rambler'. Vigorous with lovely bronze new growth and red flowers

G. juniperina. There are several forms of this low-growing plant. It gives quite a thick covering once established and growing well. Flowers range from red to yellow, depending on the form.

G. laurifolia. Deep red toothbrush flowers on a dense plant with large lobed leaves

G. 'Poorinda Royal Mantle'. Forms a dense mat of green leaves with bronze-red new growth. Flowers are red toothbrush types.

G. thelemanniana. Sends out long trailing stems, greyish leaves with red flowers

This native fuchsia *(Correa reflexa* var. *reflexa)* is in fact a small shrub that is very variable in growth habit. Some forms can grow to 1.5 m while others only reach 50 cm and spread out as groundhugging plants. All correas will attract birds to the garden with their nectar-filled, bell-like flowers. They can take partial shade and need well-drained soil.

the ground with a tight mass of clover-like leaves and red pea flowers. *K. nigricans* grows very quickly and has unusual yellow and black flowers. The running postman (*K. prostrata*) is a good prostrate grower, covering about 2 m, with green leaves and scarlet, pea-shaped flowers. *K. rubicunda* is a quick-growing plant that will climb or drape itself over the ground. The flowers are bright red.

Lippia (*Phyla nodiflora*)

A tough, spreading groundcover, especially good for hot, sunny spots. It has pink balls of flowers which attract bees.

Mazus pumilio

This is a mat-forming plant which grows close to the ground, preferring part shade and a moist position. It spreads by creeping roots, and has unusual mauve flowers.

Myoporum parvifolium

This very hardy plant has dense, tough leaves, stems that grow to 1 m or more, and starry white flowers. It will root quite readily as it spreads, hugging the ground tightly. It prefers full sun.

Native fuchsia (*Correa* spp.)

These very attractive shrubs with their lovely bell flowers are suitable for sun or part shade. Many spread out to a metre across and don't grow too high, so they can certainly be grown as groundcovers. *C. decumbens*, with red tubular flowers, grows to about 30 cm high and spreads to 1.5 m wide. *C. reflexa* var. *nummulariifolia* has light creamy green, tubular flowers and grows to 20 cm high by 1 m wide. *C.* 'Dusky Bells' is an ever-reliable one with dusky pink flowers.

Native violet (*Viola hederacea*)

The native violet is an excellent groundcover which forms a dense mat with lime green, heart-shaped leaves. It has small white and mauve violet-shaped flowers at most times of the year. It will spread very quickly and may become invasive, but you can chop it back as hard as you want. It likes part shade to full sun, but do keep it moist.

Pratia pedunculata

This is a lovely carpeting plant with small tight leaves and tiny, starry blue flowers (there is also a white-flowering variety). It likes

The Australian groundcover, *Pratia pedunculata*, performs really well in a partly shaded, moist part of the garden. It has starry blue or white flowers. Pratia creeps along, hugging the ground and sending its roots down wherever they touch the soil. It is a gentle groundcover, not particularly invasive and very pretty.

a shady spot and to be kept moist. Each plant spreads to about 50 cm wide.

Scleranthus biflorus

This unusual plant looks just like a soft green cushion and spreads over the ground or between rocks. The leaves are very tightly packed and the flowers are rather insignificant, but it is a delightfully 'pattable' plant which always causes comment. It likes full sun or part shade and will spread to 1 m.

TUFTY PLANTS

To break up the all-flat appearance of an area of ground-covers, it can be an advantage to have some clump-growing plants. These are tufty or grassy plants that will not get too high, but will help give a different natural look to the garden bed.

Dietes spp. Tall clumps of dark green, narrow leaves with beautiful mauve-white flowers, looking rather like an iris. Dietes are quick growing and flower for ages over summer. Great as a foliage contrast, and hardy in sunny spots.

Kangaroo Grass (*Themeda triandra*). This native grass grows in clumps to 1 m high, attractive and lax in habit.

Lomandra spp. Healthy-looking tussocks to 1 m high with narrow strap leaves and blue flower spikes. They are hardy plants and will grow in most soils. *L. longifolia* is one of the most reliable.

GROUNDCOVERS FOR LIGHT SHADE

Baby's tears (*Soleirolia soleirolii*). Minute, bright light green leaves

Bergenia spp. Large heart-shaped leaves, clusters of pink flowers on long stems

Boston fern (*Nephrolepis exaltata 'Bostoniensis'*). Lovely, light green, ferny foliage, spreads by runners

Clivia miniata. Clump forming, apricot-orange flowers

Ligularia spp. Dark green oval leaves

Pennyroyal (*Mentha pulegium*). Small, fragrant leaves, purplish flowers

Rainbow plant (*Coleus blumei*). Colourful foliage

Spider or ribbon plant (*Chlorophytum comosum 'Vittatum'*). Long, narrow leaves with cream stripes

Wild strawberry (*Fragaria* spp.). White flowers, deep green foliage, bonuses of small, red edible fruit

GROUNDCOVERS FOR SUNNY SPOTS

African daisy (*Dimorphotheca* spp.).
White, mauve or pink, daisy-like
flowers

Golden marguerite or chamomile
(*Anthemis tinctoria*). Yellow
daisy-like flowers

Bellflower (*Campanula poscharskyana*).
Blue flowers

Convolvulus mauritanicus. Blue flowers

Cotoneaster horizontalis. Tiny, white
rose-like flowers, red berries

Crane's Bill (*Geranium pratense*).
Mauve or pink flowers

Ivy-leaf geranium (*Pelargonium
peltatum*). Variety of colours

Nasturtium (*Tropaeolum* spp.).
Round edible leaves, brightly
coloured flowers

Phlox subulata. Pinks, whites
or mauves

Prostrate rosemary (*Rosmarinus
officinalis*). Blue flowers

Snow-in-summer (*Cerastium
tomentosum*). White flowers

Sweet violet (*Viola odorata*).
Fragrant mauve flowers

Thyme (*Thymus* spp.) Mauve flowers,
fragrant, edible leaves

Verbena (*Verbena × hybrida*)
Spreads with a mass of flowers,
variety of colours

Yarrow (*Achillea tomentosa*).
Lacy foliage and yellow flowers

**Tufty Australian plants, including
Kangaroo paw (*Anigozanthos* spp.) and
grasses (*Poa* spp.) make an excellent
change in form and texture.**

Orthrosanthus multiflorus. A beautiful, clump-forming, native plant that has starry blue flowers, needs full sun and good drainage

Patersonia spp. Native irises, growing in clumps, with strap-like leaves and tall-flowering stems in violet–mauve. They prefer a sunny, well-drained spot.

Poa spp. The common tussock grasses. *Poa labillardieri* is a fairly commonly grown grass with lovely flowerheads. There are lower growing, clump-forming poas, some with beautiful blue-grey leaves to give contrast in the garden bed.

Stipa spp. The spear grasses grow in lovely clumps, with attractive flowerheads

Wallaby grass (*Danthonia* spp.). Clump-forming grasses growing to 1 m high by half a metre wide.

Screening plants

Most of us who live in suburban areas want some kind of division between our neighbours' gardens and our own. It is fairly uncommon for houses to share their back gardens, though in inner suburbs it is a great idea. Screening plants will define a boundary, giving a sense of enclosure to your own space. Plants can also screen off a noisy road, as well as forming a buffer against pollution. Planting the boundaries is one of the first tasks to do in a brand new garden. Selecting the right plant, appropriate for the job, is half the battle, especially getting the size right. For windbreaks and screens, always check on the plant's eventual width, not just its height.

Apart from using screening plants to hide ugly spots or utility areas such as compost or a clothesline, you can also break up the regularity of a garden or create different 'garden rooms'. A long, narrow garden, for example, can be divided by screening plants into several spaces, different in character from each other, which give a feeling of space and variety.

Screening plants such as these kangaroo paws (*Anigozanthos* spp.) can define a boundary or help to create different 'garden rooms', as well as hiding ugly spots or utility areas.

SCREENING PLANTS

Common name	Botanical name	Height width (metres)	Flowering time	Flower colour	Needs pruning	Special comments
Bottlebrush	*Callistemon* spp.	3 x 2	spring	mostly red, pink, mauve	prune after flowering	Many spectacular varieties e.g. 'C. viminalis' 'Hannah Ray', C. citrinus 'Lilacinus', C. citrinus 'Splendens'
Butterfly bush	*Buddleia davidii*	3 x 2	spring/ summer	lilac	prune hard after flowering	Quick growing, fragrant flowers
Cape plumbago	*Plumbago capensis*	2–3 x 2	summer	sky blue and white variety	prune regularly to shape	Quick growing, shrub or semi-climbing plant
Coastal rosemary	*Westringia fruticosa*	2 x 1.5	long flowering especially in summer	white	clip to shape if needed	Always reliable, especially in sandy soil
Evergreen dogwood	*Cornus capitata*	3 x 2	spring	lemon–yellow bracts	only for shaping	Best in cool soils
Glossy abelia	*Abelia × grandiflora*	1 x 1.5	summer– autumn	purplish–white	prune once or twice a year	Dense foliage and autumn-coloured sepals that look good for a long time
Heath banksia	*Banksia ericifolia*	4.5 x 2	winter–spring	orange–yellow	prune lightly especially when young	Attracts birds, orange spikes
Japanese barberry	*Berberis thunbergii*	1.5–2 x 1.5	spring	yellow	prune lightly in late winter	Purple foliage, quick growth and lots of spikes
Lauristinus	*Viburnum tinus*	3 x 2	mainly spring but occasionally all year	white	prune occasionally for shape	Underrated plant, but always reliable
Lemon-scented tea tree	*Leptospermum petersonii*	5–7 x 2	spring	white	tip prune when young	Fragrant foliage, quick growing
Mock orange	*Philadelphus* 'virginale'	2–3 x 2	spring–early summer	pure white	prune after flowering	Deciduous, fragrant flowers, purity of green and white
Oleander	*Nerium oleander*	2–5 x 2	later spring– summer-autumn	red, pink, white, salmon	prune after flowering	Poisonous if large quantities are consumed, but very hardy
Pittosporum	*Pittosporum* 'James Stirling'	3 x 1.5		insignificant	light prune in Spring	Quick growing ornamental foliage is chief attribute
Port-wine magnolia	*Michelia figo*	3 x 1.5	spring–early summer	creamy yellow– white, mauve	prune lightly after flowering	Fragrant flowers, fairly slow growing
Protea	*Protea* spp.	3 x 1.5	spring–summer	pinkish	prune by picking off long flower stems	Needs well drained spot, various colours
Purple mint bush	*Prostanthera ovalifolia*	2 x 1	spring	mauve	prune lightly after flowering	Other mint bushes are equally quick growing as screen plants.
Purple paperbark	*Melaleuca nesophila*	3–4 x 2	spring– mid-summer	mauve	prune lightly	Fast growing, hardy. Many other melaleucas are good screening plants.
Purple smoke bush	*Cotinus coggygria*	3 x 2	summer	greyish– smoky	occasional pruning after flowering	Lovely autumn foliage, rich red, deciduous
Silver cassia	*Cassia artemisiodes*	2 x 1.5	winter–spring	yellow	light pruning after flowering	Should be grown more often, flowers through winter
Wiralda wattle	*Acacia retinodes*	3–6 x 3	most of year	pale yellow	tip prune when young	Quick growing, balls of flowers

Pots, tubs and hanging baskets

In recent years there has been a renaissance in growing plants in pots — everyone has room for a small clutch of containers that can be displayed in season and moved around. Bulbs are a perfect example as they can be brought inside or moved to a prominent spot outside when they are in flower, then put aside while you are waiting for the foliage to die down.

Very often pots, especially large containers, can be used to hide something unattractive, and a large ornamental pot or elegant urn can turn a dull area into something beautiful or provide a focus in a garden scene.

Everyone wants a decorative garden, and for people like me with a tiny courtyard or balcony, or those with no garden beds at all, pots and containers are the easy answer. There is a huge variety of plants to grow in them and all containers are very versatile, as they can be moved around. Whatever you choose to plant in them, whether it be one plant or a collection of different plants grouped for colour, container planting gives atmosphere and versatility to your garden, courtyard or balcony.

Be imaginative about containers for your plants. This rustic wheelbarrow with drainage holes in the base has been filled with potting mix and suits plants such as double impatiens (*Impatiens* spp.), white verbena (*V.* × *hybrida*) and variegated ivy (*Hedera canariensis* 'Variegata'). If you don't want to plant out you can always sink pots into the wheelbarrow so that they are hidden and you can easily interchange various pots in their flowering season.

How to grow happy pot plants

FEEDING

The key to success is using good quality potting mix. Don't use garden soil, as the best growing medium is a well-drained, well-aerated potting mix with fertiliser added. Feeding is another important consideration — use a liquid fertiliser every 3 weeks or a small amount of slow-release fertiliser at planting time. Remember that, in a pot, the plant's roots are restricted in looking for nutrients, so you must feed for best results.

WATERING

In hot, windy weather pots can dry out very quickly, especially small pots, putting plants under stress. Water regularly, testing whether the potting mix is dry by putting your finger 3–4 cm down into it. It is a good idea to use a rewetting agent so that the water penetrates the potting mix. This can work wonders in keeping the plants looking much better — in fact their life is extended.

PLANTING

When you plant up any container never fill the potting mix right up to the rim — you should leave a gap at the top when you have pressed the soil down so that when you water it doesn't splash out.

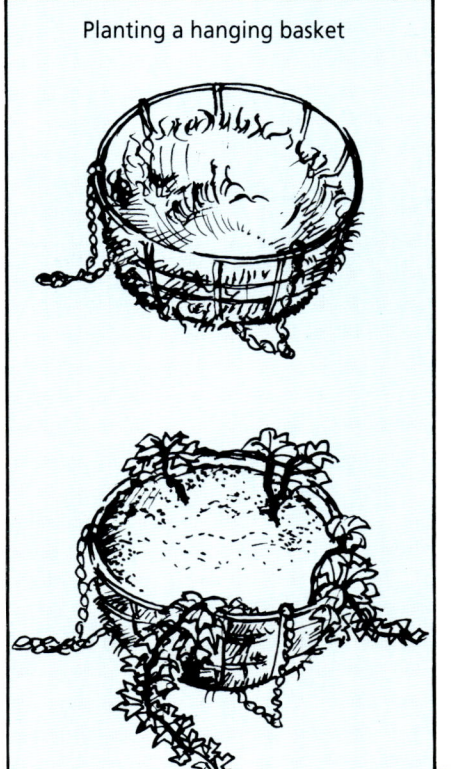

Planting a hanging basket

Line two-thirds of the basket with sphagnum moss, coconut fibre or basket liners. Fill with potting mix and a small amount of water-saving granules. Position trailing plants around the edge of the lining. eg Lobelia, pansy, begonia, English daisy, white chrysanthemum daisy Fill with potting mix to just below the edge of the basket.

Feed regularly with a liquid fertiliser. Do not let basket dry out. Dead head regularly.

Annual plants for containers

Anemone (*Anemone* spp.). Red, pink, blue and white
Begonia spp. Red, pink and white
Busy Lizzie (*Impatiens* spp.). Mixed pastels or vibrant colours
Chrysanthemum spp. Wide range of colours
Cineraria spp. Red, blue, mauve, pink and carmine
Cosmos spp. Pink, white
Easter daisy, Michaelmas daisy (*Aster* spp.). Mixed colours
English daisy (*Bellis perennis*). White, rose, red or pink
Everlasting daisy (*Helipterum* spp.). White, rose or pink
Lobelia spp. Blue, mauve or white
Monkey flower (*Mimulus* spp.). Yellow, cream, red or orange
Nasturtium (*Tropaeolum* spp.). Yellow, orange or red
Nemesia spp. Blue, orange, red or yellow
Pansy *(Viola* spp.). Mixed colours, pastels and bright
Petunia spp. Mixed colours, pastels and bright
Pinks (*Dianthus* spp.). White, pastels, red or rose
Polyanthus (*Primula* spp.). Mixed bright colours
Poor man's orchid (*Schizanthus* spp.). Mixed vibrant colours
Primrose (*Primula* spp.). Mixed pastel colours
Snapdragon (*Antirrhinum* spp.). Mixed colours
Statice (*Limonium* spp.). Blue, white and yellow
Summer forget-me-not (*Anchusa capensis*). Blue
Sweet Alice (*Alyssum maritima*). Pink, purple and white
Verbena spp. Mixed pastel and bright colours

A scrambly, lively creeper is the nasturtium (*Tropaeolum majus*), with its vibrant orange or yellow flowers. It is easy to grow from seed, and it will cover an area of 3 × 3 m quickly. Nasturtiums will grow in the sun or a partly shaded spot and require only occasional watering.

GROUPING CONTAINERS OF LOW-GROWING NATIVE PLANTS

1 *Thomasia pygmaea*. A beautiful little plant with unusual pinkish purple flowers, a rather delicate-looking plant, but with good drainage will perform well

2 *Eriostemon verrucosus*. A lovely small variety of the wax plant with graceful arching branches and masses of white flowers from pink buds

3 *Acacia cultriformis* or *A. baileyana* (prostrate form). Grafted wattles which hang down the pot, with yellow ball flowers

4 *Callistemon* 'Little John'. A neat, compact bush with emerald leaves and deep red bottlebrush flowers

5 *Hypocalymma angustifolium*. One of my very favourite Australian plants, with its soft appearance and masses of white-pink flowers up and down the stems

6 *Crowea* spp. Starry pink flowers and lime green leaves, very decorative plants

7 *Lechenaultia biloba*. Flowers of an unbelievable sky blue; as this plant needs really sharp drainage it is best grown in a container.

One of my very favourite Australian plants is the *Hypocalymma angustifolium*. In spring its weeping branches are covered with clusters of tiny white and pink flowers. In a large pot (with good potting mix for drainage), you will be guaranteed success with this lovely evergreen shrub. To keep it compact and bushy to 1 m high, prune it back hard after flowering, taking off one-third of the top growth.

A selection of geraniums for a window box

Select one or more colours, considering house colours, of trailing geraniums in whites, mauves, pinks and reds. Fragrant-leaved varieties can be included to complement the flowers as well as add interest if the window box can be reached from either inside or outside.

What to choose for containers

TREES AND OTHER LARGE PLANTS

Large plants or even trees can be grown in pots as long as they are at least 40 cm in diameter. Because their roots are confined the plants won't grow too large. Every couple of years they should be repotted into fresh potting mix with some slow-release fertiliser added for healthy growth.

People often want to know what can be grown for privacy between neighbouring houses. The suggestions below will give some height and are dense enough to provide a certain amount of screening.

TREES FOR POTS

Bottlebrush *(Callistemon* spp.*)*
Gungurru *(Eucalyptus caesia)*
  (a popular eucalypt with silver-white branches and fluffy pink flowers which needs the good drainage that can be provided in a large tub)
Heath banksia *(Banksia ericifolia)*
Japanese Maple *(Acer palmatum)*
Native rosemary *(Westringia fruticosa)*
Oleander *(Nerium oleander)*
Olive tree *(Olea europaea)*
Pittosporum 'James Stirling'
Teatree *(Leptospermum* spp.*)*

Lower growing shrubs for pots

Abelia spp. These are very reliable shrubs. One variety has glossy bronze foliage, another has golden leaves and pink-white tubular flowers which keep flowering for ages.

Bay (*Laurus nobilis*). A bay tree is a useful plant as the leaves are good for cooking or for repelling moths in cupboards, and it is a heroically hardy plant in a pot.

Cumquat (*Fortunella* spp.). Cumquats in pots are both useful and ornamental with their glossy dark green leaves and round orange fruits.

Daphne spp. and *Gardenia* spp. are good grown in pots as they can be moved around as they flower so you can enjoy the wonderful perfume.

Fuchsia spp. All fuchsias do well in pots and hanging baskets in a shady spot.

Hibiscus spp. will grow well in a pot if placed in a hot, sunny spot where they will flower best.

Hydrangea spp. For shady areas hydrangeas will always do well in pots.

Veronica (*Hebe* spp.). This group of plants is ever-reliable to grow in pots in a sunny spot.

Growing bulbs in pots

*B*ulbs are perfect in pots to decorate a sunny patio or to move around to brighten up a dull spot. You can also bring them indoors for a few days when they are in full flower so your friends can admire your gardening prowess.

When you are planting bulbs in containers put them close together, nearly touching, and use a good bulb-growing mix in the pot. Remember that any pot for bulbs should be at least 20 cm deep. Plant the bulbs at a depth of about twice their height, in the top half of the pot. Keep them in the shade for the first couple of weeks, then move them out into the sun once they have sent up a shoot. This is also the time to feed them with liquid fertiliser.

Bulbs in pots should be taken out of their containers each year after flowering and put into the garden so they flower better the next year.

BULBS TO CHOOSE FOR CONTAINER GROWING

Any of the following bulbs can be grown in garden beds, but they will give an equally pretty picture in a pot.

Anemone (*Anemone* spp.)

The red, pink, white, purple and blue flowers are all on long stems, some 30–40 cm long. 'St Brigid' types are the double-flowered forms. These bulbs do not have to be lifted every year.

In one of the best displays of anemones I have seen they were mixed with the *Primula malacoides* 'Gilham's White'. The combination worked beautifully and meant that when the bulbs had finished flowering the primulas kept on giving pleasure. The wonderful rich, bright colours of anemones also make them hard to beat for picking as a cut flower. They prefer to be massed in a sunny position. Water with liquid fertiliser as they are heavy feeders. It is probably best to treat them like annual plants and start off with new bulbs every year.

Baboon flower (*Babiana* spp.)

This very hardy South African bulb should be grown much more. The flowers look similar to freesias but are purple-blue. They last in the same position for years, like full sun and are tolerant of very dry conditions.

Bluebell (*Scilla* spp.)

There are now pink and white bluebells available, as well as the traditional blue. They are also known evocatively as the 'English wood hyacinth', with bell-shaped flowers on upright flower spikes. They will grow in dappled shade, and should be massed together in large clumps.

Cyclamen (*Cyclamen* spp.)

The familiar flowering plants for indoors are florist's cyclamen, grown especially for their large grey-green, often mottled

---

I like to grow these cyclamens (*Cyclamen hederifolium*) in a pot at my semi-shaded front entrance. They flower with an abundance of pink and white blooms in winter and really brighten up this spot. On occasions I bring them indoors but they prefer the cool outdoors where they keep flowering until October. Then they go into their dormant period because of the warmer conditions.

leaves and colourful flowers over the cooler months in southern Australia. The plants flower for months if they are shuffled from indoors to outdoors regularly, so they represent very good value as container plants for indoors. Group three or four together in a large container for a spectacular effect.

Dutch iris (*Iris latifolia*)

Irises are one of the most elegant, striking bulbs with long stems and vibrant blue or yellow flowers. They are best planted in clumps amongst other perennials or shrubs and lifted every year, especially if the summers are wet.

Grape hyacinth (*Muscari* spp.)

Another blue flower, the grape hyacinth, has smaller stems than the bluebell, but is an equally beautiful, rich blue. I prefer to grow grape hyacinths on the front border of the garden bed, mixed in with fragrant, creamy freesias — a pretty picture, and one that will continue to spread and multiply over the years.

Hyacinth (*Hyacinthus* spp.)

Hyacinths flower easily and have the added bonus of fragrance. They need sun and well-drained soil and are best in cool districts, or grown in containers so you can move them indoors to appreciate their flowers and perfume.

Ixia (*Ixia* spp.)

Ixias are also known as 'corn lilies'. They grow in clumps with slender stems and starry flowers, in colours of beautiful duck-egg blue or salmon. With good drainage and plenty of sun they will multiply quite readily.

Triteleia (*Triteleia* spp.)

This is known as the 'spring star flower' as it has masses of small, blue-mauve, star-shaped flowers which keep coming for ages amongst the grass-like foliage. Triteleias are the longest flowering of the spring bulbs.

SMALL-FLOWERING DAFFODILS — PERFECT FOR POTS

All miniature daffodils are perfect for growing in pots. Their dainty flowers can sometimes be lost in a garden bed, but in containers they can be put in an airy, sunny spot indoors while flowering, to be enjoyed at close range. Here is a short list of some you might like to consider growing in containers:

Hoop petticoat daffodils (*Narcissus bulbocodium*). The bright yellow flowers in spring resemble the old-fashioned hoop petticoats of Victorian times. The stems grow to about 15 cm, while each flower is about 4 cm long.

Miniature-flowered daffodil *Narcissus cantabricus*. A creamy white flower similar to the hoop petticoat daffodil. Flowers in winter.

Miniature-flowered daffodil *Narcissus cyclamineus*. A daffodil growing to about 20 cm high with a narrow, tube-like cup and a perianth that is swept back like a rabbit's or dog's ears in a great wind. They are charming, with lovely cultivars like 'Tête à Tête', a rich golden colour.

Narcissus 'Hawera'. A miniature triandrus hybrid, quite vigorous, with multiple flowers on each stem. They are lemon yellow with tiny cups.

Narcissus 'Jumblie' is another cultivar, dainty in shape, with bright golden petals and deeper coloured cups. It is very free flowering, with two or three flowers to each stem.

Poet's narcissus (*Narcissus poeticus*). These have a white perianth surrounding a small, orange-rimmed cup. They are usually the last of the daffodils to flower in the season.

Cascading plants for hanging baskets

Cascading plants such as trailing lobelia, ivy geranium, blue-flowering convolvulus, impatiens (for colour) and tuberous begonias are all good in hanging baskets. Keep them at eye level so you can see see them at their best, and to remind you to water them.

Alpine strawberry (*Fragaria alpina*)
Blue-flowering convolvulus (*Convolvulus mauritanicus*)
Busy Lizzie (*Impatiens* spp.). Add for colour
Fishbone fern (*Nephrolepis* spp.)
Grey-leaved gazania (*Gazania pinnata*). A mixed delight
Ivy geranium (*Pelargonium peltatum*)
Petunia spp.
Strawberry (*Fragaria* spp.)
Trailing fuchsias (selected *Fuchsia* spp.; for example *F.* 'Angel's Flight' and *F.* 'Sophisticated Lady')
Trailing lantana (*Lantana montevidensis*). The new colours of pink, white and yellow look good
Trailing lobelia (*Lobelia erinus* 'Cambridge Blue'; *L. erinus* 'Colour Cascade')
Tuberous begonias (*Begonia* × *tuberhybrida*)
Verbena (*Verbena* × *hybrida* 'Peaches and Cream')

Early in spring, the charm of miniature daffodils gives me great pleasure. The tiny cyclamineus daffodils, such as *Narcissus* 'Jumblie' have swept-back petals, and tiny golden cups (one or two per stem) about 4 cm long. They do best in pots or a rock garden, where you know where they are, and they help so much to brighten your garden before other spring flowers come out.

SOFT TREE FERN (DICKSONIA ANTARCTICA)

Walk into any fern gully in the bush and you will find a secretive, mysterious place, full of fascination. There is usually water rushing over rocks, lush green ferns spilling over the ground and, of course, tree ferns. They are one of the most common ferns found in eastern Australia and are plants with real character. With a group of tree ferns, a cluster of lower growing ground ferns and even a trickle of water in a pond nearby, you can go on a bushwalk in your own backyard.

In a shady part of the garden, a single tree fern, or a group of them, growing at different heights makes a very peaceful, satisfying sight. It's even better if you can replicate what often happens in the bush, when soft filmy ferns grow up the sides of the fibrous trunk, making an even greener, cooler effect.

You will need to keep them moist, especially in dry, windy times, by handwatering the trunks assiduously, or by an installed sprinkler system. Don't be afraid to cut back their old brown fronds, which look untidy with age.

You could hardly beat this bank of deciduous mollis azaleas (*Rhododendron japonicum* × *R. molle*) growing in a morning-sun position. They dazzle with flower colour and their fragrance wafts in the air. Mollis azaleas need a well-drained spot in partial shade, and they prefer plenty of compost or leaf mulch mixed in the planting hole.

Flowers, foliage and ferns for shady spots

Shady spots in the garden are often looked on as awkward spots which can daunt the gardener: how to add colour and interest? Often the reason for a shady area is a huge tree in the neighbours' garden that takes all the light from your own garden. Or maybe a tree that you planted in your own garden has grown much larger than you ever imagined. Well, the good news is that there are solutions to the problem of shade. There are many plants that not only tolerate deep shade, but grow well if given the right conditions, and they are perhaps some of the most beautiful plants, certainly some of my favourites.

The most obvious reasons why plants will not grow under a tree are that the tree takes so much of the moisture and food and its roots make it difficult for other plants to obtain a footing. Trying to grow plants under shade can be a bit of a battle, I admit. They will need a regular regime of mulching, watering and feeding. In such a situation, it is worthwhile trying to dig over the soil under the tree canopy, too, to open it up. If you turn the soil over, even only a few centimetres deep, and dig in some enriched mulch or well-rotted compost, plants will be better able to get their roots down. It will help to fertilise the roots of your plants, as well as the leaves, with a liquid fertiliser every few weeks over spring and summer. Mulch and compost will open up the soil and help to retain more moisture, so other low-growing (and shade-loving) plants will grow.

There is *no* advantage in building the soil up directly against the tree trunk, as this can allow rot to set in and damage the trunk. Keep the mounded soil well away from the base of the tree, even if this means setting a few bricks around its base or building a retaining wall.

Some special shade plants

Clivia (*Clivia miniata*), a perennial plant from South Africa, grows in clumps and flowers with large, bright orange, trumpet-shaped flowers. There are also new hybrids becoming available in cream and peach. Their great benefit is that they will flower in semi-shade, and the dark green, strap-like foliage always looks good, especially growing under trees. Check for snails, which like to hide under the foliage. Plants can be divided once flowering has finished, if the clump is large enough.

Peppermint-scented geranium (*Pelargonium tomentosum*) is one of my favourite 'touchy' plants. Its leaves are glorious, lime green in colour and soft and velvety in texture when you pat them — a beautiful foliage plant. In fact it is grown for its foliage alone, but it

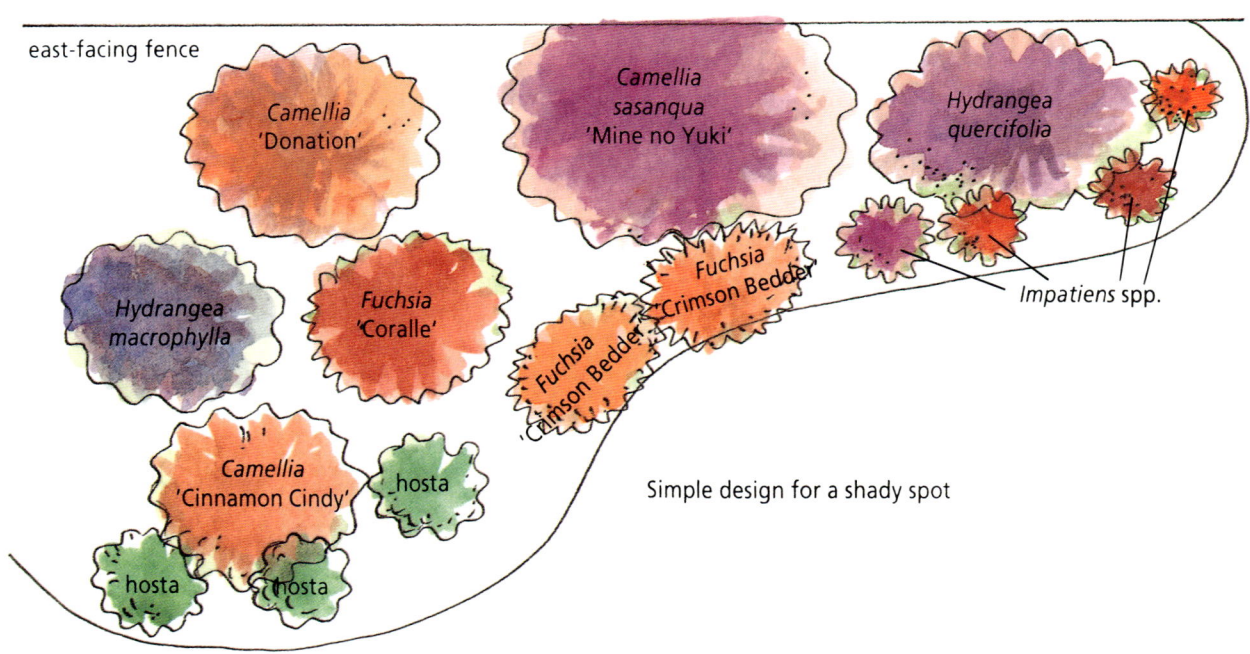

east-facing fence

Camellia 'Donation'

Camellia sasanqua 'Mine no Yuki'

Hydrangea quercifolia

Hydrangea macrophylla

Fuchsia 'Coralle'

Fuchsia 'Crimson Bedder'

Fuchsia 'Crimson Bedder'

Impatiens spp.

Camellia 'Cinnamon Cindy'

hosta

hosta

hosta

Simple design for a shady spot

If you have a spot under the shade of trees, a clump of clivias (*Clivia miniata*) will thrive. Not unlike agapanthus in appearance, with thick, strap-like leaves, they have rich orange-apricot flowers that last for ages. Protection is needed in frosty areas, and a leafy canopy overhead to shelter them from direct sun.

does have tiny, delicate, white flowers. It grows about 60 cm high and will spread quickly.

Plectranthus (*Plectranthus* spp.) used to be seen only in very old-world gardens where it was planted along the back fence line as a 'filler' plant. Nowadays there are various species and cultivars of plectranthus that are excellent to grow in shade or in a hanging basket. They can even be treated as a most useful indoor plant. The most common is *Plectranthus oertendahlii*, which has deep green leaves with purple undersides. The flowers are pale mauve spikes. It strikes easily by cutting and spreads 1 m wide by 60 cm high. Other plectranthus varieties include one with grey leaves and a more succulent light green one. All are very useful as quick-growing groundcovers for shady places.

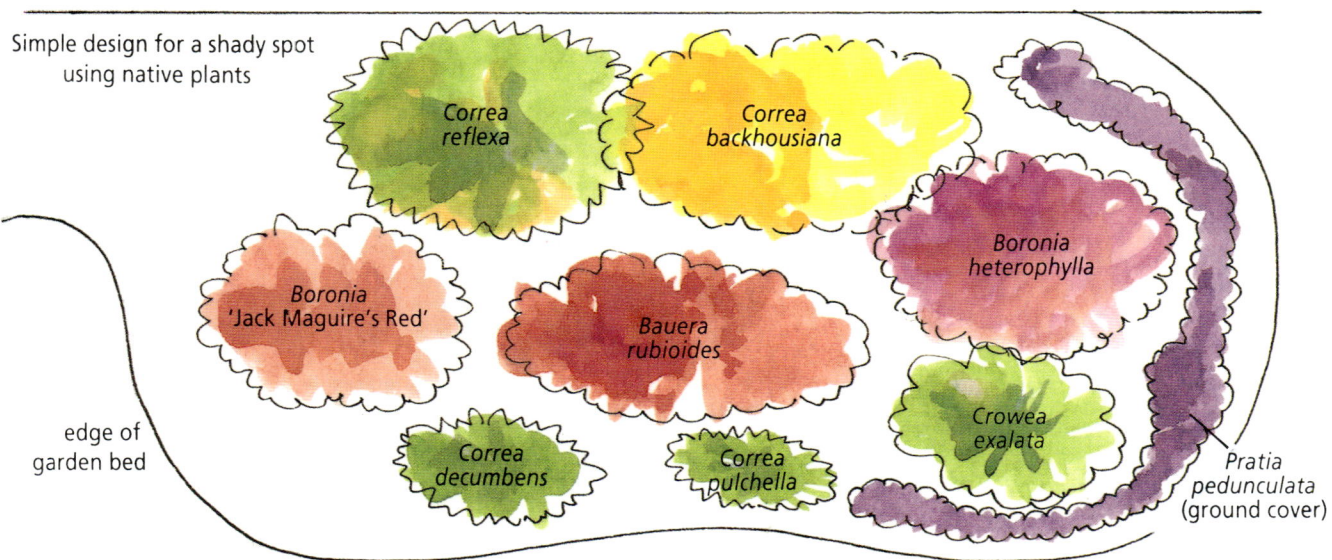

Simple design for a shady spot using native plants

Correa reflexa

Correa backhousiana

Boronia heterophylla

Boronia 'Jack Maguire's Red'

Bauera rubioides

Crowea exalata

edge of garden bed

Correa decumbens

Correa pulchella

Pratia pedunculata (ground cover)

Maples (*Acer* spp.) are deciduous trees grown for their brilliant coloured foliage, both in autumn and in spring. The best autumn colours are produced after a cold snap, but they always turn spectacular colours — oranges, reds, yellows or russets. This is the popular Japanese maple (*Acer palmatum*), but there are many varieties and it is worth searching out a favourite when they are in their autumn colour.

Acers — the beautiful maples

Members of the *Acer* family, which includes the Japanese maples and other maples from Norway, Canada and elsewhere, must be among the most beautiful trees in the world. The shape of their leaves and the delicacy of the leaf colour make them very popular trees in shady gardens, and they can also be grown in large containers in a dappled situation or on a porch or veranda. Their height, generally 3.5 – 6 m, makes them a good choice for a home garden. In a large pot they are small- to medium-growing trees, perfect for a site with filtered shade. If they are planted in a spot with too much summer sun or northerly wind to burn and dry the leaves, they will suffer.

While the autumn foliage is much admired, maples also provide a wonderful spring show with the delicate tracery of the new leaves and beautiful soft spring tones. The Japanese maples (*A. palmatum*) are particularly magnificent in autumn, turning shades of orange, red, yellow and russet. These are the most common varieties of this species. The *A. p. dissectum* cultivars have dissected leaves with very fine serrated edges. There are other maples with unusual leaves, such as the variegated *A. palmatum* 'Butterfly', which has a fine creamy white variegation in its leaves, giving a very delicate effect. Not all maples have finely dissected leaves — the maples from Norway (such as *A. platanoides* 'Crimson King') and the Canadian maples have larger leaves and are generally less likely to burn if stressed by hot winds. They, too, put on a good show with their autumn colour.

Still other maples have colourful, distinctive trunks as well as beautiful leaves. *Acer* 'Senkaki' is known as the coral bark maple, as in cooler areas the young trunk and stems have a red tinge.

Care of maples is not unduly hard, as long as they are protected from drying winds and kept well-watered. The roots are shallow, so they need thorough mulching to protect them, especially over dry summers. They are relatively slow-growing, with no real need to be pruned except for shaping.

Camellias

No garden is quite complete without a camellia or two, and indeed the camellia is one of the most popular garden plants of all. Legend has it that it was brought to China by a disciple of Buddha. Sleep overcame him while he was meditating, so he cut off his eyelids in an attempt to remain awake. Where the eyelids touched the ground, roots formed and grew up as tea plants. Tea, of course, is a drink that people have to keep them awake and energetic. The tea plant is in the same family as the camellia — its name is *Camellia sinensis* (that is, from China) and both are in the Theaceae family.

Camellias grow for years, virtually unaided — you only need to look around old gardens to see the large shrubs, verging on small trees, which they become in time. *Camellia japonica* can reach 7 m high in thirty years, but it can be kept cut back to 3–4 m high.) Their flowers are lovely, but their foliage also makes a very good background in any garden. If you choose your camellia varieties carefully, you can have some in flower from late summer right through the colder months and into spring.

CAMELLIA JAPONICA

Most commonly grown are the *Camellia japonica* varieties. These have broad, glossy, deep green leaves and masses of large flowers over many months in winter. The colours are variations of red, white or pink, and some are striped or marbled. They like a position that gets morning sun only, as hot afternoon sun can be too strong and burn the leaves — a common problem. Although they are very hardy, camellias will do best if you manage them properly. Keep them moist, especially over summer when they are

Camellia × williamsii 'Donation' is one that is always reliable in flowering and has masses of pink flowers that stay on the bush for a long time.

forming the flower buds. If they are allowed to dry out the buds will drop off or go brown and fail to form. Mulch thickly over the root area with organic mulch such as milled pine bark, mushroom compost or well-rotted animal manure. You will notice the difference.

CAMELLIA LUTCHUENSIS

Perhaps one of the more interesting species of camellia is the scented *Camellia lutchuensis*. It has small white flowers on a delicate, loose-looking bush. It is wonderful as a container plant, especially elegant in matching boxes on either side of your front door, or it can be grown as a standard on a 1-m stem.

CAMELLIA RETICULATA

Another variety of camellias — those belonging to the reticulata group — have the largest flowers, between 15 and 22 cm wide, depending on the variety. They flower from winter to spring and are quite spectacular. They will grow in a sunny spot, but need protection from wind for their large blooms to survive. One of the most popular is *Camellia reticulata* 'Dr Clifford Parks', which has very large, bright scarlet flowers.

CAMELLIA SASANQUA

The sasanqua species, like all camellias, are evergreen medium shrubs or small trees. They have smaller, pointier leaves and more vigorous growth than the others, and they flower much earlier — any time from late February through to June. These sasanquas withstand sun and grow better in areas with hot summers than the other species.

Blooming in single to semi-double forms, with contrasting rich yellow stamens in the centre, sasanquas range in colour from white and pale pinks to rosy reds and brighter cerise. They flower profusely in full bloom, with masses of buds. Individual flowers can shatter quickly, especially after a wind, but I think the fallen petals carpeting the ground like snowflakes look very beautiful.

Sasanqua camellias are great in pots, ideal as a hedge (planted 1.5 m apart) or as screens against fences and as wind-breaks, because they are quick growing and withstand sun. They are ideal to train as an espalier against a wall as their loose, pendulous branches easily adapt to being fanned.

Favourite varieties of japonica camellias

Camellia japonica 'Betty Sheffield Supreme'. White to blush pink with a pink margin on each petal

C.j. 'Brushfields Yellow'. Pale yellow inner petals and creamy white outer petals

C.j. 'China Doll'. White to silvery pink flowers, a good pot plant

C.j. 'C.M. Wilson'. Silvery pink petals, another ideal tub plant

C.j. 'Cornish Snow'. A miniature flower with a silvery pink bud that opens to ivory white

C.j. 'Debutante'. Clear pink flowers on a vigorous bushy plant

C. x williamsii 'Waterlily'. Double pink flowers

Some favourite sasanquas

I prefer whites and pinks in camellia colours, and the following are amongst my favourites.

Camellia sasanqua 'Jennifer Susan'. A loose, informal grower with pale pink petals

C.s. 'Mine no Yuki'. Semi-double white

C.s. 'Plantation Pink'. Single pink with prominent stamens

C.s. 'Setsugekka' or 'Wavy White'. Large, single, creamy white

C.s. 'Sparkling Burgundy'. Dark lavender, flowers early

C.s. 'Yuletide'. Single red

Miniatures

Small is beautiful in the case of recent releases of camellia hybrids. They are sasanqua camellias and are grown for their miniature flowers. They are quite delightful, very delicate and petite, with masses of flowers, each only 4–5 cm across. 'Little Liane' is a beauty, pure white with a fleck of pink; 'Blush', white with a pink edge and good for making a hedge; 'Paradise Pearl', a double white flushed pink; and 'Paradise Hilda', a double pink that flowers over a long season. Other miniature-flowering varieties include 'Baby Bear', 'Cinnamon Cindy', 'Fragrant Pink', 'Snowdrop' and 'Wirlinga Princess'.

HOW TO GROW CAMELLIAS

Camellias have virtually no pests or diseases to watch out for. A caterpillar that gets into a leaf and rolls it over may affect the foliage, but you can easily spot these. Get rid of them by squeezing with a tissue between your fingers or spray with pyrethrum.

Camellias love organic matter, so keep adding compost and mulch to the soil. They will reward you plentifully with flowers, so when they finish flowering give them some fertiliser to build up their strength.

Camellias respond well to pruning, though it may not be necessary as they keep their shape very well — just picking their flowers may be enough. If you take off any spent flowers, the bud behind the flower will grow more fully. If you want to prune your camellia to make a thicker bush, for instance for a hedge, do this after flowering at the end of spring. Old bushes can be rejuvenated by cutting them back and giving them a good feed.

PROPAGATION

Camellias will propagate well from cuttings. Take semi-hardwood cuttings, with the stem tip green and the base hard and brown, at the end of the growing season from December to January. Shorten them to about 10 cm long and put into a propagating mix of coarse sand and peat moss or coconut fibre. Camellias can also be grown from a leaf bud cutting. Use a hormone rooting powder to help the cuttings root quickly.

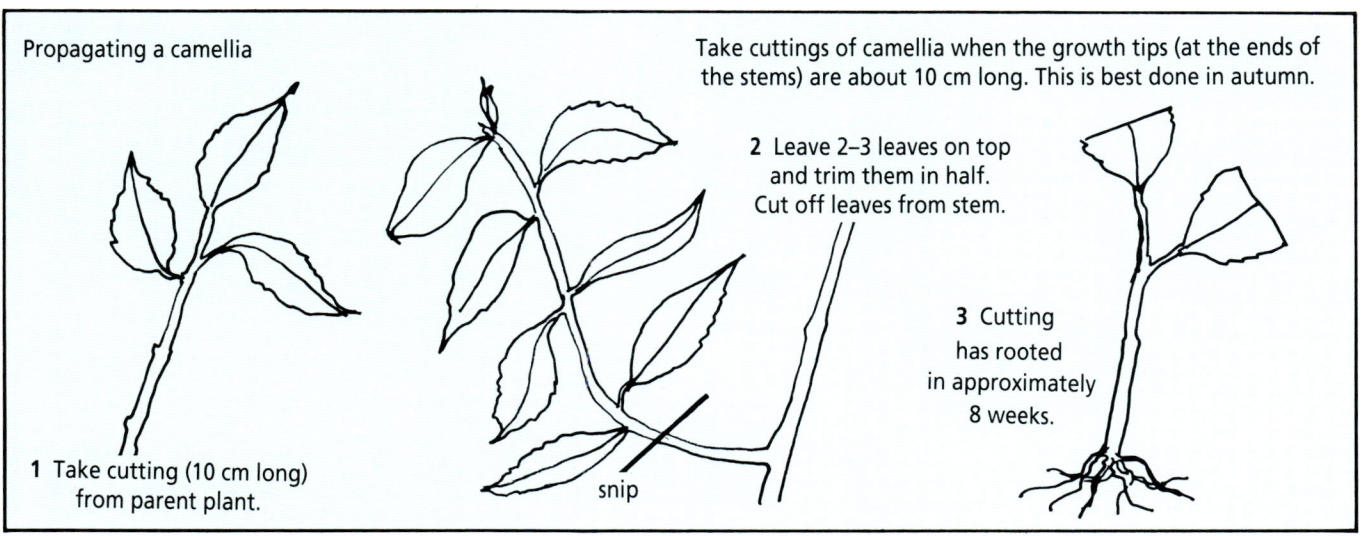

Propagating a camellia

Take cuttings of camellia when the growth tips (at the ends of the stems) are about 10 cm long. This is best done in autumn.

1 Take cutting (10 cm long) from parent plant.

snip

2 Leave 2–3 leaves on top and trim them in half. Cut off leaves from stem.

3 Cutting has rooted in approximately 8 weeks.

Some camellias for containers

C. Williamsii 'Donation'. Many
    flowers in pink
C.j. 'Drama Girl'. Deep salmon pink
C.j. 'Elegans'. Very large flowers,
    peach-coloured
C.j. 'Magnoliiflora'. Blush pink
    flowers

FLOATING FLOWERS

*Try floating one perfect camellia, or
a few different coloured ones, in a
shallow bowl with candles especially
designed to be used in water. They
are just as pleasing as an outdoor
decoration, floating in a bird bath or
garden pool.*

Camellias will grow in containers. A pot about 40 cm wide will usually be big enough. Using a good quality potting mix is very necessary. Pots can easily be neglected and the shallow roots of your pot plants will dry out quickly, so make sure they are kept moist.

Camellias and candles floating in a decorative bowl

Ferns

Not all plants must have flowers to be beautiful. Ferns are one of the loveliest plants and they never flower. They depend on lush green foliage in different shapes, textures and tones to give a wonderful effect in shady places in the garden.

To grow ferns properly you must provide them with some shade, especially in the afternoon. They will grow well in morning sun and in areas with filtered afternoon sun. In too much shade they will grow straggly; in too much sun their fronds will burn. In positions with filtered light, provided either by a canopy of trees or shade cloth overhead, they will grow strongly.

Of course, ferns can be grown in a glasshouse or bush house, but we are very fortunate in Australia as most will survive successfully in shaded parts of the open garden. Tree ferns, for instance, which we take so much for granted in our gardens and in

Maidenhair ferns (*Adiantum* spp.) are among the most delicate-looking of all ferns and they will grow into a spectacular display in a pot or basket. Keep them moist, in a well-drained mix, and cut off any brown fronds that appear at the base. Feed them with a half-strength liquid fertiliser over spring and summer and the plants will respond with many more lime-green fronds.

The mini fernlets on the ends of the fronds can be cut off and grown in propagating mix.

bulbil or
mini fernlet

Propagating
bulbils from
Asplenium bulbiferum

the bush, are prized specimens in the United States and England as they are so difficult to grow in those countries.

Most ferns will need some kind of protection from the hot sun from midday onwards, and from hot, drying winds all day. Choose a southerly or easterly aspect, or grow them under protection of bushy trees or shrubs. Shade cloth (the knitted variety is the best quality) gives 70 per cent shade protection and is an ideal way to protect ferns.

Ferns will be very content if your soil is well drained and not too heavy. Clay soils or mountain soil can be too heavy, compacting around the roots, so you should mix in some sandy loam and/or compost to help drainage. Use as much well-rotted compost as you have, plus some old, decayed, cow manure, and this is usually all the fertiliser they will need. They will benefit from a mulch of leaf mould.

FERNS IN BASKETS

Many ferns display well in baskets hanging from cross beams, especially when they produce a wealth of fronds or a mass of rhizomes like furry brown fingers. Use a good quality potting mix and keep the ferns moist. A misting spray is probably the most convenient way to provide humidity around the foliage.

FERNS ON BACKING BOARD MOUNTS

Elkhorn and staghorn ferns (*Platycerium* spp.) and bird's nest ferns (*Asplenium nidus*) can all be mounted on a piece of hard wood or tree fern square to hang on a shaded wall. They should be firmly wired on, as they eventually grow very large and heavy. In their native habitat bird's nest ferns grow in rock crevices or on tree forks where they get excellent drainage, so you must try to provide the same conditions. Put some leaf litter or sphagnum moss behind the leaves of these mounted ferns to help keep them moist. It is normal for bird's nest ferns to have rotting leaves in their crown, where they collect and provide some nutrients for the fern's growth. People often talk of putting banana skins behind their staghorn ferns, but I don't encourage this practice as the skins may attract European wasps and other pests. All that is really necessary are some rotting leaves or a handful of compost.

PLANTING AND REMOVING TREE FERNS

To plant a tree fern such as *Dicksonia antarctica*, dig a hole so that about a third of the trunk is in the ground. Backfill, pressing the soil around so that it is stable, and water in well. If your tree fern is brought from a nursery it will have a certificate from your state conservation department. If it has old fronds, cut them off right to the base in the centre of the trunk (don't leave little stubs that can cause any new fronds to twist).

I am often asked whether it is possible to move tree ferns. It is, though it is quite strenuous work as the fibrous roots grow thick and dense at the base. You can cut through the trunk and move it that way, but do realise that the bottom bit will not grow new fronds, only the top portion. You may have to cut off fronds and wait for new ones to grow from the centre, but this won't take long.

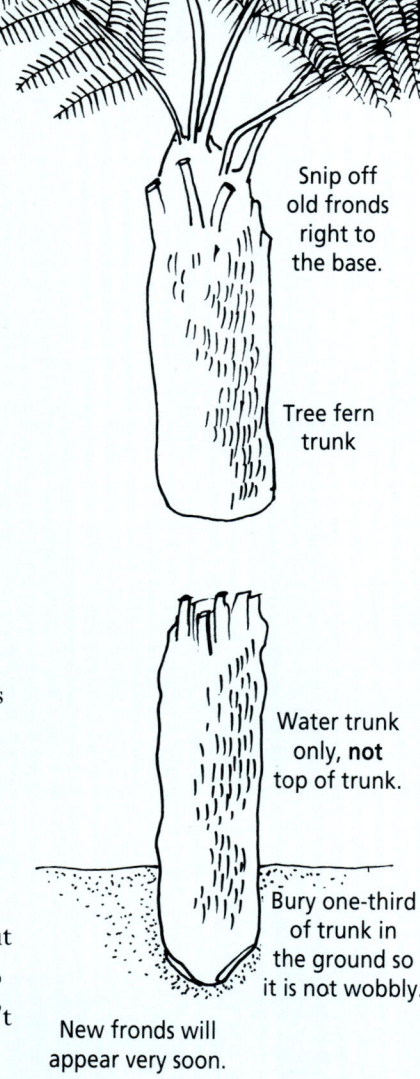

Planting a tree fern

Snip off old fronds right to the base.

Tree fern trunk

Water trunk only, **not** top of trunk.

Bury one-third of trunk in the ground so it is not wobbly.

New fronds will appear very soon.

Some favourite ferns

Asplenium 'Island Beauty'. A recently introduced hybrid with lush, waxy-looking leaves, very hardy. Another hybrid is *Asplenium* 'Maori Princess'.

Bird's nest fern (*Asplenium nidus*). A lovely fern that resembles a nest with its fronds radiating from the centre. It can grow very large, and is excellent in a pot or basket.

Brake fern (*Pteris spp.*). This ground fern has beautiful erect fronds and forms quite a large clump. The tender brake fern (*Pteris tremula*) is an easy, fast-growing one.

Blechnum spp. There are several varieties of this ground-covering fern available. They have erect fronds and are generally hardy and tough.

Drynaria spp. Although frost tender, this is a spectacular fern to show off in a basket where its thick, fleshy rhizome can be seen.

Elkhorn and staghorn (*Platycerium* spp.). These make excellent ferns for hanging baskets or for mounting on a backing board as a wall specimen.

Hare's foot fern (*Davallia* spp.). This fern is excellent for growing in hanging baskets where the rhizomes, which are very conspicuous with their brown, papery, hairy scales, can grow through the wire.

King fern (*Todea barbara*). This versatile fern has a large, fibrous trunk that grows slowly to 1 m high, with 2-m-long fronds. It is useful to fill up those gaps in the shady garden.

Maidenhair fern (*Adiantum* spp.). There are many species of these lovely ferns. They look delicate, often with leaves that are fan shaped, and most are quite hardy outdoors or in pots to be brought indoors in a brightly lit spot.

Mother spleenwort (*Asplenium bulbiferum*). This lovely fern, also known as the hen and chicken fern, is excellent in pots or baskets with hanging fronds, often with tiny plantlets at their ends which can be propagated.

Rainbow fern (*Culcita dubia*). This fern has masses of soft pale green fronds and is very hardy. It spreads by a creeping rhizome to cover an area of up to 1 m.

Rough tree fern (*Cyathea australis*). A very hardy fern with a trunk that can grow many metres high (10–12 m). It has lovely long green fronds that can spread to 4 m and, if kept moist, will take a little more sunlight than other tree ferns.

Soft tree fern (*Dicksonia antarctica*). A commonly grown tree fern with a lovely soft fibrous root trunk that can slowly grow to 15 m. The fronds are a beautiful soft green as they unroll from the centre.

Fuchsias

I remember as a little girl thinking fuchsias looked just like dancing ballerinas. They are suitable to grow in many parts of the country if given the right conditions. There are so many different ways to display these plants — as garden shrubs, in hanging baskets and in pots.

Fuchsias need light but not direct sunlight, as well as protection from the hot afternoon sun that may burn them. Fresh air is vital, which is why they don't do well as indoor plants. They are best grown in dappled sun under trees. Some large trees, however, will compete for nutrients and water so in-ground fuchsias might miss out. In that kind of spot it is probably best to transplant them into containers.

A perfect site for fuchsias is a garden bed on the east side of the house where they receive morning sun and afternoon shade. There they can be mixed with other plants that like similar conditions, such as hydrangeas, begonias and azaleas. They will also grow well in a shade house where direct sun cannot scorch the leaves.

Fuchsias appreciate soils that are well drained; they dislike having their roots sitting in water. You will need to add humus in the form of compost to clay soils to open up the soil. In sandy soil compost will help retain more moisture so they do not dry out. Never sit a fuchsia in a container in a saucer filled with water; they cannot stand wet feet. Nevertheless, fuchsias need plenty of water and their roots should not be allowed to dry out or the leaves and flowers will drop off. For this reason mulching and a heavy penetration of water around the roots is vital. Fuchsias growing in baskets or pots may need watering once a day, if not more, depending on the weather.

Make sure water actually drains out of the holes in the container — it is again a matter of good drainage. If a fuchsia dries out, the best remedy is to dunk it entirely in a bucket of water, leaving it to soak for an hour or at least until the bubbles stop rising.

Fuchsias are heavy feeders and it is important to feed them regularly. Every four to six weeks give them fertiliser that is a balance of nitrogen, phosphorus and potassium; there is a

The dainty, ballerina-like flowers of a typical fuchsia (*Fuchsia* 'Rose of Castile'). There is a huge range of colours to select from. They flower over summer and into autumn and there are shrub and hanging basket varieties.

TRAINING FUCHSIAS AS STANDARDS

Fuchsias trained as a standard look terrific. You can buy standard fuchsias, of course, but it's tremendously rewarding to do it yourself, even though it takes some effort and patience. First, choose or grow a cutting or small plant with a straight stem, staking and tying the stem to keep it straight. Remove any side shoots from the main stem, but leave any leaves, as they will keep the stem stronger as it grows. Let your burgeoning standard grow to at least 30 cm, or up to 90 cm high if you want. Now pinch out the tips of the main stem, so it bushes out and develops side shoots, and eventually a 'head' will have developed on the top of the stem. This may take 2–3 years, and then you will have a beautiful flowering plant.

commercial fertiliser high in potash which is especially formulated for flower colour.

If you find that the leaves of your fuchsias are looking yellow, especially the young leaves and tips, it is usually caused by lack of iron and can be remedied by chelates of iron. Always water a plant before fertilising and after pruning, and do not feed again until new shoots show.

HOW TO GROW AND MAINTAIN FUCHSIAS

- Soil: light, friable soil which is well drained. For pots and containers use a good quality potting mix; they will not tolerate their roots constantly sitting in water.
- Feeding: for fuchsias in containers, when repotting in spring add a small handful of slow-release fertiliser and some blood and bone to each pot.
- Watering: they hate to dry out over summer and if let do so they will drop their leaves very quickly. Keep moist, watering daily on hot days.

PRUNING AND PINCHING BACK

Most fuchsias need training and pruning to save them from becoming leggy and unruly — luckily they are easy to prune. To encourage a good bushy plant, keep pinching out the top growths so that side shoots are produced. Pinching is simply nipping out the top pair of leaves, the fleshy growing tip, with thumb and forefinger. This forces extra side shoots to develop. After many years, some fuchsias will grow large, leggy and very woody if left neglected. If you want to bring them back to a more compact, free-flowering plant, get out the secateurs and cut them back hard, even just above ground level. Feed, then wait for the new growth. This is best done in late winter or when any frost danger has passed. An extra hard prune every year is important as fuchsias only flower on new wood. Even if a plant still has a few flowers on it, it will look much better if pruned.

Some of my favourite fuchsias

Fuchsia 'Angel's Dream'. Pink and white, a lax grower, good basket and standard, always a good performer

F. 'Coralle'. Mine never seems to finish flowering with masses of tangerine tubular flowers, a real highlight in a dull place

F. 'Crimson Bedder'. Noted for its crimson red leaves and low growth — good for a basket or the edge of a garden bed

F. 'Lisa'. Soft, smoky blue with big double flowers, either as a basket or upright

F. 'Lord Byron'. Doesn't suffer from pests, scarlet and purple colour

F. magellanica. Tiny red and purple flowers, an old-fashioned species from which most modern cultivars are bred

F. 'Sophisticated Lady'. A good trailing fuchsia for baskets or window boxes

F. 'Swingtime'. Easy to grow, free of disease, sharp red and white colours

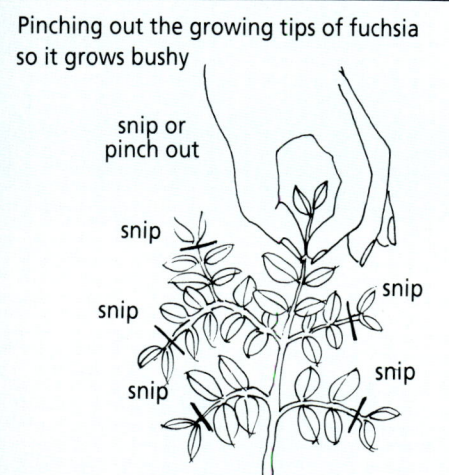

Pinching out the growing tips of fuchsia so it grows bushy

snip or pinch out

snip

snip

snip

snip

snip

PROPAGATION

Fuchsias can be raised by seed, but remember that if seeds are collected from hybrids the result may not be true to type. For exact replicas of the parent plant, the best way to propagate is by cuttings. The best propagating medium is a mix that is porous and open, such as washed river sand, vermiculite, perlite and peat moss or coconut fibre.
Take softwood cuttings from the soft green tips of the stems. Cut just below one or two pairs of leaves and place the cuttings into the propagating mix in a pot. Cover the pot with a plastic bag that will give extra humidity and heat.
While the cuttings are striking roots, keep the pot in the shade with plenty of light and moisture. You can take cuttings from spring through to early autumn and they will strike within three to six weeks, ready to be transferred to individual pots.

Hellebores

Amongst the most beautiful of all winter-flowering plants are the hellebores (*Helleborus* spp.) or Lenten roses. They have unusual flowers ranging in colour from greenish white to deep pink with spots of maroon or plum colours, and they flower in mid-winter right through to spring. They are also wonderful foliage plants, with evergreeen leaves forming clumps to about 30 cm high. If individual leaves become tattered, it's an easy matter for the fastidious gardener to cut them off.

Hellebores are very hardy and wonderful to grow in the shade of trees or in a massed group. They make a great under-planting for camellias, rhododendrons and large trees such as claret ash or liquidambar, where they will be protected by the tree's leafy canopy in summer.

Of the many varieties of hellebores, the *H. orientalis* hybrids are the easiest to grow, given cool, moist spots in dappled shade. They keep their leaves all year and will grow bountifully if given heaps of compost around their roots and any sort of organic matter to keep them cool and moist. I usually give them plenty of well-rotted animal manure which makes their leaves green and lush.

Another popular helleborus is *H. corsicus*, which forms mounds of grey-green leaves with masses of pale, lime-green, cup-

Lenten roses (*Helleborus* spp.) are perennial plants that form clumps of evergreen leaves in a semi-shaded position. They are valued for being long-flowering and very useful as cut flowers. *H. orientalis* is most commonly seen with mauve flowers or in a greenish white form, but there are other varieties worth searching for. They will develop seeds after flowering has finished (over winter and into spring), which can then be sown to increase their numbers.

shaped flowers. They will grow in moderate shade or in sunnier spots if kept well mulched.

With a similar colour — that special lime green — *Helleborus foetidus* has clusters of small, bell-shaped flowers on tall stems. It has the unfortunate common name of stinking hellebore. There is also the green hellebore (*H. viridis*), another very 'collectable' plant. In fact, once you start with one hellebore, you may well go on to search out all the others, though some will take some seeking out.

The common *H. orientalis* self-seeds quite readily after flowering, and you should collect the abundant black seeds and sow them as soon as they form. You can sow them in seed-raising mix in trays, or directly into the ground with plenty of compost mixed in. If you want, you can cut all the foliage back to ground level in May and smother the ground with well-rotted animal manure. Don't be afraid; they will come up again, as fresh as new-born babies.

Hellebores make terrific cut flowers, especially for posies. The old idea was to burn the base of the stem before using them in an arrangement, but I find that cutting just 2 cm off the stem every few days makes them last longer.

Hostas

*T*here's always some spot in the garden that gets only partial sun, maybe underneath the apple tree where dappled light gets through, or down the side of the house which only gets morning sun. Morning sunlight, or filtered sunlight through a leafy canopy, is a good place to grow many plants that prefer the shade. This includes plants grown for their foliage, such as hostas and hellebores, many of which have fabulous foliage, either dense green or with unusual markings.

Hostas are extremely beautiful foliage plants. They will tolerate most soil types but do best in well-composted, moist soils in partial shade. They form neat clumps, with their beautiful leaves growing from a crown at the surface of the soil. Some varieties have leaves the size of dinner plates, and some reach about 60 cm high.

HOW TO GROW HOSTAS

The only trick with hostas is to keep snails and slugs away from them, as their leaves seem to be the most delectable food for those creatures. Hostas can be grown in containers, provided they are kept out of the scorching sun and kept moist. Feed them with a small amount of animal manure and a teaspoon of slow-release fertiliser. Mass them together either in a garden bed or a large pot which you can bring onto the verandah when they are at their best. Since they are perennials, hostas die down at the end of autumn, but don't worry, the leaves will pop up out of the ground and unfurl beautifully in spring and remain growing through summer.

Hydrangeas

*M*ost people would know a hydrangea. My grandmother grew these shrubs in the shady part of the garden and she brought great bunches of flowers inside to use as cut flowers. With their great globular flowerheads on long stems, they flower on and on over summer and make a great display in a vase, especially at Christmas time and on into January.

In a garden designed for colour through the seasons,

My favourite hostas

Hosta fortunei comes in various forms. *H. fortunei* 'Albopicta' has soft green and yellow, variegated leaves that open yellow and cream in the centre with a deeper green border which becomes completely green by late summer. *H. fortunei* 'Aurea' has more delicate leaves that are yellow–green at first and then become a superb light green.

Hosta plantaginea has pale green, glossy leaves with tall spikes of fragrant white flowers.

Hosta sieboldiana is probably the most dramatic of the hostas, with its large waxy leaves of a grey–green colour. The flowers hide amongst the leaves.

There are many other hostas with narrow variegations on the edge of the leaves, or a deep midrib of cream with green edges. They have tall spikes of ball-shaped flowers and a few varieties are fragrant, another bonus. Once you have discovered the delights of hostas, you will want to start a collection. There are numerous species and cultivars available, so check out specialist mail-order catalogues.

hydrangeas will certainly lift a shaded or partly sunny spot over summer. They can be massed together under tall trees in the garden or given pride of place on a porch or terrace in a decorative tub or pot, where they will give many months of pleasure. I like to see several of them grouped with some thought to a pleasant blending of colours.

Hydrangeas are wonderfully useful plants in any garden — and this is nothing to be sneezed at. If a plant can fill a difficult position in the garden, why not grow it? The good old hydrangea grows and flowers in a shady spot and only complains if left unwatered over a dry period. Even then the plant will tell you, as its leaves droop down in a complaining manner, that it needs a good, deep watering to revive. The large, oval, light green leaves can easily burn around the edges if given too much sun, so morning sun is all they can usually take.

The commonly grown varieties, the mop tops, are the Hortensia variety and usually grow to 1–1.8 metres high. Their large flowerheads, which are really a collection of individual flowers, are glorious, like big balls all over the plant.

One of the most eye-catching is *Hydrangea paniculata*, which has extra large, cone-shaped inflorescences of creamy white flowers right through summer and autumn. There is a cultivar of *H. paniculata* called 'Grandiflora' which has massive creamy panicles. I have seen it grown as a spectacular standard with one trunk trained up to a metre or so high and a ball of flowers at the top.

H. quercifolia, commonly known as the oakleaf hydrangea, is one of my favourites. It not only has attractive flowers, but also appealing deeply lobed foliage, resembling oak leaves. These turn red and russet colours in autumn, and the bush seems to keep its leaves through winter, unlike the other truly deciduous ones. The foliage may be a high point, but the flowers are also spectacular, in panicles of white that flower from summer until mid-autumn. This outstanding shrub will grow between 1.5–2 m high.

There is even a hydrangea that climbs, so if you have a wall or fence that needs covering this is a splendid choice. It is *H. petiolaris* — a particularly attractive climber.

Lacecaps or 'hen and chicken' hydrangeas are yet another variety well worth growing in any garden. They are similar in growth habit to the mop-top types, but their flowers are large and flat, with fertile flowers in the middle surrounded by a ring of

Hydrangeas are propagated by hardwood cuttings taken in winter. This is the attractive foliage of *Hydrangea quercifolia*.

coloured florets. *H. macrophylla* 'Blue Wave' is a beauty, with a ring of colours around a lovely blue. For those wanting a white flower there is 'Veitchii'.

PRUNING

Pruning hydrangeas is really quite simple. Immediately after flowering in autumn or in winter, cut shoots that have flowered back to two fat buds within a few centimetres of the old wood. Leave the shoots that have not flowered this season unpruned (or at the most just shorten them back a little) as they will flower early next season.

TAKING CUTTINGS

Hydrangeas will grow from softwood tip cuttings up to 10 cn long taken in spring or summer, or in winter take hardwood cuttings 20–25 cm long after the plants have dropped their leaves. Put them in pots or heel them directly into the ground, where they should take root in 6–8 weeks.

Some hydrangea species

H. arborescens 'Grandiflora'. Pure white flowers, often large enough to weigh down the branches; known in America as 'Hills of Snow', a beautiful shrub to 2 m. The flowers age from white to pale green.

H. aspera subsp. *sargentiana*. A rarely seen species, growing to 2 m tall, with huge, distinctive leaves to 30 cm long and white or pinkish flowers

H. paniculata 'Grandiflora'. A very hardy plant with creamy-white panicles of flowers that turn slightly pink as they age over summer into autumn.

H. petiolaris. The climbing hydrangea which self-clings, so can grow up to 6–7 m on a wall or tree, white lacecap flowers and vivid green leaves

H. quercifolia. Large oak-like leaves, and beautiful white panicles of flowers

THE COLOUR OF HYDRANGEAS

Most people know that the colour of some hydrangeas depends on the type of soil they grow in. Back in the 18th century, when these colour variations were first noticed, it was thought that the flowers took their colour from nearby objects which cast a shade. Later, in the 19th century, after much experimentation, it was discovered that if hydrangeas were watered with a solution of alum (the double sulphate of aluminium and potassium), the flowers would turn blue. Iron filings mixed in the soil also proved successful in changing flowers to blue. My grandmother used to put used wads of steel wool under her hydrangeas; a canny friend keeps a bucket filled with old nails and water and pours the liquid around the plants. There is also a commercially available bluing powder available from nurseries and garden centres which can be watered in around the plant's roots from July and August.

Acid soils produce blue flowers when they are able to absorb the iron in the soil; that is, if the soil has a pH of 5.5 or below, iron and aluminium are easily absorbed. However in alkaline soils with a higher pH, the lime and chalk imprisons the iron, which cannot be absorbed by the plant, so a blue colour is hard to obtain. For pink flowers, which will occur naturally in alkaline soils, you can use fertilisers high in phosphorus, which neutralises the aluminium in the soil. White flowers will not change their colour.

PICKING AND DRYING HYDRANGEA FLOWERS

As a cut flower, hydrangeas are hard to beat, as they will last in water for many months. Put them into the vase with a mixture of half water and half glycerine so that the preserving process begins then. It is best to pick mature blooms, as the early flowerheads don't last. There may even be a shortage of hydrangeas as cut flowers in florists and markets, since large numbers are sold by Australian growers to markets in Japan and the United States, where they are highly prized.

If you want to dry some hydrangeas, hang the cut flowers upside down in a well ventilated spot in the shed or garage. They will dry in the air and keep a certain amount of colour in the petals. They also dry if you put them in a vase with a little water and, though they may become brittle, they will last for months in dried flower arrangements.

Needing protection from direct sunlight, hydrangeas grow well in the semi-shade or with an easterly facing aspect with morning sun. Pictured here is a lacecap hydrangea, *Hydrangea macrophylla* 'Veitchii', with a lovely flat head of flowers. The small, fertile flowers are in the centre with large, sterile flowers on the outside. It flowers from mid to late summer and likes plenty of mulch and moisture around its roots in dry times.

Impatiens

*T*here is no need to go overboard, but most gardeners do love a splash of colour over the summer months. Annual plants are so easy to grow and certainly provide just the dash of colour to finish off a garden. If you would like to find a colourful perennial to do this job, you might try impatiens. From spring onwards, impatiens are most rewarding. Once the danger of frost has passed, these remarkable plants come to the fore. They are very vibrant — luscious pinks, tangerine oranges, bright whites, purples and reds that hit you in the eye. There are also many varieties of double-flowered impatiens, with compact growth and delightful small flowers that are massed with petals. These look like miniature roses and come in soft pastels, white or red.

Each year wholesale growers release new colours, so keep a look out for them. For instance, oranges, reds and mauves — all bold colours — are coming back along with ruby, purple and white. The pastel shades will always be popular, too, and white creates a very cool look against the lush green foliage.

THE BEST WAY TO GROW IMPATIENS

Over the warmer months impatiens should be watered very regularly — if they dry out the flowers and leaves crumple. Watering is especially important if you are growing your impatiens in a hanging basket where air movement round the roots evaporates the water very quickly. Check the water regularly, and remember to water every morning.

In early spring, feed impatiens with a good dose of animal manure, and during their growth and flowering time feed with a liquid fertiliser.

If you are a keen gardener, nip out one or two shoots every fortnight or so, so that the plant will remain bushy and not grow straggly. Pruned gradually like this (only a few shoots at a time), it will be hardly noticeable. On the other hand, if you have let your impatiens become straggly, with stems growing hither and thither, take courage and cut it back. Using secateurs, cut all growths back by at least 10 cm all around, give it a feed and then wait for more flowers.

You can get a couple of seasons out of impatiens if you cut them back in early spring, say September, or to avoid frosts. Don't keep plants for too long; throw them away after three or four years. They grow so easily and quickly you won't be left with much of a gap.

NEW GUINEA HYBRIDS

Why not try something different: the shape of the flower of a New Guinea hybrid impatiens is very different from the ordinary busy lizzie (Impatiens walleriana) that is commonly grown. The flowers of the New Guinea types are large, up to 8 cm across, and shaped like a butterfly. Very often their leaves are highlights also, sometimes variegated or backed with mauve, contrasting well with the flowers. New Guinea impatiens were bred for a compact growth habit, and for masses of flowers. This makes them ideal for hanging baskets, pots and well-drained garden beds.

The beautiful New Guinea impatiens flower in vibrant colours over summer and autumn, if grown in a shady or partially shaded area. They can be cut back when flowering has finished — this is best done after any frosty weather — then feed them up well so they flower on again.

Native plants for shade

BORONIA MUELLERI 'Sunset Serenade'

All boronias are lovely, notably for their fragrance (see *B. megastigma* and *B. heterophylla*, pages 5–6), but there are others that are stunning for their profusion of flowers. This boronia is a favourite of mine, with its masses of pale pink, starry flowers in spring. It prefers to grow in dappled shade and will grow to little more than 1 m high and wide.

Boronias do need good drainage, plus a deep mulch of compost and leaf litter so their surface roots are kept cool. Prune them after flowering in spring so they keep compact and you will be very pleased with the results.

NATIVE FUCHSIA (*Correa* spp.)

There are many species of correa, which is one of my favourite native plants. I like *C.* 'Dusky Bells', *C.* 'Marian's Marvel, *C. pulchella* and *C. reflexa*. They will all grow and flower well in light shade, provided the soil is well drained. Correas are all frost hardy and one of the bonuses of growing them is that birds love them for their nectar-filled flowers. A group of different correas (called native fuchsia because of their hanging, bell-shaped flowers) is a wonderful asset in any garden, whether native or mixed planting.

For a partly shaded position, the native fuchsias (*Correa* spp.) are always very useful. This one, *Correa* 'Dusky Bells' grows to 75 cm high and spreads to 2 m wide. It has masses of pale pink, tubular flowers which are bird attracting. Correas are one of my favourite native plants, because they are hardy and free flowering — at home in any garden.

Boronia muelleri 'Sunset Seranade' grows well in shaded spots and it is covered with pale pink, starry flowers in spring. It is one of the best boronia cultivars and will grow to a little more than 1 m high. It has no fragrance but is worth growing for its bounteous flowers.

Commonly called the river rose, *Bauera rubioides* is an evergreen shrub growing to 1.5 m high, with a loose, spreading habit. It is quite a sight in spring with masses of flowers, either in white or pink. If the shrub becomes straggly, prune the stems by one third after flowering. Grow this plant in a well-drained position and keep it moist in dry times.

RIVER ROSE (*Bauera rubioides*)

This bauera will grow with very little sun, its natural habitat being in shade, but it will grow in sun as well. It is native to the Grampians area in western Victoria, where it grows in dense thickets in moist shady spots along creek and river beds. It hits you in the eye when you see it en masse. Its flowers resemble a simple single rose, hence its common name. The flowers are pink masses on the stems (though there is also a white form), and it forms clumps which are sometimes a little straggly but look good in an informal garden. The plant grows about 1 m high and spreads to about 2 m across. Baueras will take to most types of soil, but they prefer lots of moisture.

Rhododendrons

*I*n the late 19th and early 20th centuries rhodendrons became extremely popular — a 'rhododendron mania' swept through the gardening world as a result of many new species being introduced from China and the Himalayas by the great plant hunters E. H. Wilson, George Forrest and F. Kingdon Ward. A huge new range of colours and species of rhododendrons inspired many gardeners to grow them. They have established themselves as one of the hardiest and most pleasurable plants to grow.

Rhododendron 'White Pearl' is a vigorous, upright shrub reaching 4–5 m high. The pink trusses opening from white buds are a spectacular sight in late spring. Keep this plant moist and well mulched in summer when flower buds are forming.

A selection of beautiful rhododendrons

Rhododendron davisii. White flowers

R. 'Fragrantissimum'. Even though it is a little straggly, a magnificent perfume with white flowers.

R. 'Anne Teese'. Pink form of 'Fragrantissimum', may be hard to obtain, but worth looking out for

R. 'Mrs G. W. Leak'. Two-tone pink, growing to 2 m

R. 'Mount Everest'. Lovely white, growing to 1 m

R. 'Ross Maude'. Pink and absolutely massed with flowers

R. 'Sappho'. White with dark blotch

R. 'Unique'. Peachy cream colour, medium grower to 1 m, compact even without flowers

R. 'Unknown Warrior'. A waxy, cerise-red, grows to 1.5 m

R. 'White Pearl'. A big shrub to 7 m, lovely flowers which cover the bush

R. *yakushimanum*. Small hybrids that will even grow in full sun, rose pink, fading to white.

Rhododendrons are variable plants, growing as a tree or shrub, with leathery leaves and flower buds on the end of the branches. They are always a fine sight when in full flower, especially from September through to December.

Azaleas are also members of the genus *Rhododendron* and both plants are always popular as spring-flowering shrubs in traditional gardens where colour is paramount. Both plants prefer a cool, moist soil, so their roots do not dry out, and will grow well in a shady spot. Rhododendrons are not fussy things — they do not need pruning (unless they grow too big for the spot in the garden, in which case you can prune them as you wish). All they require is good compost around their roots or in the planting hole and mulch to insulate the soil, so their roots don't bake in summer.

The biggest problem that home gardeners find with rhododendrons is that they die from wet feet — poor drainage is usually the problem. In heavy soils where water can sit around, it will be necessary to improve the drainage. Or you can plant your rhododendron on a mound, a fairly smart practice, as then water can drain away freely.

Fertilise with a complete fertiliser, so there is enough nitrogen for a green colour all over the leaf (yellowing leaves mean a nitrogen deficiency). If leaves show signs of yellowing but with green veins, you have iron deficiency. Spray iron chelates on the foliage, or sprinkle iron sulphate on the soil and water in.

Mulch will help retain water in the soil, and this is vital over summer to autumn when the rhododendron is forming its flower buds for the following season. Don't let them dry out at all at this stage.

Once the rhododendron flowers have withered and finished, remove the spent flowers by simply putting your hand over the spent flower and twisting firmly so it breaks cleanly from the stem. A clean cut with secateurs will nip them off just as well. By doing this, the growth bud (which is clearly seen at the base of the point where the flower has developed) can grow out straight and vigorously.

Rhododendrons, and their relatives the azaleas, always look their best if planted as a bank with others of differing heights and colours. Under the half-shade of tall trees, they will create a lovely woodland effect if massed together.

PRUNING AN OVERGROWN PLANT

It is much easier to prune a young plant in spring to keep it compact than to wait until the plant is overgrown. You can certainly prune a large bush, but it may take several years to rejuvenate and get back to a good shape, as you may cut back into old wood. It will grow back, however, so be confident. Prune in early spring or immediately after flowering.

Rhododendrons can be moved quite easily, even when they are large. The best time is in autumn through to early spring, even when flowers buds are aboard, provided of course that you don't plant into wet, badly drained soil. Dig the new hole comfortably deep and wide enough to take the plant and mix plenty of compost into the bottom of it. Before you dig the plant up, make sure the soil is thoroughly soaked. Then dig as much of the root ball up as possible.

VARIETIES

Mollis azaleas are the deciduous varieties; many are fragrant and they range in colours from red, orange, cream and yellow. They are very beautiful, especially in a massed planting.

The Vireya group of rhododendrons are quite different, especially as they have vibrant bright flowers.

Last but not least, there is a real beauty, *Rhododendron lochae*, the Australian native species, which has tubular crimson-red flowers in summer. If you have no other rhododendron in your garden, this is the one worth planting.

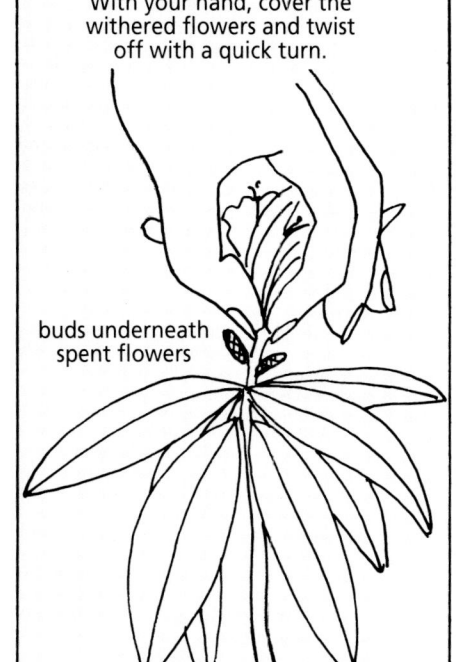

Pruning rhododendrons

With your hand, cover the withered flowers and twist off with a quick turn.

buds underneath spent flowers

Plants that like it hot and dry

*I*t is often stated that Australia is the driest continent on earth, and this is something that no Australian gardener can afford to ignore, for we need to understand the consequences for our gardens. Of course most people live on the coastal belt of eastern Australia, where there may be dry seasons but they can be reasonably confident that relief will eventually come with rain. There are, however, plenty of people living in the country where rainfall is often much less than 500 mm a year, and a drought is not an uncommon occurrence.

Coming from Mildura in the Sunraysia district, I am well aware of the hazards that low rainfall (250 mm in a good year), searing hot winds and temperatures well over 35°C for weeks and weeks can bring to a garden. My parents are fortunate in having plenty of water for their Mildura garden, but conditions like these make gardening a real challenge.

Low rainfall and high temperatures are familiar conditions in much of inland Australia. They make it hard to grow plants that need lots of moisture, and gardens need to be restricted in size simply to save this precious commodity. Although we city people are insulated, to a degree, from these extreme conditions, we should not be complacent about water use.

There are various ways in which you can be water conscious yet have a beautiful garden. Careful selection of plants that (once established) don't require loads of water is most important. Australian native plants carefully chosen for their dry-tolerance and the growing requirements in your area will do well, as any keen

A great survivor, this lion's ear (*Leonotis leonurus*) is able to cope with hot, dry conditions. It is not commonly found in gardens, but deserves to be grown more often. If the tan-orange colour doesn't sit well in your pastel garden, it will look good combined with grey-leaved plants and amongst mauve and lilac perennials.

native-plant grower or Society for Growing Australian Plants member will know. Other plants — trees, shrubs and perennials — from overseas can be grown if they relate to our climate. Many plants from California and the Mediterranean area will adapt well because very often they are used to the same dry, hot conditions.

Mulching any garden to keep the moisture in the soil is vital. I often say that I have never seen a really good garden that is not mulched — plants certainly respond well. Mulches can be lucerne hay, pea straw, hay, mushroom compost, seaweed mulch (now available commercially in bags), coconut fibrous material, compost, or anything that you can find locally. Even stones or pebbles grouped around the base of trees will act as mulch. Mulch breaks down, adding organic material to the garden, so it needs to be replenished every eighteen months or so, but you will notice the difference in the way your plants respond.

Mind you, I have my reservations about large wood chips used as a mulch, as all too often I've noticed that young plants are 'set back' in their initial growth when this is used. This is usually the effect of nitrogen 'draw-down', which simply means that freshly laid pinebark chips or sawdust mulch uses up nitrogen from the soil as it breaks down. If you must use bark or wood chip mulch, it is a very good idea to counteract this effect by first applying plenty of blood and bone to give extra nitrogen.

It makes sense to group plants together according to their water needs, so put plants with high water needs, such as rhododendrons, hydrangeas and impatiens, together and those which need less water near each other. This will help you to rationalise your watering regime. You should analyse the way you water, too — there is no point in watering leaves, for example. Put the water right where it is needed, at root level. Irrigation systems are an excellent idea, as long as the automatic timer doesn't water unnecessarily. Hand watering may be time consuming but I do enjoy it as a relaxing task, especially as you can direct water to where it is most beneficial.

There are many plants, very many of them native plants, that are tough John Wayne types in the garden when it comes to hot and dry conditions. Not only are there trees, but also plenty of medium-growing shrubs and smaller plants. Some of my choices for suitable plants follow, but if you live with this sort of climate it is always worth checking your local nursery or con-servation department for local plant lists.

SEDUM — A BUTTERFLY ATTRACTER

Plant names have interesting origins and I am often fascinated by them; indeed the names can add much to my enjoyment of the plants. One such plant is the hardy perennial called sedum or stonecrop.

It is a succulent plant with large juicy leaves and stems and very easy to grow. Its mauve-pink flowers are in a large head, about 15 cm across, and are long lasting on the bush. The plant grows up to 40 cm high.

Over late summer and autumn Sedum spectabile *is one of the most popular garden plants for people with a cottage garden bent.*

This plant should be dotted around the front of the garden bed, or in a herbaceous border planting, for its colour and for its amazing attraction to butterflies and bees. Always a welcome addition to the garden, sedum is rarely

Suitable trees for hot and dry places

*T*hese trees are in my 'tough customer' list, not only for their stout constitutions, but also for their attractiveness.

• Fuchsia gum (*Eucalyptus forrestiana*). I noticed these fuchsia gums (*E. forrestiana*) growing as a roadside planting in western Victoria where I used to teach years ago. They caught my eye because they were a small tree, bushy rather than tall, to 5 m high, and were growing really well in a fairly hot, dry spot in the country. They are called fuchsia gums because of the large red buds which hang like bells and the yellow flowers. The fruits are red and last well on the tree so that for many months there is a point of interest. They prefer a sunny spot and are well suited to inland areas.

• Jacaranda (*Jacaranda mimosifolia*). With its fine fern-like leaves and clusters of beautiful mauve-blue flowers in early summer, the jacaranda is one of the most attractive trees. They do grow into a large tree, eventually reaching about 15 m high with a spreading canopy that gives lovely shade in summer. When we grew jacarandas in the Sunraysia district, where frost can be severe for several months, we had to protect them with a shade cloth tent until they grew to 1.5 m and out of reach of frosts. Now they are huge trees and quite a highlight. The flowers look stunning against the blue skies of early summer and I love it when the flowers drop to spread like a blue carpet.

• Redcap gum (*Eucalyptus erythrocorys*). This was one of my first propagation successes: collecting the seed from the parent plant of this red-capped gum, growing and planting it in Mildura. And what a delight it was when it finally flowered four years later. It is a glorious gumtree, coping with hot and dry conditions extremely well, though it prefers sandy, well-drained soils and doesn't do well in the gluggy heavy soils of the east coast. It grows to about 7 m high and in autumn flowers with spectacular bright yellow, even lime-coloured blooms that pop out from large buds with a red cap. Birds are attracted to it and honeyeaters cackle away in the flowers as they search out the copious nectar.

seen without its attendant visitors. The plants love to grow in full sun and are excellent in dry positions in a garden. Back to the origin of its name. In Roman times they would plant sedums on the roofs of their houses in the belief they would keep away lightning. I have read that the name comes from the Latin word sedo, meaning 'calm'.

Just looking at these easy-to-grow, uncomplicated flowers may be a means of calming a gardener, though I am not sure about growing them on my pitched roof!

Here's a plant that thrives in hot, dry conditions. There are many varieties of Stonecrop (*Sedum* spp.) to choose to grow in a pot. They are also easy to grow in well-drained, sandy soil, and have succulent leaves on stems that can easily be propagated by taking 10 cm cuttings.

TREES FOR HOT, DRY CONDITIONS

Common Name	Botanical Name	Height & Width	Comment	Country of origin
Athel tree	*Tamarix aphylla*	6 x 10 m	Fine leaves, soft pink flowers	Africa, Asia
Bushy yate	*Eucalyptus lehmanii*	5 x 8 m	Unusual lime green flowers	Australia
Carob tree	*Ceratonia siliqua*	5 x 10 m	Excellent shade and hedge tree, pods provide fodder	Mediterranean area
Common olive	*Oleo europaea*	3 x 6 m	Useful for hedge or windbreak	Mediterranean region
False acacia	*Robinia pseudoacacia*	10 x 15 m	Very fast growing, deciduous	North America
Green mallee	*Eucalyptus viridis*	3 x 10 m	Lovely small tree, snow-white flowers	Australia
Honey locust	*Gleditsia triacanthos*	12 x 15 m	Yellow ferny leaves	Australia
Kurrajong	*Brachychiton populneus*	6 x 15 m	Showy, creamy bellflowers	Australia
Mulga	*Acacia aneura*	3–6 x 3 m	Yellow flowers	Australia
Native pine	*Callitris spp.*	6 x 10 m	Fine, cypress-like foliage	Australia
Pepper tree	*Schinus molle*	10 x 15 m	Drooping ferny leaves, very attractive evergreen tree	South America
Raspberry jam wattle	*Acacia acuminata*	6– 10 m x 5 m	Handsome tree, yellow flower spikes	Australia
Red-cap gum	*Eucalyptus erythrocorys*	3–7 m x 2 m	Brilliant yellow flowers	Australia
Red-flowering gum	*Eucalyptus ficifolia*	4–7 m x 5 m	Beautiful, striking flowers	Australia
Red-flowered mallee	*Eucalyptus erythronema*	3 x 10 m	Beautiful pink–white trunk	Australia
Silver cassia	*Cassia artemisiodes*	1 x 2.5 m	Yellow buttercup flowers	Australia
Strickland's gum	*Eucalyptus stricklandii*	6 x 12 m	Fast-growing, bright yellow flowers	Australia
Swamp mallet	*Eucalyptus spathulata*	2 x 7 m	Beautiful smooth bark, often brown-olive	Australia
Weeping myall	*Acacia pendula*	6 x 10 m	Pendulous habit — an attractive willow-like tree	Australia
Weeping pittosporum	*Pittosporum phillyreoides*	5 x 7 m	Hanging branches—very attractive tree	Australia
White cedar	*Melia azedarach*	5 x 12 m	Fragrant lilac flowers	Australia

With fine, ferny foliage and trusses of blue–mauve flowers, the *Jacaranda mimosifolia* makes a fine shade tree for warm climates.

• Weeping pittosporum (*Pittosporum phillyreoides*). I first saw these trees growing in the Mungo National Park and was very impressed by their obvious ability to grow in incredibly arid and tough conditions, as this is deep in the western corner of New South Wales where rainfall is very low. They are also beautiful trees, growing to about 7 m high, and with a very shapely spread of 2 m. They have pendulous branches, hanging almost down to the ground, and creamy-yellow flowers in spring. These are followed by small, round, orange seed pods with red seeds which are also an attractive feature. This pittosporum is well worth growing and is quite easy to propagate from seed.

Shrubs and woody plants for dry conditions

*T*hese shrubs should thrive in hot, dry conditions once they are established.

• Abelia (*Abelia* x *grandiflora*). Although the glossy-leaved abelia may be commonly grown, it always looks good. It flowers for ages with white bells with a pink tinge, growing to 1–2 m x 1.5 m high.

• *Alyogyne huegelii*. There is hardly a time when this native plant is without flowers, and in full flower the purple hibiscus-like blooms are profuse over the bush. It grows to approximately 2 m × 1.5 m and is very hardy, needing a sunny position.

• *Calothamnus quadrifidus.* Sometimes called 'one-sided bottlebrush', this hardy member of the genus is known for its attractive (usually red) stamens, arranged in bundles on one side of the stem. This species has fine, pine-like leaves, and forms a compact bush growing to 1.5 m.

• Flowering quince or japonica (*Chaenomeles japonica*). This is an incredibly tough plant, a bit taller than 1 m, with reddish orange, pink or white flowers. You will often see japonicas as lone survivors in old gardens, where they have lived bravely on through years of neglect. The flowers on their bare, thorny branches make spectacular cut flowers.

- Lavender (*Lavandula* spp.). There are many species, with the French and Italian varieties suiting dry areas best (see pages 9–11). They grow to 90 cm–1 m high, depending on the variety.
- Lion's ear (*Leonotis leonurus*). Plants are often named very curiously, and the common name for 'Lion's ear' has always had me guessing. Its flowers, carried on tall rigid stems, encircle the stem completely. Each individual flower is funnel-shaped and, apart from being soft and velvety, I can see no similarity between these flowers and a lion's ear. Maybe the name was influenced by the colour of the flower — a very vibrant orange, arresting to say the least. The Lion's ear plant originates from central and southern Africa, so perhaps in its natural surroundings it blends in with its animal namesake. Like many other southern African plants, this one has adapted well to southern Australian con-ditions. It grows very well, reaching 1–1.5 m high, given any reasonable soil and a hot, sunny position.
- Jerusalem sage (*Phlomis fruticosa*). This is an incredibly hardy plant for dry or coastal conditions. It has furry, greyish green leaves and yellow, sage-type flowers that last for months. It has been used around gardens for years and will just keep on surviving. It grows to 90 cm–1 m high.
- Rock rose (*Cistus* spp.). There are many *Cistus* species well worth growing in dry gardens, many with very showy flowers. The plants grow to 90 cm–1 m high.
- Rosemary (*Rosmarinus officinalis*). This familiar shrub with aromatic foliage and blue-mauve flowers is easy to grow, as a shrub or hedge to 1 m high. There is also a prostrate variety (*Rosmarinus prostratus*).
- Rue (*Ruta graveolens*). Rue's ferny, blue-green leaves have a strong, bitter aroma, but it is a pretty plant with yellow flowers and very hardy, especially in lime soils, growing to 90 cm–1 m high.
- Yucca (*Yucca* spp.). These very attractive, architectural plants with sword-like leaves and tall spikes of cream-white flowers were often used in Victorian gardens and are at last coming back into fashion. Some varieties are large; others grow in pots. All are good value because they need less water. They grow to 1–2 m high by 1 m wide. Butterflies are attracted to this plant.

PERENNIALS THAT LIKE IT HOT

Achillea spp. These come in many colours and are low growing. The family includes the popular yarrow (*Achillea millefolium*).

Chamomile (*Anthemis tinctoria*). A mound-forming plant with white daisy flowers

Coastal daisy (*Erigeron karvinskianus*) Always has tiny, daisy-like flowers

Cranesbill (*Geranium* spp.). Low-growing, spreading species with attractive foliage and flowers

Day lily (*Hemerocallis* spp.). Clump forming and bright in colour

Euphorbia spp. There are many varieties of this excellent plant

Mullein (*Verbascum* spp.). Rosettes of leaves with a spike of yellow-cream flowers, up to 2 m high

Pineapple lily (*Eucomis comosa*). Clump forming with spikes of white or greenish white flowers

Pride of Madeira (*Echium fastuosum*). Beautiful spikes of mauve-blue flowers, bee attracting

Red hot pokers (*Kniphofia* spp.). Brilliant orange colours, with other varieties available, clump forming

Sage (*Salvia* spp.). Many beautiful varieties, hardy for sun and dry (see pages 150–1)

Stonecrop (*Sedum* spp.). Stunning plants with succulent leaves and flowers, attractive to butterflies (see pages 144–5)

CLIMBERS

Bougainvillea glabra
'Magnifica Traillii'.
Creeping or climbing fig
(*Ficus pumila*).
Honeysuckle (*Lonicera japonica*)
Ivyleaf pelargonium
(*Pelargonium peltatum*).
Maidenhair creeper
(*Muehlenbeckia complexa*)
Perennial pea (*Lathyrus latifolius*)

(For more on climbers, see
pages 85–98)

A sprawling shrub with beautiful spikes
of blue flowers, Pride of Madeira
(*Echium fastuosum*) is well suited to
a hot, dry spot.

Grey-leaved plants for dry positions

• *Arabis caucasica*. Grows into a neat, low mat of grey leaves
• *Brachyglottis greyi* (formerly *Senecio*). A beautiful plant with felty grey leaves and yellow daisy flowers, on a bush that grows 1–1.5 m high. It grows well on the coast and will tolerate dry conditions.
• Chamomile (*Anthemis punctata* ssp. *cupaniana*). Grows into a wide, low mound with silvery, fern-like leaves, very hardy
• Catmint (*Nepeta mussinii*). Grows in thick clumps with soft lavender spikes flowering for ages. Its leaves have a pleasant fragrance. This plant thrives in hot dry places, and takes alkaline soils.
• Cineraria (*Senecio* 'Dusty Miller'). A remarkably tough plant with lovely, lacy, silvery-grey leaves. Has heads of small yellow flowers, grows to about 90 cm high, and will grow in poor soil, tolerates sea winds, salt and heat as well as dry conditions.
• *Dianthus* spp. Many varieties are sun and drought tolerant, and good to grow on the edge of the garden bed. Can be cut back after flowering.
• *Eromophila* spp. These are all very hardy plants with pink, red, yellow or green flowers. *E. glabra* has silvery grey leaves and very persistent tubular flowers. It is well suited to hot, dry inland areas.
• Silver wormwood (*Artemisia arborescens*). Once grown prolifically as a hedge in many farm gardens, this thrives on neglect. It will respond well to an annual cutback. Its leaves are soft and felty to touch and have a 'healing' type of smell, quite lovely.
• Snow-in-summer (*Cerastium tomentosum*). Forms a very dense carpet of grey leaves which give a good contrast as a ground-cover or plant to spill over a border or bank. Called snow-in-summer for the masses of single white flowers in summer.
• Strawflower or everlasting daisy (*Helichrysum bracteatum*). There are various forms of these golden everlastings, all with beautiful heads of flowers that are made up of papery bracts. Like *H.* 'Dargon Hill Monarch' they are very showy, and well worthwhile in any garden.
• Woolly lamb's tail (*Verbascum bombycilferum*). Common name

comes from its 2-m high woolly stem with single, lemon yellow flowers coming through. They self-seed readily. The flower spikes appear from large rosettes of greyish-green leaves.

Salvias: sage stuff

Most people would know the fiery red of the salvia: it is one of the most popular annual bedding plants. Over summer many local councils plant masses of salvias in prominent positions, and passersby cannot fail to be struck by their strong, vibrant colour. The common red salvia is *Salvia splendens*, and this is the one that most people think of. But there are over 500 other species in the genus, most of them quieter coloured, including the edible sage so commonly used for cooking.

S. splendens is invariably grown as an annual to be dug up when flowering finishes in late autumn. Salvias are, however, true perennials in their natural state in the country of Brazil. They have bright green foliage, the plant growing to about 60 cm high with 5 cm long terminal spikes as the inflorescence. The true flower is insignificant — the spectacular scarlet colours are bracts surrounding it. This explains why salvias have such a long-lasting display. In this 'annual' range there are new forms and colours being introduced with purple, mauve, pink, claret and white making a change from the ordinary red.

Apart from this well-known one there are many very beautiful salvias that should not be ignored. They are shrubby enough to fill a gap in a perennial garden or to combine with other shrubs in a sunny spot. There are many different flower colours and different leaf variations to create interest. And as one gardener who loves salvias says, there is virtually no time in the year when there is not a salvia flowering.

Gardeners appreciate their hardiness and long-flowering characteristics, and have found that searching them out in nurseries and old gardens has been very rewarding for some of the more unusual varieties.

Salvia species

Bog sage (*Salvia uliginosa*). Although most salvias grow best in well-drained spots, this one will grow in moist conditions as well as drier spots, hence its name. It is a good herbaceous perennial with

When massed in a background border, the tall, slender blue flower spikes of *Salvia farinacea* 'Blue Bedder' look much like lavender. It is a long-flowering plant for sunny to semi-shaded positions and will stand up to hot conditions very well. Pinch it back regularly to keep it compact, taking off any spent flowers.

a graceful habit and delightful sky blue flowers on long (1.5 m) stems. It spreads rapidly, so unless you want it everywhere, cut it back frequently and dig the roots up to keep it under control.

Clary sage (*Salvia sclarea*). This plant is a native of Europe and Asia. It has lovely, very prominent bracts in shades of pink and white and its leaves are very aromatic; indeed the whole plant has an intense, penetrating fragrance. The oil from Clary sage is used for massage, relaxation and aromatherapy, allegedly to relieve stress and clear the eyesight.

Mealy sage (*Salvia farinacea*). This sage loves the heat, being a native of Texas and New Mexico, and is tolerant of dry soil. The graceful stems are a feature, with spikes to 1 m of violet-blue flowers which resemble lavender. 'Indigo Spires' is a beauty for gardeners looking for blue flowers.

Mexican bush sage (*Salvia leucantha*). Sadly this splendid plant, once commonly seen in gardens, must have gone out of fashion. It should not be forgotten as it has a lovely soft appearance with velvet-like green leaves with white felt on their undersides. The flowers are very attractive — long, lavender–purple and shaped like a cat's paw. This is an evergreen shrub from Mexico growing to 90 cm high.

Fruit salad plant (*Salvia dorisiana*). So-called for its large, light green leaves, which are felty to touch and have a refreshing fragrance similar to fresh fruit. It flowers in the winter and the one outside my window is a mass of rich pink flowers that look well against the lime green leaves. Although my plant gets no special favours, it withstands dry times and just needs a clipping back if it gets out of hand.

Salvia canariensis. This wonderful grey-leaved shrub from the Canary Islands grows to 1.5 m high and is particularly useful as a feature in permanent plantings. It has lance-shaped, hairy, grey leaves and mauve flowers. Many of the salvias have grey leaves, which is usually a sign that they can stand extremes of temperature and sunlight. Give this one plenty of room to spread.

S. guaranitica (syn. *S. ambigens*). A perennial growing in a bush to 1.5 m high, this sage has beautiful, clear blue flowers that seem to go on and on. Mix it with other colours in the garden — whites, yellows or silver leaves — to bring out those colours.

S. involucrata 'Bethellii'. This sage is in continuous flower for months over spring. It grows to 1.75 m high with reddish pink stems and deep, rose pink flowers in large heads of flowers. It is very attractive and suits either a sunny or shady spot.

Index

Note: Bold page numbers indicate photographs.